Breaking Into The Trade Game

A SMALL BUSINESS GUIDE TO EXPORTING

Co-sponsored by the
U.S. SMALL BUSINESS ADMINISTRATION
AND AT&T

Dear Small Business Exporter:

As the Administrator of the U.S. Small Business Administration (SBA), I clearly see the increasing importance of exporting for the future growth and health of this Nation's businesses. Ninety-five percent of the world's population is outside the borders of the United States. American products and services are in demand by people in many other countries; our small businesses must learn the most effective means to sell to them.

The SBA and AT&T are pleased to provide small businesses with this second edition of *Breaking Into the Trade Game: A Small Business Guide to Exporting*. Part I provides a thorough overview of the export process. We added a new chapter to address the "information superhighway" and how to use it to improve your chances of succeeding in far-away markets. We also updated and expanded the workbook to get you started on writing an international marketing plan. Part II gives you an "at-your-fingertips" source of telephone numbers and places to contact for further assistance in exporting your products and services.

Familiarize yourself with the contents of this *Guide*. Keep a copy close by as you travel along the exciting and profitable road to overseas markets. I wish you great success!

Sincerely,

Philip Lader
Administrator

Gail J. McGovern
Vice President & General Manager -
Business Services

Room 15A09
55 Corporate Drive
Bridgewater, NJ 08807

Dear Small Business Exporter:

Once again, AT&T is delighted to team up with the U.S. Small Business Administration to bring you **Breaking Into The Trade Game**: A Small Business Guide to Exporting.   This guide has proven to be extremely useful in the past and we hope you find this revised edition a valuable addition to your library.

AT&T is committed to your success, the success of small businesses in general, and to the efforts of small businesses expanding into global markets.   And it will continue to support you with the information and resources you need to accomplish your goals.

We wish you continued success, because at AT&T we recognize the crucial role that businesses like yours play in providing jobs, contributing to a robust U.S. economy and, consequently, helping to narrow the trade gap.   In fact, making significant progress within the global marketplace is a critical factor that will impact positively on the way America fares as it approaches the 21st century.

To your continued global success.

Sincerely,

Gail McGovern

The second edition of *Breaking Into The Trade Game: A Small Business Guide to Exporting* was produced under the guidance of Giordano A. Chiaruttini, Deputy Assistant Administrator, Office of International Trade, U.S. Small Business Administration. Kathy Parker, Export Development Specialist, was managing editor. A special thanks to our volunteer interns who made countless telephone calls and provided valuable editorial support: Fernando d'Arteaga, Louis Dagostino, Alan Kirk, Amy Reding, and Rick Rodman. Sheldon Snook and Jean Smith, Office of International Trade; Ray Williams, SBA District Office, Kansas City, Missouri; and Sid Lawrence, International Trade Director, National SCORE Office, also provided valuable editorial support.

The International Marketing workbook was adapted from Developing Your International Business Plan, written at the Lake Michigan College Small Business Development Center (SBDC) and International Business Center. The materials and worksheets were adapted from the Oregon SBDC publication, "Your International Business Plan" at Portland Community College. The Lake Michigan College SBDC is partially funded under Cooperative Agreement No. SB-2M-00092-09 by the U.S. Small Business Administration.

Cover design by Signal Communications, Bethesda, Maryland.

INTRODUCTION

The U.S. Small Business Administration's (SBA) Office of International Trade (OIT) developed this *Guide* in 1993 to assist your business to develop international markets. The second edition, with updates and new information, is intended to help take your company into the second half of the 1990s. The new edition contains new information on how to maximize your international opportunities through the use of high-technology equipment to facilitate global information transfers and communications. The *Guide* answers questions and takes some of the mystery out of exporting. The U.S. government has worked hard to provide small businesses, like yours, with the tools to succeed in the international marketplace because we understand that small businesses are vital to the health of the U.S. economy. More than 99 percent of all businesses in the United States are small firms, which employ 57 percent of America's private work force. Between 1990 and 2005, small firms are expected to create about 66 percent of all new jobs.

The Trade Promotion Coordinating Committee (TPCC), chaired by the Secretary of Commerce, combines the efforts of nineteen federal agencies, all offering some type of export assistance for American businesses, to create a National Export Strategy. The *National Export Strategy* makes the expansion of American sales abroad a high priority and recommends concrete actions to accomplish this expansion. Two years ago, the TPCC identified three essential ingredients that small business exporters need to be successful. They are *access to capital, advice and information* and *training*.

The U.S. government has reshaped its international trade programs to better respond to each of these small business needs:

- The TPCC has a nationwide toll-free number for information on export counseling, seminars/conferences, export financing, technical assistance and overseas buyers (*see* Section 1, Part II of this *Guide*).

- The SBA, the U.S. Department of Commerce (DOC) and the Export-Import Bank of the United States (Ex-Im Bank) have international trade personnel currently located at four Export Assistance Centers (EACs) in major U.S. cities and will open eleven more by the end of calendar year 1995; EACs offer you federal export marketing and trade finance assistance in convenient one-stop locations (*see* Chapter 3).

- The SBA has a new, short-term financing program called the Export Working Capital Program (EWCP) for financing your export transactions; the program is harmonized with Ex-Im Bank's Working Capital Guarantee to provide a seamless product to all our customers as their export financing needs increase (*see* Chapter 6).

- The SBA made 1,161 loans nationally to exporters for more than $481 million in FY 1994.

- The SBA Office of International Trade (OIT), maintains a Washington, D.C. staff which serves as the focal point for coordinating the delivery of SBA's export assistance programs.

- The SBA, through the Service Corps of Retired Executives (SCORE) program, utilizes 850 volunteers with international trade experience who provide one-on-one counseling to actively exporting and new-to-export businesses, with a total of 13,000 SCORE volunteers nationwide.

- The SBA supports over 900 Small Business Development Centers (SBDCs). There are approximately 38 SBDC designated as international trade centers; all SBDCs provide export counseling, referral and/or training.

- The SBA coordinates the Export Legal Assistance Network (ELAN), a nationwide group of international trade attorneys who provide free initial consultations to small businesses on export related matters.

- The Department of Commerce (DOC) has 68 district export assistance offices throughout the United States and 120 overseas posts, representing 95 percent of the world market for U.S. products and services (*see* Section 1, Part II).

- The DOC International Trade Administration in Washington, D.C. has industry-specific specialists monitoring export opportunities for U.S. products and services in every sector, from abrasive products to zippers (*see* Section 1, Part II).

- The DOC sponsors 51 District Export Councils (DECs), comprised of nearly 1,700 business and trade experts available on a volunteer basis to help U.S. firms develop export strategies.

- The DOC Minority Export Development Consultants Program supports more than 107 Minority Business Development Centers throughout the United States.

- The U.S. Department of Agriculture (USDA) Foreign Agricultural Service (FAS) maintains a $30 million budget for export promotion of U.S. commodities through trade fairs and other activities.

- Like the DOC, the USDA employs country specialists who focus on a range of products from oilseeds to poultry (*see* Section 3, Part II).

- In addition to specialists located at the EACs, the Ex-Im Bank has trained specialists in 24 states and in Puerto Rico through its City/State program to provide export financing assistance to small businesses.

- The Ex-Im Bank provided over $15 billion in 1994 in authorized loans, guarantees and insurance to support U.S. exports, with 11.3 percent of Ex-Im Bank's authorizations going to support small business exports.

The SBA and other federal, state and local government agencies are ready to assist you in opening new avenues of opportunity in the international marketplace. With their help, and with the information contained in this *Guide*, you will discover that access to international markets is possible and profitable.

The explosion of global competition and new market opportunities has made timely information essential for the small business exporter. Keep this *Guide* close by for reference and resource information; your business will be certain to benefit.

OVERVIEW

BECOMING A SMALL BUSINESS EXPORT SUCCESS STORY

Small businesses in the United States have gained international exposure and greatly increased their profits through exporting during the 1990s. However, success has not come without hard work. Learning the rules of the trade game can be demanding. An important step is planning through writing an international marketing plan. And, one of the most pressing needs of small businesses to export is finding the capital to fulfill orders as they come in. Consider the case of C.S. Johnson Co., an Illinois company. Company president Alexander Balc, Jr. tells his story:

> *"Established in 1921, C.S. Johnson Co. developed an international reputation as the premier company designing, engineering and manufacturing concrete batching and mixing plants capable of producing high volume, high quality concrete. C.S. Johnson manufactured equipment has mixed concrete for most of the major hydro-electric dams and navigational lock and dam projects in the United States, beginning with the Hoover Dam.*
>
> *C. S. Johnson Co.'s success and reputation in the United States created its entree into the international market. Johnson manufactured equipment mixed and batched the concrete for the largest hydroelectric project in the world to date, the Itaipú Dam in Brazil, containing in excess of 15 million cubic meters of concrete. In international competition, we have prevailed against multi-billion dollar companies from Japan, Italy, Germany and Korea. The timely assistance of the Small Business Administration has helped this small central Illinois company compete as a major player in the international marketplace. With major hydro development projects and navigational projects winding down in the U.S., the major thrust for C.S. Johnson is in the international marketplace. This export business for C.S. Johnson creates and sustains jobs for U.S. citizens with imported dollars.*

In 1991, my partner Allen Seeland and I bought the C.S. Johnson business with the goal of establishing a major presence in the international marketplace. We invested heavily and have successfully met our goal. Unfortunately, the process took twice as long, and was far more costly, than we had planned. As we moved into September of 1994, we were awarded two major contracts: a $3.4 million contract for two concrete batch plants for the Tunnels for the Xiaolangdi Dam, and a $2.3 million contract for a concrete batch plant for the Three Gorges Dam in The Peoples Republic of China. Subsequently, we were awarded additional contracts for related equipment for the Xiaolangdi Dam.

Our ability to perform on the Xiaolangdi Project has confirmed C.S. Johnson's presence in the international marketplace. We are now successfully competing against some of the largest international companies in our field.

C.S. Johnson's participation in the Small Business Administration's Export Working Capital Program is an extremely positive experience and virtually life saving for the C.S. Johnson business. Without this guarantee it would be nearly impossible for the C.S. Johnson Company to meet its contractual commitments on a $3.4 million dollar contract.

Not meeting our commitments on this contract would have meant heavy financial penalties, thus severely impairing our ability to achieve accelerated growth in the international marketplace. We were granted a guarantee by the Small Business Administration based on the potential and promise of the Xiaolangdi Dam contract coupled with C.S. Johnson's ability to deliver projects of this magnitude in spite of its difficult and straitened circumstances. The result of this guarantee is that our cash flow pump was primed, and we could accelerate rather than curtail production. We will meet our contractual commitments, thereby laying a solid foundation for increased sales and participation in the international marketplace."

Breaking Into The Trade Game: A Small Business Guide to Exporting can assist your company's international efforts. This *Guide* highlights the export success stories of many small businesses. It is both a comprehensive how-to manual and reference book providing you with the contacts and resources to ease your entry into markets around the world.

Part I: The eight chapters of **Becoming an Export Success Story** take you through the exporting process with stories of small businesses from around the United States that have found exporting to be an exciting and profitable way to expand their business.

Chapter 1: Making the Export Decision includes an international marketing workbook to assess your company's export readiness, business goals and commitment.

Chapter 2: Making the Connection explains how communications can facilitate exporting worldwide and how to increase profits by traveling on the new "information superhighway."

Chapter 3: Identifying International Markets explains how to conduct foreign market research and the resources available to assist you.

Chapter 4: Foreign Market Entry discusses methods of distributing your product abroad with an emphasis on exporting.

Chapter 5: The Export Transaction details the steps involved in making trade happen, including setting prices, negotiating the sale and determining legal aspects of exporting.

Chapter 6: Export Financing outlines government and private sector financing resources and methods of payment.

Chapter 7: Transporting Goods Internationally focuses on moving goods overseas, including packaging and labelling.

Chapter 8: Strategic Alliances and Foreign Investment Opportunities explores other methods of market entry beyond exporting, such as joint ventures and off-shore manufacturing facilities.

Part II: The Exporter's Directory is a comprehensive directory of contacts and information sources to assist you as you take your business into the trade game.

BREAKING INTO THE TRADE GAME

A SMALL BUSINESS GUIDE TO EXPORTING

PART I

BECOMING AN EXPORT SUCCESS STORY

CHAPTER 1

MAKING THE EXPORT DECISION

Exporting is crucial to America's economic health. Increased exports mean business growth, and business growth means bigger profits for U.S. companies resulting in more jobs for American workers. Yet only a small percentage of potential exporters take advantage of these opportunities. It is critical for U.S. businesses to think globally. Your decision to read this book shows you are interested in exporting. You may have already discovered your company is competing internationally—foreign-owned companies are competing with you in your "domestic" markets. The division between domestic and international markets is becoming increasingly blurred. In a world of 5.5 billion people, global communication networks, next-day air freight deliveries worldwide and CNN, it no longer makes sense to limit your company's sales to the local or even the national market. Your business cannot ignore these international realities if you intend to maintain your market share and keep pace with your competitors.

Making the export decision requires careful assessment of the advantages and disadvantages of expanding into new markets. Once the decision is made to export, an international marketing plan is essential. This chapter presents the advantages and disadvantages of exporting and offers a method to evaluate your company's readiness to export. The remaining chapters of this book guide you through the steps necessary to master the "trade game."

ADVANTAGES AND DISADVANTAGES OF EXPORTING

Consider some of the specific advantages of exporting.
Exporting can help your business:
* enhance domestic competitiveness
* increase sales and profits
* gain global market share
* reduce dependence on existing markets
* exploit corporate technology and know-how
* extend the sales potential of existing products
* stabilize seasonal market fluctuations
* enhance potential for corporate expansion
* sell excess production capacity
* gain information about foreign competition

In comparison, there are certain disadvantages to exporting. Your business may be required to:

- develop new promotional material
- subordinate short-term profits to long-term gains
- incur added administrative costs
- allocate personnel for travel
- wait longer for payments
- modify your product or packaging
- apply for additional financing
- obtain special export licenses

These disadvantages may justify a decision to forego direct exporting at the present time, although your company may be able to pursue exporting through an intermediary. If your company's financial situation is weak, attempting to sell into foreign markets may be ill-timed. The decision to export, for all small business exporters featured in this *Guide*, was based on careful analysis and planning.

THE NEED FOR AN INTERNATIONAL MARKETING PLAN

Behind most export success stories is a plan. Whether formally written, or sketched out informally at a meeting of your management team, an international marketing plan is an essential tool to properly evaluate all the factors that would affect your company's ability to go international.

An international marketing plan should define your company's:

- readiness to export;
- export pricing strategy;
- reason for exporting;
- potential export markets and customers;
- methods of foreign market entry;
- exporting costs and projected revenues;
- export financing alternatives;
- legal requirements;
- transportation method;
- overseas partnership and foreign investment capabilities; and
- corporate commitment to the exporting process.

Creating an international marketing plan helps to define your company's present status, internal goals and commitment, and it is also required if you plan to seek export financing assistance. Preparing the plan in advance of making export loan requests from your bank will save time and money. Completing and analyzing an international marketing plan helps you anticipate future goals, assemble facts, identify constraints and create an action statement. The plan should also set forth specific objectives, an implementation timetable and milestones to gauge your success.

INTERNATIONAL MARKETING PLAN WORKBOOK

The purpose of the International Marketing Plan workbook is to prepare your business to enter the international marketplace. Ask yourself: Should I expand my company through exporting? Do I have any products or services* I can export? This workbook will lead you step-by-step through the process of exporting your product to an international market.

The workbook is divided into sections. Each section should be completed before you start the next. After you have completed the entire workbook, you will be ready to develop an international marketing plan to export your product. The remaining chapters of this *Guide* will assist you in determining where and how to find the resources to begin exporting successfully.

*When **products** are mentioned, **services** should be assumed also.

PLANNING

Why complete this workbook and write a plan?

Six reasons it will be worth your time and effort:

1. Careful completion of this workbook will help evaluate your level of commitment to exporting.
2. The completed workbook can help you assess your products' potential for the global market.
3. The workbook gives you a tool to help you better manage your international business operations successfully.
4. The completed workbook will help you communicate your business ideas to persons outside your company. It is an excellent starting point for developing an international financing proposal.
5. Businesses are managed more successfully when operating from a business plan.
6. A plan forces the business to stay focused on primary objectives and provides a measuring tool of results as each step is achieved.

Can't I hire someone to do this for me?

No! Nobody will do your thinking or make decisions for you. This is your business. If the marketing plan is to be useful, it must reflect *your* ideas and efforts.

Why is planning so important?

The planning process forces you to look at your future business operations and anticipate what will happen. This process better prepares you for the future and makes you more knowledgeable about your business. Planning is vital for marketing your product in an international marketplace and at home.

Any firm considering entering into international business transactions must understand that doing business internationally is not a simple task. It is stimulating and potentially profitable in the long-term but requires much preparation and research prior to the first transaction.

In considering products or services for the international market,
a business needs to be:
1. Successful in its present domestic operation.
2. Willing to commit its resources of time, people and capital to the export program. Entry into the international market may take as long as two years of cash outflow to generate profit.
3. Sensitive and aware of the cultural differences in doing business in other countries.

Approach your export operations in the same way you would your domestic operations—using sound business fundamentals. Developing an international marketing plan helps you assess your present market situation, business goals and commitment, which will increase your opportunities for success.

A marketing plan is a process, not a product. It must be revised on a continual basis as your knowledge increases about international markets. You will be surprised how much easier it is to update a marketing plan after the first one is written. Planning is a continuous process. Plus, after a revision or two you will know more about your international business market opportunities to export products.

GOAL SETTING

Identifying business goals can be an exciting and often challenging process. It is, however, an important step in planning your entry into the international marketplace. The following exercise is an additional step to help clarify your short- and long-term business goals.

STEP 1: Define long-term goals.

A) What are your long-term goals for this business in the next 5 years?

Examples: increase export sales by ____% annually or ____% market share or ____% profitability or return on assets.

_____

_____

_____

_____

_____

_____

_____

_____

_____

_____

_____

_____

_____

_____

GOAL SETTING *continued*

B) How will the international trade market help you reach your long-term goals?

_____

_____

_____

_____

_____

_____

_____

STEP 2: *Define short-term goals.*

A) For your international business, what are your first year goals?

Examples: select a sales/distribution outlet in the export markets chosen; develop relationships with agents/distributors; participate in trade shows or trade missions in chosen market(s).

_____

_____

_____

_____

_____

_____

_____

GOAL SETTING *continued*

B) What are your two-year goals for your international business products/services?

Example: Modify product for metric definition; expand international opportunities from initial penetration of a market to other similar markets.

_____

_____

_____

_____

_____

_____

_____

STEP 3: Develop an action plan with timelines to reach your short-term goals.

_____

_____

_____

_____

_____

_____

_____

IDENTIFYING PRODUCTS WITH EXPORT POTENTIAL

List below the products your company sells which you believe have export potential. Write down why you believe each product will be successful in the international marketplace. The reasons should be based on your current knowledge, rather than any research.

PRODUCTS/SERVICES

1. _____

2. _____

3. _____

REASONS FOR EXPORT SUCCESS

1. _____

2. _____

3. _____

Based on reasons for export success, select one or more products you believe might have the best prospects for exporting.

Decision Point: These products have export potential.

YES   NO

If YES, go on to next steps.

STEP 1: Select the most exportable products to be offered internationally.

To identify products with export potential, you need to consider products that are sold successfully in the domestic market. The product should fill a targeted need for the purchaser in export markets according to price, value to customer/country and market demand.

What are the major products my business sells?

1. _____

2. _____

3. _____

IDENTIFYING PRODUCTS WITH EXPORT POTENTIAL *continued*

What product(s) do you feel have the best potential for international trade?

1. _____

2. _____

3. _____

STEP 2: Evaluate the product(s) to be offered internationally.

What makes your product(s) attractive for an overseas market?

1. _____

2. _____

3. _____

Why do you believe international buyers will purchase your company's products?

1. _____

2. _____

3. _____

DETERMINING YOUR COMPANY'S EXPORT READINESS

PROS AND CONS OF MARKET EXPANSION

Brainstorm a list of pros and cons for expanding your market internationally. Based on your current assumptions about your company, your company's products and any market knowledge, determine your probability of success in the international market.

PROS

1. _____
2. _____
3. _____
4. _____
5. _____

CONS

1. _____
2. _____
3. _____
4. _____
5. _____

PROBABILITY OF SUCCESS

0%	25%	50%	75%	100%

YOUR BUSINESS/COMPANY ANALYSIS

STEP 1: Why is your business successful in the domestic market? Give specific reasons. What is your company's annual growth rate?

_____

_____

_____

_____

STEP 2: What are the **competitive advantages** *of your products or business over other domestic and international businesses?*
List them:

_____

_____

_____

_____

_____

STEP 3: What is your level of commitment and that of your company's top management to expanding into international markets? How much preparation time, planning and resources are you willing to commit to implementing an export program?

_____

_____

_____

_____

INDUSTRY ANALYSIS

STEP 1: Determine your industry's growth for the next three years.

Talk to people in the same business or industry, research industry-specific magazines, attend trade fairs and seminars, use the National Trade Data Bank (NTDB).

_____

_____

_____

STEP 2: Research how competitive your industry is in the global markets.

Utilize the NTDB, obtain import/export statistics from the Bureau of the Census, contact U.S. Small Business Administration (SBA), the U.S. Export Assistance Center (EAC) or the U.S. Department of Commerce (DOC) district office in your area.

_____

_____

_____

STEP 3: Find out your industry's future growth in the international market.

Contact a U.S. EAC or Small Business Development Center (SBDC) or contact a DOC country or industry desk in Washington, D.C. (*see* Part II, *The Exporter's Directory*).

_____

_____

_____

INDUSTRY ANALYSIS *continued*

4: Research federal or state government market studies that have been conducted on your industry's potential international markets.

Obtain on the NTDB, or through a U.S. EAC, SBA, your state international trade office, or a DOC country or industry desk in Washington, D.C.

_____

_____

_____

STEP 5: Find export data available on your industry.

Contact your SBA district office or SBDC or SCORE representative, or a U.S. Export Assistance Center.

_____

_____

_____

DEVELOPING YOUR EXPORT MARKETING PLAN

Read Chapters 2 and 3 of this *Guide* before completing this section.

STEP 1: Select the best countries to market your product.

Since the number of world markets to be considered by a company is very large, it is neither possible nor advisable to research them all. Thus, your firm's time and money are spent most efficiently by using a sequential screening process.

Your first step in this process is to select the more commercially attractive countries for your product. Preliminary screening involves defining the physical, political, economic and cultural environment. Research the NTDB for DOC Country Commercial Guides for each country in which there is a Foreign Commercial Service presence. In addition, the NTDB has Department of State country reports and the Central Intelligence Agency's *World Factbook*.

(1) Select 3 countries you think have the best market potential for your product;

(2) Review the market factors for each country;

(3) Research data/information for each country;

(4) Rate each factor on a scale of 1–5 with 5 being the best; and

(5) Select a target market country (C) based on your ratings (R).

MARKET FACTOR ASSESSMENT	COUNTRY	RATING	COUNTRY	RATING
Demographic/Physical Environment:				
• Population size, growth, density				
• Urban and rural distribution				
• Climate and weather variations				
• Shipping distance				
• Product-significant demographics				
• Physical distribution and communication network				
• Natural resources				

DEVELOPING YOUR EXPORT MARKETING PLAN *continued*

MARKET FACTOR ASSESSMENT	COUNTRY	RATING	COUNTRY	RATING
Political Environment:				
• System of government				
• Political stability and continuity				
• Ideological orientation				
• Government involvement in business				
• Attitudes toward foreign business (trade restrictions, tariffs)				
Competitive Environment:				
• Other competitive offerings				
• Uniqueness of your product/service				
• Pricing of competitive products (non-tariff barriers, bilateral trade agreements)				
• National economic and developmental priorities				
Economic Environment:				
• Overall level of development				
• Economic growth: GNP, industrial sector				
• Role of foreign trade in the economy				
• Currency: inflation rate, availability, controls, stability of exchange rate				
• Balance of payments				
• Per capita income and distribution				
• Disposable income and expenditure patterns				
Social/Cultural Environment:				
• Literacy rate, educational level				
• Existence of middle class				
• Similarities and differences in relation to home market				
• Language and other cultural considerations				

DEVELOPING YOUR EXPORT MARKETING PLAN *continued*

MARKET FACTOR ASSESSMENT	COUNTRY	RATING	COUNTRY	RATING
Market Access:				
• Limitations on trade: high tariff levels, quotas				
• Documentation and import regulations				
• Local standards, practices, and other non-tariff barriers				
• Patents and trademark protection				
• Preferential treaties				
• Legal considerations for investment, taxation, repatriation, employment, code of laws				
Product Potential:				
• Customer needs and desires				
• Local production, imports, consumption				
• Exposure to and acceptance of product				
• Availability of linking products				
• Industry-specific key indicators of demand				
• Attitudes toward products of foreign origin				
• Competitive offerings				
Local Distribution and Production:				
• Availability of intermediaries				
• Regional and local transportation facilities				
• Availability of manpower				
• Conditions for local manufacture				

Indicators of population, income levels and consumption patterns should be considered. In addition, statistics on local production trends, along with imports and exports of the product category, are helpful for assessing industry market potential. Often, an industry will have a few key indicators or measures that will help determine the industry strength and demand within an interna-

DEVELOPING YOUR EXPORT MARKETING PLAN *continued*

tional market. A manufacturer of medical equipment, for example, may use the number of hospital beds, the number of surgeries and public expenditures for health care as indicators to assess the potential for its products.

What are the projected growth rates for the three countries selected over the next 3–5 years?

_____

_____

STEP 2: Determine Projected Sales Levels.

Much of this information can be obtained from an industry trade association for your particular industry.

What is your present U.S. market percentage?

_____

_____

What are the projected sales for similar products in your chosen international markets for the coming year?

_____

_____

What sales volume will you project for your products in these international markets for the coming year?

_____

_____

What is the projected growth in these international markets over the next five years?

_____

_____

22

DEVELOPING YOUR EXPORT MARKETING PLAN *continued*

STEP 3: *Identify Customers Within Your Chosen Markets.*

What companies, agents or distributors have purchased similar products?

_____

_____

What companies, agents or distributors have made recent requests for information on similar products?

_____

_____

What companies, agents or distributors would most likely be prospective customers for your export products?

_____

_____

STEP 4: *Determine Method Of Exporting.*

How do other U.S. firms sell in the markets you have chosen?

_____

_____

Will you sell direct to the customer?

1. Who will represent your firm?

_____

_____

2. Who will service the customers' needs?

_____

_____

23

DEVELOPING YOUR EXPORT MARKETING PLAN *continued*

STEP 5: Building A Distributor or Agent Relationship.

Plan to travel to the country in question as many times as is necessary to build a successful relationship.

Will you appoint an agent or distributor to handle your export market? Consider legal advice from the Export Legal Assistance Network (ELAN). A free initial consultation is available by request through an SBA District Office, SBDC, SCORE or U.S. Export Assistance Center.

_____

_____

1. What facilities does the agent or distributor need to service the market?

_____

_____

2. What type of client should your agent or distributor be familiar with in order to sell your product?

_____

_____

3. What territory should the agent or distributor cover?

_____

_____

4. What financial strength should the agent or distributor have?

_____

_____

DEVELOPING YOUR EXPORT MARKETING PLAN *continued*

5. What other competitive or non-competitive lines are acceptable or not acceptable for the agent or distributor to carry?

_____

_____

6. How many sales representatives does the agent or distributor need and how often will they cover the territory?

_____

_____

Will you use an export management company to do your marketing and distribution for you?   YES   NO

If yes, have you developed an acceptable sales and marketing plan with realistic goals you agree to?

YES   NO

Comments:

_____

_____

MARKETING YOUR PRODUCT/SERVICE

Given the market potential for your products in international markets, how is your product or service distinguished from others—attractive or competitive?

1. What are your product's advantages? _____

_____

2. What are your product's disadvantages? _____

_____

3. What are your competitors products' advantages?_____

_____

4. What are your competitors products' disadvantages? _____

_____

What needs does your product fill in a foreign market?

_____

What competitive products are sold abroad and to whom?

_____

How complex is your product? What skills or special training are required to:

1. Install your product? _____

_____

2. Use your product? _____

_____

3. Maintain your product? _____

_____

MARKETING YOUR PRODUCT/SERVICE *continued*

4. Service your product? _____

_____

What options and accessories are available?

_____

_____

_____

1. Has an aftermarket been developed for your product?

_____

_____

2. What other equipment does the buyer need to use your product?

_____

_____

3. What complementary goods does your product require?

_____

_____

If your product is an industrial good:

1. What firms are likely to use it?

_____

_____

2. What is the useful life of your product?

_____

_____

MARKETING YOUR PRODUCT/SERVICE *continued*

3. Is use or life affected by climate? If so, how?

_____

_____

4. Will geography affect product purchase; for example transportation problems?

_____

_____

5. Will the product be restricted abroad; for example tariffs, quotas or non-tariff barriers?

_____

_____

If the product is a consumer good:

1. Who will consume it? How frequently will the product be bought?

_____

_____

2. Is consumption affected by climate?

_____

_____

3. Is consumption affected by geography; for example, transportation problems?

_____

_____

MARKETING YOUR PRODUCT/SERVICE *continued*

4. Will the product be restricted abroad; for example, tariffs, quotas or non-tariff barriers?

_____

_____

5. Does your product conflict with traditions, habits or beliefs of customers abroad?

_____

_____

SUPPORT FUNCTIONS

To achieve efficient sales offerings to buyers in the targeted markets, you should address several concerns regarding products, literature and customer relations.

STEP 1: Identify product concerns.

Can the potential buyer see a functioning model or sample of your product that is substantially the same as would be received from production?

YES   NO

Comments:

_____

_____

What product labelling requirements must be met? (Metric measurements, AC or DC electrical, voltage, etc.) Keep in mind that the European Community now requires 3 languages on all new packaging and Mexico requires labels in Spanish under the North American Free Trade Agreement.

_____

_____

When and how can product conversion requirements be obtained?

_____

_____

Can product be delivered on time as ordered?

YES   NO

This is especially important since letters of credit are unforgiving when it comes to delivery promise dates.

Comments:

_____

_____

SUPPORT FUNCTIONS *continued*

STEP 2: *Identify literature concerns.*

If required, can you produce product literature in a language other than English?

YES   NO

Do you need a product literature translator to handle the technical language?

YES   NO

What special concerns should be addressed in sales literature to ensure quality and informative representation of your product? Keep in mind that translations should reflect the linguistic nuances of the country where the literature will be used.

_____

_____

STEP 3: *Identify customer relations concerns.*

What is delivery time and method of shipment?

_____

_____

What are payment terms?

_____

_____

What are the warranty terms? Will inspection/acceptance be required?

_____

_____

Who will service the product when needed?

_____

_____

SUPPORT FUNCTIONS *continued*

How will you communicate with your customer . . . through a local agent or fax? Via Internet?

_____

_____

Are you prepared to give the same order and delivery preference to your international customers that you give to your domestic customers?

YES   NO

MARKETING STRATEGY

In international sales, the chosen "terms of sale" are most important. Where should you make the product available: at your plant; at the port of exit; landed at the port of importation; or delivered free and clear to the customer's door? The answer to this question involves determining what the market requires, and how much risk you are willing to take.

Pricing strategy depends on "terms of sale" and also considers value-added services of bringing the product to the international market.

STEP 1: Define International Pricing Strategy.

How do you calculate the price for each product?

_____

_____

What factors have you considered in setting prices?

_____

_____

Which products' sales are very sensitive to price changes?

_____

_____

How important is pricing in your overall marketing strategy?

_____

_____

What are your discount policies?

_____

_____

MARKETING STRATEGY *continued*

What terms of sales are best for your export product?

_____

_____

STEP 2: Define promotional strategy.

What advertising materials will you use?

_____

_____

What trade shows or trade missions will you participate in, if any?

_____

_____

What time of year and how often will foreign travel be made to customer markets?

_____

_____

STEP 3: Define customer services.

What special customer services do you offer?

_____

_____

What types of payment options do you offer?

_____

_____

How do you handle merchandise that customers return?

_____

_____

SALES FORECAST

Forecasting sales of your product is the starting point for your financial projections. The sales forecast is extremely useful, so it is important you use realistic estimates. Remember that sales forecasts show the expected time the sale is made. Actual cash flow will be affected by delivery date and payment terms.

STEP 1: Fill in the units-sold line for markets 1, 2, and 3 for each year on the following worksheet.

STEP 2: Fill in the sales price per unit for products sold in markets 1, 2 and 3.

STEP 3: Calculate the total sales for each of the different markets (units sold x sales price per unit).

Step 4: Calculate the sales (all markets) for each year—add down the columns.

Step 5: Calculate the five year total sales for each market— add across the rows.

SALES FORECASTS—FIRST FIVE YEARS

	1	2	3	4	5
Market 1					
Units Sold					
Sale Price/Unit					
Total Sales					
Market 2					
Units Sold					
Sale Price/Unit					
Total Sales					
Market 3					
Units Sold					
Sale Price/Unit					
Total Sales					
Total Sales					
All Markets					

COST OF GOODS SOLD

The cost of goods sold internationally will differ from cost of goods sold domestically if significant product alterations will be required. These changes will affect costs in terms of material, direct and indirect labor costs.

Pass Through Costs

To ascertain the costs associated with the different terms of sale, it will be necessary to consult an international freight forwarder. For example, a typical term of sale offered by a U.S. exporter is cost, insurance and freight (CIF) port of destination. Your price can include all the costs to move the product to the port of destination and other costs necessary to complete the export transaction. However, many of these costs are incurred by the exporter to provide a service to the importer. For example, you can price your product *Ex Works* and let your customer worry about getting the product to their destination from your factory or warehouse. However, most exporters arrange many of the details (transportation, insurance, etc.) for their customers. These costs should be identified separately on the invoice and *Passed Through* with little or no markup.

A typical cost work sheet will include some of the following factors. These costs are in addition to the material and labor used in the manufacture of your product.

export packing	forwarding
container loading	export documentation
inland freight	consular legalization
truck/rail unloading	bank documentation
wharfage	dispatch
handling	bank collection fees
terminal charges	cargo insurance
ocean freight	other misc.
bunker surcharge	telex
courier mail	demurrage
tariffs	import duties

To complete this worksheet, you will need to use data from the sales forecast. Certain costs related to your terms of sale may also have to be considered. For example, include cost of capital if you are extending payment terms.

COST OF GOODS SOLD *continued*

STEP 1: Fill in the units-sold line for market 1, 2, and 3 for each year.

STEP 2: Fill in the cost per unit for products sold in markets 1, 2, and 3.

STEP 3: Calculate the total cost for each of the products—(units sold x cost per unit).

STEP 4: Calculate the cost of goods sold—all products for each year—add down the columns.

STEP 5: Calculate the five-year cost of goods for each market—add across the rows.

COST OF GOODS SOLD—FIRST FIVE YEARS

	1	2	3	4	5
Market 1					
Units Sold					
Cost Per Unit					
Total Cost					
Market 2					
Units Sold					
Cost Per Unit					
Total Cost					
Market 3					
Units Sold					
Cost Per Unit					
Total Cost					
Cost of Goods Sold					
All Markets					

INTERNATIONAL MARKETING EXPENSES

To determine marketing costs for your export products, you should include costs that apply only to international marketing efforts. For example, costs for domestic advertising of service that do not pertain to the international market should not be included. Examples of most typical expense categories for an export business are listed below. Some of these expenses will be first-year, start-up expenses; others will occur every year.

STEP 1: Review the expenses listed below. These are expenses that will be incurred because of your international business. There may be other expense categories not listed—list them under "other expenses."

STEP 2: Estimate your cost for each expense category.

STEP 3: Estimate any domestic marketing expense included that is not applicable to international sales. Subtract these from the international expenses.

STEP 4: Calculate the total for your international overhead expenses.

EXPENSE

COST

	Market 1	Market 2	Market 3	Total Yr 1
Legal Fees				
Accounting Fees				
Promotional Material				
Travel				
Communication				
Equip/Fax/PC Modem				
Advertising Allowances				
Promotional Expenses (e.g., trade shows, etc.)				
Other Expenses				
Total Expenses				
Less Domestic Expenses Included Above, if any				
Total International Marketing Expenses				

PROJECTED INCOME STATEMENT—YEARS 1 TO 5, ALL MARKETS

You are now ready to assemble the data for your projected income statement. This statement will calculate your net profit or net loss (before income taxes) for each year.

STEP 1: Fill in the sales for each year. You already have estimated these figures; just recopy them on the work sheet.

STEP 2: Fill in the cost of goods sold for each year. You already have estimated these figures; just recopy on the work sheet.

STEP 3: Calculate the Gross Margin for each year (Sales minus Cost of Goods Sold).

STEP 4: Calculate the Operating Expenses specifically associated with the international marketing program for each year.

STEP 5: Allocate the International Division's portion of the firm's overall domestic operating expenses (International's portion of lighting, office floor space, secretarial pool, etc.)

PROJECTED INCOME STATEMENT—YEARS 1 TO 5, ALL MARKETS *continued*

	1	2	3	4	5
International Sales					
Cost of Goods Sold					
Gross Margin					
International Operating Expenses					
Legal					
Accounting					
Advertising					
Travel					
Trade shows					
Promotional Material					
Supplies					
Communication Equipment					
Interest					
Insurance					
Other					
International Division's Domestic Expense Allocation					
Total International Operating Expenses					
Net Profit Before Income Taxes					

BREAK-EVEN ANALYSIS

The break-even is the level of sales at which your total sales exactly cover your total costs, which includes non-recurrent fixed costs and variable costs. This level of sales is called the Break-Even Point (BEP) sales level.

In other words, at the BEP sales level, you will not make a profit. If you sell more than the BEP sales level, you will make a net profit. If you sell less than the BEP sales level, you will have a net loss.

To calculate the break-even point, costs must be identified as being either fixed or variable. *Fixed expenses* are those which the business will incur regardless of its sales volume—they are incurred even when a business has no sales—and include such expenses as rent, office salaries and depreciation. *Variable expenses* change directly and proportionately with a company's sales and include such expenses as Cost of Goods Sold, sales commissions, etc. Some expenses are *semi-variable* in that they vary somewhat with sales activity but are not directly proportionate to sales. Semi-variable expenses include utilities, advertising and administrative salaries. Semi-variable expenses ideally should be broken down into their fixed and variable components for an accurate break-even analysis. Once a company's expenses have been identified as either fixed or variable, the following formula is used to determine its break-even point.

$$\text{Break-Even Point} = \frac{\text{Total Fixed Expenses}}{1 - \dfrac{\text{Total Variable Expenses}}{\text{Sales Volume}}}$$

Note: In addition to a break-even analysis, it is highly recommended that a profit and loss analysis be generated for the first few actual international transactions. Since there are a great number of variables relating to costs of goods, real transactions are required to establish actual profitability and minimize the risk of losses.

TIMETABLE

This is a worksheet that you will need to work on periodically as you progress in the workbook. The purpose is to ensure that key tasks and objectives are identified and completed to ensure accomplishment of your stated goals.

STEP 1: Identify key activities.

By reviewing other portions of your marketing plan, compile a list of tasks that are vital to the successful operation of your business. Be sure to include travel to your chosen market as applicable.

STEP 2: Assign responsibility for each activity.

For each identified activity, assign one person primary responsibility for the completion of that activity.

STEP 3: Determine scheduled start date.

For each activity determine the date when work will begin. You should consider how the activity fits into your overall plan as well as the availability of the person responsible.

STEP 4: Determine scheduled finish date.

For each activity determine when the activity must be completed.

ACTION PLAN

PROJECT/TASK	PERSON	START DATE	FINISH DATE

SUMMARY

STEP 1: Verify completion of previous pages.

You should have finished all the other sections in the workbook before continuing any further. You are now ready to summarize the workbook into an exporting plan for your company.

STEP 2: Identify your international marketing plan audience.

What type of person are you intending to satisfy with this plan? A banker? The company's chief executive officer? The summary should briefly address all the major issues that are important to this person. You may want to have several different summaries, depending on who will read the marketing plan.

STEP 3: Write a one-page summary.

You will now need to write no more than a page summarizing all the previous work sheets you have completed.

Determine which sections are going to be most interesting to your reader. Write one to three sentences that summarize each of the important sections. Keep in mind that this page will probably be the first read by this person. It is extremely important the summary be brief yet contain the information most important to the reader. This section should make the reader want to read the rest of your plan.

Summarize the sections in the order that they appear in the workbook.

INTERNATIONAL MARKETING PLAN SUMMARY

_____

_____

_____

_____

_____

_____

_____

_____

_____

_____

_____

_____

_____

_____

_____

_____

_____

_____

_____

_____

_____

_____

_____

_____

_____

_____

_____

_____

_____

_____

PREPARING AN EXPORT PRICE QUOTATION

Setting proper export prices is crucial to a successful international sales program; prices must be high enough to generate a reasonable profit, yet low enough to be competitive in overseas markets. Basic pricing criteria—costs, market demand, and competition—are the same for domestic and foreign sales. However, a thorough analysis of all cost factors going into producing goods for export, plus operating expenses, result in prices that are different from domestic ones (remember freight costs, insurance, etc., are *pass through costs* identified separately and include little or no markup).

Marginal cost pricing is an aggressive marketing strategy often used in international marketing. The theory behind marginal cost concludes that if the domestic operation is making a profit, the nonrecurrent annual fixed costs are being met. Therefore, only variable costs and profit margin should be used to establish the selling price for goods that will be sold in the international market (this strategy is used for domestic pricing as well. This results in a lower price for international goods yet maintains the profit margin. The risk of this strategy becomes apparent when the domestic operation becomes unprofitable and cannot cover the fixed costs, as each incremental sale could result in a larger loss for the company. This is a complex issue that can yield substantial benefits to a company with manageable risks. Some effort should be made by management to understand this pricing strategy.

COST FACTORS

In calculating an export price, be sure to take into account all the cost factors for which you, the exporter, are liable.

1.   Calculate direct materials and labor costs involved in producing the goods for export.

2.   Calculate your factory overhead costs, prorating the amount of overhead chargeable to your proposed export order.

3.   Deduct any charges not attributable to the export operation, especially if export sales represent only a small part of total sales.

4.   Be sure operating expenses are covered by your gross margin. Some of these expenses directly tied to your export shipments may include:

travel expenses	catalogs, slide shows, video presentations
promotional material	export advertising
commissions	transportation expenses
	(usually *pass through costs*)
packing materials	legal expenses*

PREPARING AN EXPORT PRICE QUOTATION *continued*

office supplies*	patent and trademark fees*
communications*	taxes*
rent*	insurance*
interest*	provision for bad debts
market research	credit checks
translation costs	product modification
consultant fees	freight forwarder fees
	(usually *pass through* costs)

5.   Allow yourself a realistic price margin for unforeseen production costs, operating expenses, unavoidable risks and simple mistakes that are common in any new undertaking.

6.   Also allow yourself a realistic profit or markup.

OTHER FACTORS TO CONSIDER

Market Demand—As in the domestic market, product demand is the key to setting prices in a foreign market. What will the market bear for a specific product or service? What will the estimated consumer price for your product be in each foreign market? If your prices seem out of line, try some simple product modifications to reduce the selling price, such as simplification of technology or alteration of product size to conform to local market norms. Also keep in mind that currency valuations alter the affordability of goods. A good pricing strategy should accommodate fluctuations in currency, although your company should quote prices in dollars to avoid the risks of currency devaluations.

Competition—As in the domestic market, few exporters are free to set prices without carefully evaluating their competitors' pricing policies. The situation is further complicated by the need to evaluate the competition's prices in each foreign market an exporter intends to enter. In a foreign market that is serviced by many competitors, an exporter may have little choice but to match the going price or even go below it to establish a market share. If, however, the exporter's product or service is new to a particular foreign market, it may be possible to set a higher price than normally charged domestically.

*These items will typically represent the expenses of the total operation, so be sure to prorate these to reflect only the operating expenses associated with your export operation.

WORKSHEETS

EXPORT PROGRAMS & SERVICES

This worksheet helps you identify organizational resources that can provide programs and services to assist you in developing your international business plan and increase your export sales.

ORGANIZATIONS

SERVICES	SBA Office	USDOC Office	SBDC	USEAC	Trade Associaton	University/ Comm. College	World Trade Centers
Readiness to Export Assessment							
Market Research Studies							
Counseling							
Training Seminars							
Education Programs							
Publications							
Export Guides							
Databases							
Trade Shows							
Financing							

EXPORT COSTING WORKSHEET

QUOTE PREPARATION

Pricing is a reflection of all costs incurred and influenced by the competitiveness of the marketplace. The quotation must first determine the domestic *ex works** costs and then identify the additional costs incurred to sell overseas.

EXPORT COSTING WORKSHEET

Reference Information
1. Our Reference _____   2. Customer Reference _____

Customer Information:
3. Name _____   5. Cable Address _____
4. Address _____   6. Telex No. _____
_____   7. Fax No. _____

Product Information _____   ### SIC Code _____
8. Product _____   12. Dimensions _____ x _____ x _____
9. No. of Units _____   13. Cubic Measure _____ (sq.in.)
10. Net Weight _____ (unit)   14. Total Measure _____
11. Gross Weight _____   15. H.S. No. _____

Ex Works *Costs*
16. Direct Materials _____
17. Direct Labor _____
18. Factory Burden_____
19. Cost of Goods_____

20. Selling Expenses _____ (should be less than domestic
    sales)
21. General Expenses _____ (includes cost of money
    borrowed)

*Ex works means that the seller fulfills his delivery obligation to the buyer when he has made the goods available at his factory, warehouse or other place of business.

EXPORT COSTING WORKSHEET *continued*

22. Administrative
    Expenses _____
23. Export Marketing Costs (product changes,
    labeling) _____
24. Profit Margin _____
25. *Ex Works* Price _____

Additional Exporting Costs:

26. Foreign sales commission (if applicable)
27. Special export packing costs (typically 1 to 1.5 percent above *ex works* price)
28. Special labeling and marking (to protect from moisture, theft, rough handling)
29. Inland freight to pier (normal domestic common carrier; should also carry insurance)
30. Unloading charges (include demurrage, if any)
31. Terminal charges (include wharfage, if any)
32. Consular documents (includes Shippers Export Declaration [SED], export license and/or certificate of origin)
33. Freight (port-to-port)—determined by freight forwarder
34. Freight forwarder fees (*must* be included)
35. Export insurance (insurance for transit risk; also for credit risk, if credit-worthiness of buyer is unknown
36. Cost of credit (include credit reports, letter of credit costs, amendments, if any)

37. Total additional exporting costs _____

QUOTE = Ex Works Price + Total of additional exporting costs

MAKING THE CONNECTION

Computers and telecommunications can make exporting faster, easier and more profitable. State-of-the-art communications will be even more important in the years ahead, because a flood of innovations has created the "information superhighway" that has changed the way of doing business internationally. Staying current with technical innovations can help you keep your competitive edge.

As an exporter, you need to deal with the time-zone differences between your location and your customer's. You should be as prompt as your in-country competitors when providing after-sales support to your customers. Finally, you want to minimize barriers created by cultural and language differences.

THE ESSENTIALS: PHONE SYSTEM AND FAX

At a minimum, your business should have an adequate telephone system and a facsimile machine. Telephone features should be adequate to support worldwide communications. Some specific features might include:

- the ability to store and dial automatically the numbers you call most frequently. Because overseas calls typically involve dialing at least 14 digits—a special prefix (usually 011) followed by a country code, a city code and then the local number—automatic dialing can save you time.
- conferencing capability—adding one or more parties can be useful in closing a business deal. Communications can be more effective when you, your overseas client and your overseas agent can be linked by a conference call.
- time-delay fax transmission to take advantage of non-peak telephone rates.

Answering Machines and Voice Mail

Competition at the local level can be intense in countries where you plan to sell your product. Closing the time gap between your U. S. offices and those of your customers and agents overseas can save you time and money. These people should have the option of contacting you outside of normal business hours. An answering machine may be sufficient, or you may choose an automated service provided by your local telephone company or a personal answering service. Also, you should be able to retrieve your messages from any place in the world.

Another option is voice mail which allows callers to leave messages for specific employees. More advanced systems can now respond in several languages and guide callers to price quotes or service information, even when your business is closed for the day or weekend. A word of caution: voice messaging is much less common abroad than in the United States and may not always leave a favorable impression on an international customer.

By the turn of the century, new technology will include digital services that can receive voice and written messages in other languages and translate them for you—or simultaneous translations while you are holding a telephone conversation with a party in another country.

Facsimile (FAX) Machines

FAX machines are essential to conducting international business. They are invaluable for the speedy transmission of drawings, diagrams and documents. To cut costs, you may want to have a fax machine capable of storing messages for electronic transmission later, when rates are lower. Machines of that type can usually also broadcast the same fax to several different pre-programmed locations.

With a modem and suitable fax software you can send and receive faxes of documents or invoices directly from your computer. You can broadcast materials from your computer to a list of recipients automatically, at a pre-programmed time. You can receive legible faxes on your computer screen, although conversion to a computer-readable format for additional processing requires Optical Character Recognition (OCR) software, which may require some editing of characters within the scanned text.

> *Rick Champon, owner of Produce Trading Corporation in Merritt Island, Florida, uses a computer-based fax program to send and receive paperwork directly from his computer and a regular fax machine provide additional support. Champon regularly faxes bills of lading to steamship companies and stores the boilerplate forms in his computer. All he has to do is fill in the information for a particular shipment and push a button to send the fax. He does the same with invoices and purchase orders. The appropriate letterheads are stored as images in his computer, and he pulls in the necessary data from his billing and order-entry systems to produce a particular invoice or purchase order in final form.*

If your international fax traffic becomes heavy, you may need a second fax machine. Your phone lines can be arranged so that calls will go to the backup machine if the first line is busy, ensuring that your customers always get through. When you are doing business worldwide, the communications door to your business should be wide open 24 hours a day.

PERSONAL COMPUTERS, MODEMS AND SOFTWARE POWER

You can now call clients in Europe, see their face on your computer screen (while yours can be seen on theirs), share a blueprint on your screens, collaborate on altering or editing it, sign an agreement and dispatch copies to offices around the world. That sort of videoconferencing and computer interfacing will be more common in the years ahead. When international travel is not feasible, you may be able to provide professional and timely after-sales service by using computer-based communications to keep your company ahead of the competition.

In a small firm, a basic personal computer with modem will meet most of your business needs. A personal computer can handle accounting, word processing and store data on your customers and international transactions. Check with a reputable computer store to help determine your business' needs.

Modems—Your Link to the World Market

Your computer, equipped with a modem, becomes a powerful export tool that enables you to communicate with other computers, send and receive e-mail, gather data from libraries around the world and exchange faxes. With a modem and the appropriate software, you can tie into the Internet, an interconnected network of 30 million users of personal and mainframe computers worldwide. Modems can transmit information at differing speeds; the faster the transmission, the lower your costs.

The Internet and World Wide Web

The Internet is a rapidly growing world-wide network of computer users and networks that allows you to: (a) send and receive e-mail; (b) "download" information from libraries and databases throughout the world; and (c) join in electronic discussion groups. The Internet can also help you to sell your product, as Mubashir Cheema of Sparco Communications found:

> *Sparco Communications of Starkville, Mississippi sells 80 percent of its electrical supplies via the Internet. Sparco's 45,000-item catalog can be searched and orders placed via*

> *e-mail (mailserver@sparco.com). "We have at least 500 orders from abroad every day," says General Manager Mubashir Cheema. "You'd be surprised how many people abroad access the Internet."*

To use the Internet, you need a computer and modem and an on-line service that offers Internet access. Getting around the Internet on your own can be difficult. For that reason, you may find it helpful to use software that simplifies your data search. Commercial applications of the Internet are expanding rapidly and will continue to do so in the future. Companies are putting "home pages" on the World Wide Web that provide access to information that includes pictures, audio and even video. Marketing products and services through the Internet and other online computer communications can be profitable, especially for small businesses with limited resources.

Software that combines communication via modem and related functions—such as keeping track of your customers and your contacts with them—is becoming more accessible. These programs can remind you to make calls, place the calls for you and place a complete history of prior contacts with your customers on your computer screen as you communicate with them on-line. With the conversation completed you can dispatch a fax or an e-mail message confirming your agreements.

Power Tools in Action

With computer and modem you can communicate more effectively via e-mail. By using one of the many on-line services, you can send text messages to customers around the world. You will also have your own electronic address and a "mailbox" from which you can collect your messages wherever you are. Some e-mail services offer a text-to-speech capability that can "read" your mail to you. An advantage of e-mail over fax is that e-mail messages are in computer-compatible form, and can be further manipulated, incorporated into documents or relayed from your computer. Your e-mail box can receive messages even when your computer and modem are turned off.

Export-Focused On-Line Services

Trade leads from international companies seeking to buy or represent U.S. products are gathered by US&FCS officers worldwide and are distributed on-line through the Department of Commerce's Economic Bulletin Board. There is a nominal annual fee and a connect-time charge. Another source of trade leads is the World Trade Centers (WTC) Network, where you can advertise your product or service on an electronic bulletin board transmitted globally.

The U.S. Small Business Administration (SBA) supports services available by modem, such as *SBA OnLine*, an electronic bulletin board that expedites information and assistance to the small business community. SBA Online offers information on managing and expanding your business, software for small businesses and gateways to other on-line services, including other federal bulletin boards and Internet e-mail. Mailboxes for different industry sectors and different topic areas, such as international trade, are available to exchange mail with other small businesses to share information.

The SBA also supports **UNINET™**, a new overseas partnering service for small firms competing in global technology markets. UNINET, operated by UNISPHERE, a joint venture broker, is on the Internet, with full image, voice and text, employing the World Wide Web. Participants are small and mid-sized firms in telecommunications, information, environmental, energy and medical technologies. UNINET facilitates finding partners for joint research and development, licensing, co-production, teaming and other types of relationships. Its multimedia presentations, product literature, facility tours, and other material can all be presented to a world-wide audience on the Internet.

> *Cortex Vision Systems of Durham, NC has sold equipment in three countries to customers identified through UNINET. The firm manufactures infrared security surveillance systems which are used in perimeter protection. Cortex has also identified several potential licensees through UNINET.*

Trade Point USA, located in Columbus, Ohio, is the U.S. site for an electronically linked global network of over 50 Trade Points. Through partnerships with electronic service providers, they can help you uncover trade leads, track international shipments and access databases covering U.S. manufacturers and services.

The *International Trade Data Network (ITDN)* has satellite offices throughout the country, many with electronic bulletin boards offering information useful to exporters. Many state commerce departments offer on-line services that help businesses link up with the World Trade Centers (WTC) Network, which posts international offers to sell and buy. The *National Trade Data Bank (NTDB)*, a CD-ROM subscription service of the U.S. Department of Commerce's STAT-USA, is also available on the Internet (*see* Chapter 3 for more about these services).

Electronic Banking

Your communicating computer can expedite the financial tasks of your export business. Many banks provide electronic access to your business balances and statements. Forward-looking banks now route letters of credit, collection on consignment agreements, as well as wire transfer acknowledgments directly to your computer.

> *"With Trade Advantage, a comprehensive PC-based trade system, your company can initiate and monitor import, export and standby letters of credit, collections, and acceptances," says Newark, New Jersey-based First Fidelity Bank's Laureen K. Carlson.*

With the right banks in the loop, your overseas customers can wire letters of credit to your bank, and you can electronically transfer funds to agents or employees abroad.

> *"At CoreStates Bank in Philadelphia, PA, we're offering international collection services electronically," reports Carole Verona, "such as export letter of credit payments, reimbursement collection services, documentary draft collection services, and electronic reporting of export and intra-company cross-border payments. Automated electronic services allow customers to create, send and change letters of credit on their PCs, as well as to create international drafts via the PC."*

Electronic Data Interchange

By the year 2000, 70 percent of all business transactions are expected to be conducted via Electronic Data Interchange (EDI), the electronic transfer of transaction information from computer to computer in an agreed-upon standard format. Importers, for example, can clear the many documents required by the U.S. Customs Service by modem, sending only the data needed to fill in forms rather than the complete form. In 1975, the U.S. Transportation Data Coordinating Committee (TDCC) created a standard called TDCC, used for the electronic transmission of air cargo documentation.

EDI is most useful when the information exchanged is fully integrated into your business' order-entry, delivery and inventory systems. Because EDI allows you to forego entering information manually—doing everything computer-to-computer—it can put your business ahead of your competition. If your communications resources are limited, there are service bureaus that can handle EDI for you.

Tracking Shipments Electronically

Most air express companies now offer free computer software with which you can track your shipments. The software provides access to electronic information, for example, on where your shipment is located, when it was delivered, whether delayed in customs and who received the shipment. Freight forwarders and trucking companies also benefit from electronic tracking, as they move goods and services across international borders.

Frontiers in International Telecommunications

The Internet is just one example of the communications revolution. Today, using ordinary telephone lines, you can see as well as talk with your customer; tomorrow, with more bandwidth, you will be able to showcase your product, and video conferencing will be commonplace. Today, user-friendly software allows you and your overseas customers to collaborate on computer screens; tomorrow, those sessions will be even easier as artificially intelligent computer "agents" expedite your collaboration by seeking needed data from networks or databases. Today, satellites bring advanced communications services to previously isolated areas throughout the globe; tomorrow, even smaller satellite dishes will let you download video business training sessions and information on highly specialized market opportunities in full color from around the world.

What lies ahead is a world where you can reach anyone, anywhere, anytime with interactive multimedia services. Even if you are just now deciding whether to "break into the trade game," you should keep that vision before you. Now you will need to identify the best export markets. Chapter 3, "Identifying International Markets," will help you do this.

CHAPTER 3

IDENTIFYING INTERNATIONAL MARKETS

To succeed in exporting, you must first identify the most profitable international markets for your products or services. Without proper guidance and assistance, however, this process can be time consuming and costly—particularly for a small business.

The U.S. federal government, state governments, trade associations, exporters' associations and foreign governments offer low-cost and easily accessible resources to simplify and speed your foreign market research. This chapter describes those resources and how to use them.

FEDERAL GOVERNMENT RESOURCES

Many government programs and staff are dedicated to helping you, the small business owner, assess whether your product or service is ready to compete in a foreign market. The U.S. government created the Trade Promotion Coordinating Committee (TPCC) in 1990 to consolidate and coordinate the export promotion and trade finance functions of 19 federal agencies. The resulting clear focus on increasing exports has resulted in new strengths in federal export promotion and trade finance programs.

U.S. Export Assistance Centers (EACs)

EACs were authorized by Sec. 202 of the Export Enhancement Act of 1992 and implemented by recommendation of the TPCC's report *Toward a National Export Strategy*. They are designed to provide the U.S. exporting community a single point of contact for all federal export promotion and finance programs. EACs can deliver services directly or refer clients to appropriate public and private sector partners. The Centers integrate representatives of the Small Business Administration (SBA), the Department of Commerce (DOC) and the Export-Import Bank of the United States (Ex-Im Bank) and additional federal agencies at certain sites. Depending upon site-specific needs and feasibility, the Centers are co-located convenient to or in facilities with private and other public sector partners already servicing the exporting community.

Co-located federal agencies concentrate on assisting export-ready firms in all areas of export promotion and trade finance. EAC staff assess and service a company in accordance with standard criteria to determine its stage of export readiness.

Companies considered to be in the start-up stage are referred by the Center counselor to a local resource partner for business start-up assistance and basic "How-to-Export" classes. Resources appropriate for this type of counseling are the SBA's Service Corps of Retired Executives (SCORE) and the Small Business Development Centers (SBDCs).

The U.S. Small Business Administration

Many new-to-export small firms have found the counseling services provided by the SBA's SCORE volunteers particularly helpful. Through your local SBA District office, you can gain access to more than 850 SCORE volunteers with experience in international trade.

> *"SCORE," says Marion Stuart, owner of Learning Wrap-ups, a Unitah, Utah-based teaching aids firm, "has been an incredible support system." Stuart, a former schoolteacher, had developed a hand-held teaching aid for children, but she had no business or marketing experience. So she turned to SCORE for assistance. Learning Wrap-ups is now marketing 21 different teaching aids for math, English, foreign languages and other educational skills throughout the world; exports now account for 15 percent of her sales, most to Western Europe and Australia.*

Two other SBA-sponsored programs are available to small businesses needing management and export advice: SBDCs and Small Business Institutes (SBIs) are affiliated with colleges and universities throughout the United States.

SBDCs offer counseling, training and research assistance on all aspects of small business management.

The SBI program provides small business owners with intensive management counseling from qualified business students who are supervised by faculty. SBIs provide advice on a wide range of management challenges facing small businesses—including finding the best foreign markets for particular products or services.

The U.S. Department of Commerce

The DOC's International Trade Administration (ITA) is a valuable source of advice and information. International trade specialists can help you locate the best foreign markets for your products.

"We have actually been exporting for 15 years, but it's only in the last 3 years that we have targeted our company's export potential," says Dennis Hilling, of Stackhouse Athletic Equipment, a Salem, Oregon-based institutional sporting goods manufacturer. "In the spring of 1994 we participated in a Department of Commerce trade mission to South America as a first targeted effort. By the end of 1994, export sales were 10 percent of our total sales and the total of our growth for that year."

The *United States and Foreign Commercial Service (US&FCS)* helps U.S. firms compete more effectively in the global marketplace with trade specialists in 69 U.S. cities, including in the Export Assistance Centers, and in 70 countries worldwide. US&FCS specialists provide information on foreign markets, agent/distributor location services, trade leads and counseling on business opportunities, trade barriers and prospects abroad.

Check the Department of Commerce's National Trade Data Bank (NTDB) for the US&FCS Country Commercial Guides for each country in which there is a Foreign Commercial Service presence. In addition, the NTDB has Department of State country reports and the Central Intelligence Agency's *World Factbook*.

These are valuable sources for identifying international markets for your exportable products or services.

District Export Councils (DECs) are another useful ITA-sponsored resource. The 51 District Export Councils located around the United States are comprised of 1,800 executives with experience in international trade who volunteer to help small businesses export. Council members come from banks, manufacturing companies, law offices, trade associations, state and local agencies and educational institutions. They draw upon their experience to encourage, educate, counsel and guide potential, new and seasoned exporters in their individual marketing needs.

The United States Department of Agriculture

If you have an agricultural product, you may want to investigate the U.S. Department of Agriculture's (USDA) *Foreign Agricultural Service (FAS)*. With posts in 80 embassies and consulates worldwide, the FAS can obtain specific overseas market information for your product. The FAS also maintains sector specialists in the United States to monitor foreign markets for specific U.S. agricultural products. The FAS Trade Assistance and Planning Office (TAPO) can assist you in finding out more about the export programs of the USDA.

The United States Export-Import Bank

Country desk officers at The United States Export-Import Bank (Ex-Im Bank) can provide you with information about a country's political and economic risk.

State Economic Development Offices

Most state commerce and economic development offices have international trade specialists to assist you. Many states have trade offices in overseas markets.

> *"We made our first trip to Japan with the help of the Alabama state trade development office," says Anand Chitlangia, president of Birmingham-based Nidek Medical. "After attending the 'Made in USA' fair, we began successfully selling our oxygen concentrators in Japan." Exporting since 1987, Nidek's export sales now account for 60 percent of its total revenue. The company currently exports to Asia, the Middle East, Western Europe and Latin America. Most of their export sales are done through exclusive distributors.*

Port authorities are a wealth of export information. Although traditionally associated with transportation services, many port authorities around the country have expanded their services to provide export training programs and foreign-marketing research assistance. For example, the New York-New Jersey Port Authority provides extensive services to exporters including XPORT, a full-service export trading company. XPORT, created in 1982, is the first publicly sponsored U.S. trading company. XPORT specializes in assisting small- to medium-size businesses in New York and New Jersey, to introduce their products in world markets. Among the services XPORT can offer are market research, transportation of products, contacting local distributors and market entry strategies.

> *Ruine Design Associates, Inc., New York, designers of furniture, custom lighting and accessories, have increased their export sales from 0 to 30 percent of gross sales since their first XPORT-assisted exhibit in Japan three years ago. The response from the Japanese was astounding. "They didn't know Americans could design," indicated Paul Ruine, president and head designer of Ruine. "XPORT became the lens that allowed us to see what we couldn't see before." Their entry into Japan was through XPORT's Tokyo office. Ruine*

Design Associates is now selling in Brazil, Germany, Taiwan, Hong Kong, Mexico, Canada, Spain and Holland.

Foreign Embassy Commercial Sections
Talk to the Commercial Attache assigned to the embassy of the country to which you wish to export.

PRIVATE SECTOR RESOURCES
In addition to government-supported resources, private sector organizations can also provide invaluable assistance.

Exporters' Associations
World Trade Centers, import-export clubs and organizations such as the American Association of Exporters and Importers and the Small Business Exporter's Association can aid in your foreign market research.

Trade Associations
The national Federation of International Trade Associations lists over 150 organizations in the United States to help new-to-export small businesses enter international markets. Many of these associations maintain libraries, databanks and established relationships with foreign governments to assist in your exporting efforts.

More than 5,000 trade and professional associations currently operate in the United States; many actively promote international trade activities for their members.

The Telecommunications Industry Association is just one association which leads frequent overseas trade missions and monitors the pulse of foreign market conditions around the globe. Whatever your product or service, a trade association probably exists that can help you obtain information on domestic and foreign markets.

Chambers of Commerce, particularly state chambers, or chambers located in major industrial areas, often employ international trade specialists who gather information on markets abroad.

HOW TO GATHER FOREIGN MARKET RESEARCH
Now that you know where to begin your research, you should next identify the most profitable foreign markets for your products or services. You will need to:
* classify your product;

- find countries with the largest and fastest growing markets for your product;
- determine which foreign markets will be the most penetrable;
- define and narrow down those export markets you intend to pursue;
- talk to U.S. customers doing business internationally; and
- research export efforts of U.S. competitors.

Classifying your product

The *Standard Industrial Classification (SIC)* code is the system by which the U.S. government classifies its goods and services. Knowing the proper code for your product or service can be useful in collecting and analyzing data available in the United States.

Data originating from outside the United States—or information available from international organizations—are organized under the *Standard International Trade Classification (SITC)* system, which may assign a different code to your product or service.

Another method of classifying products for export is the *Harmonized System (HS)*. Knowing the HS classification number, the SIC and the SITC codes for your product is essential to obtaining domestic and international trade and tariff information. DOC and USDA trade specialists can assist in identifying the codes for your products. The codes are listed on the *National Trade Data Bank (NTDB)*. The U.S. Bureau of the Census (USBC) can help identify the HS number for your product.

Finding countries with the largest and fastest growing markets for your product

At this stage of your research, learn where your domestic competitors are exporting. Trade associations can often provide data on where companies in a particular industry sector are exporting their products. The three largest markets for U.S. products are Canada, Japan and Mexico. Yet these countries may not be the largest markets for your product.

Three key U.S. government databases can identify those countries which represent significant export potential for your product: *SBA's Automated Trade Locator Assistance System* (SB*Atlas*), *Foreign Trade Report FT925* and the U.S. Department of Commerce's *National Trade Data Bank (NTDB)*.

SB*Atlas* is offered only by the U.S. Small Business Administration and provides current market information to SBA clients on world markets suitable for their products and services. This valuable research tool supplies small business exporters with information about where their products are being bought and sold and which countries offer the largest markets. The country reports detail products imported and exported by various foreign nations. Data are supplied by the DOC's USBC and member nations of the United Nations, and presented in an easy-to-read report format. This information can be obtained through a SCORE counselor at SBA District Offices, at EACs, SBDCs and SBIs. This service is free to requesting small businesses.

Foreign Trade Report FT925 gives a monthly country-specific breakdown of imports and exports by SITC number. Available by subscription from the Government Printing Office, the FT925 can also be obtained through EACs, DOC ITA offices, or downloaded from the National Trade Data Bank.

The NTDB, a CD-ROM subscription service of the Department of Commerce's STAT-USA, is a trade library of more than 190,000 documents on export promotion and international economic information from more than 20 federal sources. With the NTDB, you can conduct databank searches on markets, tariffs and non-tariff barriers, importers, logistics and product information. The NTDB can be purchased by subscription and used with a CD-ROM reader, or can be used at Export Assistance Centers, many DOC ITA offices and at nearly 1,000 federal depository libraries throughout the United States. The NTDB is also available on the Internet (*see* Chapter 2).

Once you learn the largest markets for your products, determine which are the fastest growing. Find out what demographic patterns and cultural considerations will affect your market penetration.

Several publications, most available on the NTDB, provide geographic and demographic statistical information pertinent to your product: *The World Factbook*, produced by the Central Intelligence Agency; *World Population*, published by DOC's USBC; *The World Bank Atlas*, available from the World Bank; and the United Nations *International Trade Statistics Yearbook*. Volume Two of this U.N. publication (available at many libraries) lists international demand for commodities over a five-year period.

DETERMINING THE MOST PENETRABLE MARKETS

Once you have defined and narrowed a few prospective foreign markets for your product, you will need to examine them in detail. At this stage you should ask the following questions:

- how does the quality of your product or service compare with that of goods already available in your target foreign markets?

- is your price competitive in the markets you are considering?
- who are your major customers?

Answering these questions may seem overwhelming at first, but many resources are available to help you select which foreign markets are most conducive to selling your product. Use the workbook in the first part of this guide to assist you.

The DOC's ITA can link you with specific foreign markets. ITA offices are part of the US&FCS and communicate directly with FCS officers working in U.S. embassies worldwide.

FCS staff and in-country market research firms produce in-depth reports on selected products and industries that can answer many of your questions regarding foreign market penetration.

You can also order a *Comparison Shopping Service (CSS)* report through ITA district offices. The report is a low-cost way to conduct research without having to leave the United States.

SBA's and DOC's *Export Legal Assistance Network (ELAN)* provides new exporters with answers to their initial legal questions. Local attorneys counsel small businesses on a one-time basis to address their export-related legal questions. These volunteer attorneys can address questions pertaining to contract negotiations, licensing, credit collections procedures and documentation. There is no charge for this one-time service, available through SBA or DOC district offices.

The *Trade Opportunities Program (TOP)* of the DOC can furnish U.S. small businesses with trade leads from foreign companies that want to buy or represent their products or services. These trade leads are available in electronic form from the DOC's Electronic Bulletin Board (*see* Section 8). Participating companies must pay a modest fee to gain access to this service.

Other important issues about the target foreign markets you should explore are:

- political risk considerations,
- the cultural environment and
- whether any product modifications, such as packaging or labelling, will make the product more "exportable."

Identifying market-specific issues is easily accomplished by contacting foreign government representatives in the United States. Commercial posts of foreign governments located within embassies and consulates can assist you in obtaining specific market and product information.

American Chambers of Commerce (AmChams) abroad can also be an invaluable resource. As affiliates of the U.S. Chamber of Commerce, 84 AmChams, located in 59 countries, collect and disseminate extensive information on foreign markets (*see* Part II, Section 7). While membership fees are usually required, the small investment can be worth it for the information received.

Another fundamental question to ask country-specific experts is what market barriers, such as tariffs or import restrictions, exist for your product. You should consult specialists at the U.S. Trade Representative (USTR) office on trade barriers. Trade barriers can include non-tariff barriers.

Tariffs are taxes imposed on imported goods. In many cases, tariffs raise the price of imported goods to the level of domestic goods. Often tariffs become barriers to imported products because the amount of tax imposed makes it impossible for exporters to sell their products profitably in foreign markets.

Non-tariff barriers are laws or regulations that a country enacts to protect domestic industries against foreign competition. Such non-tariff barriers may include subsidies for domestic goods, import quotas or regulations on import quality.

To determine the rate of duty, you will need to identify the Harmonized Tariff section which corresponds to the product you wish to export. Each country has its own schedule of duty rates corresponding to the section of the Harmonized System of Tariff Nomenclature, I–XXII.

DEFINING WHICH MARKETS TO PURSUE

Once you know the largest, fastest growing and most penetrable markets for your product or service, you must then define your export strategy.

Do not choose too many markets. For most small businesses, three foreign markets will be more than enough, initially. You may want to test one market and then move on to secondary markets as your "expertise" develops. Focusing on regional, geographic clusters of countries can also be more cost effective than choosing markets scattered around the globe.

After you have identified the best export markets, your next step will be to determine the best way to distribute your product abroad. Chapter 4, "Foreign Market Entry," discusses distribution methods.

FOREIGN MARKET ENTRY

Having determined the best international markets for your products, you now need to evaluate the most profitable way to get your products to potential customers in these markets.

There are several methods of foreign market entry including exporting, licensing, joint venture and off-shore production. The method you choose will depend on a variety of factors including the nature of your particular product or service and the conditions for market penetration which exist in the foreign target market.

Exporting can be accomplished by selling your product or service directly to a foreign firm, or indirectly, through the use of an export intermediary, such as a commissioned agent, or an export management or trading company. Your company can also employ different methods of market entry for each country, so that they can be most effective in reaching each particular market:

> *"We have a mix of approaches, including in-country agents, strategic alliances and in-country representatives to reach into various markets," says Susan Corrales-Diaz, president of Systems Integrated, an Orange, California computer systems business involved in exporting for over 7 years. "Small business can effectively compete in the expanding global economy by maintaining a variety of exporting relationships." SI's export sales represent about 30 percent of total sales; their largest foreign customer is China.*

International joint ventures can be a very effective means of market entry. Joint ventures overseas are often accomplished by licensing or off-shore production. Licensing involves a contractual agreement whereby you assign the rights to distribute or manufacture your product or service to a foreign company or individual. Off-shore production requires either setting up your own facility or sub-contracting the manufacturing of your product to an assembly operator.

Licensing and off-shore production are discussed in Chapter 8, "Strategic Alliances and Foreign Investment Opportunities."

EXPORTING

Of the various methods of foreign market entry, exporting is most commonly used by small businesses. Start-up costs and risks are limited, and profits can be realized early on.

There are two basic ways to export: direct or indirect. The direct method requires your company to find a foreign buyer and then make all arrangements for shipping your products overseas. If this method seems beyond the scope of your business' in-house capabilities at this time, do not abandon the idea of exporting. Consider using an export intermediary.

> *American Cedar, Inc., a Hot Springs, Arkansas, producer of cedar products reports that 30 percent of its product sales now comes from exporting: "We displayed our products at a trade show, and an export management company found us. They helped alleviate the hassles of exporting directly. Our products are now being distributed throughout the European Community from a distribution point in France," says American Cedar president Julian McKinney.*

INDIRECT EXPORTING

Many small businesses like American Cedar have been exporting indirectly by using an export intermediary. There are several kinds of export intermediaries you should consider.

Commissioned agents

Commissioned agents act as "brokers," linking your product or service with a specific foreign buyer. Generally, the agent or broker will not fulfill the orders, but rather will pass them to you for your acceptance. However, they may assist, in some cases, with export logistics such as packing, shipping and export documentation.

Export Management Companies (EMCs)

EMCs act as your "off-site" export department, representing your product—along with the products of other companies—to prospective overseas purchasers. The management company looks for business on behalf of your company and takes care of all aspects of the export transaction. Hiring an EMC is often a viable option for smaller companies that lack the time and expertise to break into international markets on their own.

EMCs will often use the letterhead of your company, negotiate export contracts and then provide after-sales support. EMCs may assist in arranging export financing for the exporters, but they do not generally guarantee payment to the manufacturers. Some of the specific functions an EMC will perform include:

- conducting market research to determine the best foreign markets for your products;
- attending trade shows and promoting your products overseas;
- assessing proper distribution channels;
- locating foreign representatives and/or distributors;
- arranging export financing;
- handling export logistics, such as preparing invoices, arranging insurance, customs documentation, etc.; and
- advising on the legal aspects of exporting and other compliance matters dealing with domestic and foreign trade regulations.

EMCs usually operate on a commission basis, although some work on a retainer and some take title to the goods they sell, making a profit on the markup. It is becoming increasingly common for EMCs to take title to goods.

Export Trading Companies (ETCs)

ETCs perform many of the functions of EMCs. However, they tend to be demand-driven and transaction-oriented, acting as an agent between the buyer and seller. Most trading companies source U.S. products for their overseas buyers. If you offer a product that is competitive and popular with the ETC buyers, you are likely to get repeat business. Most ETCs will take title to your goods for export and will pay your company directly. This arrangement practically eliminates the risks associated with exporting for the manufacturer.

ETC Cooperatives

ETC cooperatives are U.S. government-sanctioned co-ops of companies with similar products who seek to export and gain greater foreign market share. Many agricultural concerns have benefited from ETC cooperative exporting, and many associations have sponsored ETC cooperatives for their member companies. The National Machine Tool Builders' Association, the Outdoor Power Equipment Institute and the National Association of Energy Service Companies are a few examples of associations with ETC co-ops. Check with your particular trade association for further information.

The Export Trading Company Act of 1982

This legislation encourages the use and formation of EMCs/ETCs by changing the antitrust and banking environments under which these companies operate. The Act increases access to export financing by permitting bank holding companies to invest in ETCs and reduces restrictions on trade finance provided by financial institutions. Under the Act, banks are allowed to make equity investments in qualified ETCs.

Foreign Trading Companies

Some of the world's largest trading companies are located outside the United States. They can often be a source of export opportunity. United States & Foreign Commercial Service (US&FCS) representatives in embassies around the world can tell you more about trading companies located in a given foreign market.

Exporting through an Intermediary—Factors to Consider

Working with an EMC/ETC makes sense for many small businesses. The right relationship, if structured properly, can bring enormous benefits to the manufacturer, but no business relationship is without its potential drawbacks. The manufacturer should carefully weigh the pros and cons before entering into a contract with an EMC/ETC.

Some advantages include:
- Your product gains exposure in international markets—with little or no commitment of staff and resources from your company.
- The EMC/ETC's years of experience and well-established network of contacts may help you to gain faster access to international markets than you could through establishing a relationship with a foreign-based partner.
- Using an intermediary lowers or eliminates your export start-up costs, and, therefore, the risks associated with exporting. You can negotiate your contract with an EMC so that you pay nothing until the first order is received.
- Your intermediary will guide you through the export process step-by-step. Over time, you will develop your own export skills.

Some disadvantages of exporting through an intermediary include:
- You lose some control over the way in which your product is marketed and serviced. Your company's image and name are at stake. You will want to incorporate any concerns you may have into your contract,

and you will want to monitor closely the activities and progress of your intermediary.

- You may lose part of your export-sales profit margin by discounting your price to an intermediary. However, you may find that the economies of scale realized through increased production offset this loss.

- Using an intermediary can result in a higher price being passed on to the overseas buyer or end-user. This may or may not affect your competitive position in the market. The issue of pricing should be addressed at the outset.

Export Merchants/Export Agents

Export merchants and agents will purchase and then re-package products for export, assuming all risks and selling to their own customers. This export intermediary option should be considered carefully, as your company could run the risk of losing control over your product's pricing and marketing in overseas markets.

Piggyback Exporting

Allowing another company, which already has an export distribution system in place, to sell your company's product in addition to its own is called "piggyback" exporting.

Piggyback exporting has several advantages. This arrangement can help you gain immediate foreign market access. Also, all the requisite logistics associated with selling abroad are borne by the exporting company.

How to Find Export Intermediaries

Small businesses often report that intermediaries find them—at trade fairs and through trade journals where their products have been advertised—so it can often pay to get the word out that you are interested in exporting.

One way to begin your search for a U.S.-based export intermediary is in the *Yellow Pages* of your local phone directory. In just a few initial phone calls, you should be able to determine whether indirect exporting is an option you want to pursue further.

The National Association of Export Companies (NEXCO) and the National Federation of Export Associations (NFEA) are two associations that can assist in your efforts to find export intermediaries. The *Directory of Leading Export Management Companies* is another useful source (*see* Part II, The Exporter's Directory).

The U.S. Department of Commerce (DOC)'s Office of Export Trading Company Affairs (OETCA) can also assist in providing information on how to locate ETCs and EMCs, as well as ETC cooperatives in the U.S. The office, under a joint public/private partnership, compiles the *Export Yellow Pages*, which provides the names and addresses of EMCs/ETCs, as well as other export service companies, such as banks and freight forwarders. Manufacturers, or producers, can also be listed in the guide free of charge; 50,000 copies are distributed worldwide annually. Contact your local DOC district office or U.S. Export Assistance Center for information on being listed or for a free copy of the directory. The directory is also on the National Trade Data Bank.

Locating the best export intermediary to represent you overseas is important. Do your homework before signing an agreement.

DIRECT EXPORTING

While indirect exporting offers many advantages, direct exporting also has its rewards: although initial outlays and the associated risks are greater, so too can be the profits.

Direct exporting signals a commitment on the part of company management to fully engage in international trade. It may require that you dedicate a staff person or even several personnel to support your export efforts, and company management may have to travel abroad frequently.

Selling directly to an international buyer means that you will have to handle the logistics of moving the goods overseas.

Different Approaches to Direct Exporting

Sales Representatives/Agents

Like manufacturers' representatives in the United States, foreign-based representatives or "agents" work on a commission basis to locate buyers for your product. Your representative most likely will handle several complementary, but non-competing, product lines. An agent is, generally, a representative with authority to make commitments on behalf of your firm. Be careful, therefore, about using the terms interchangeably. Your agreement should specify whether the agent/representative has legal authority to obligate the firm.

Distributors

Foreign distributors, in comparison, purchase merchandise from the U.S. company and re-sell it at a profit. They maintain an inventory of your product, which allows the buyer to receive the goods quickly. Distributors often provide after-sales service to the buyer.

Your agreement with any overseas business partner—whether a representative, agent or distributor—should address whether the arrangement is exclusive or non-exclusive, the territory to be covered, the length of the association,
and other issues. (*see* Chapter 5, *The Export Transaction*, for additional information on negotiating agent/distributor agreements.)

Finding overseas buyers for your products need not be more difficult than
locating a representative here in the United States. It may require, however,
an investment of time and resources to travel to your target market to meet
face-to-face with prospective partners. One way to identify those interested in
your product is to tap the DOC's Agent/Distributor Service. This program
provides a customized search to identify agents, distributors and representatives for U.S. products based on the foreign companies' examination of the
U.S. product literature.

Other sources of leads to find foreign agents and distributors are trade
associations, foreign chambers of commerce in the United States and
American chambers of commerce located in foreign countries.

Many publications can be useful. The Manufacturers' Agents National
Association also has a roster of agents in Europe (*see* Part II, The Exporter's
Directory).

Foreign government buying agents

Foreign government agencies or quasi-governmental agencies are often
responsible for procurement. In some instances, countries require an in-country
agent to access these procurement opportunities. This can often represent significant export potential for U.S. companies, particularly in markets where
U.S. technology and know-how are valued. Foreign country commercial
attaches in the United States can provide you with the appropriate in-country
procurement office.

Retail sales

If you produce consumer goods, you may be able to sell directly to a foreign retailer. You can either hire a sales representative to travel to your target
market with your product literature and samples and call on retailers, or you
can introduce your products to retailers through direct-mail campaigns. The
direct-marketing approach will save commission fees and travel expenses. You
may want to combine trips to your target markets with exploratory visits to
retailers. Such face-to-face meetings will reinforce your direct marketing.

Direct sales to end-user

Your product line will determine whether direct sales to the end-user are a viable option for your company. A manufacturer of medical equipment, for example, may be able to sell directly to hospitals. Other major end-users include foreign governments, schools, businesses and individual consumers.

HOW TO FIND BUYERS

Advertise in Trade Journals

Many small businesses report that foreign buyers often find them. An ad placed in a trade journal or a listing in the DOC's *Commercial News USA* can often yield innumerable inquiries from abroad. *Commercial News USA* is a catalog-magazine featuring U.S. products and distributed to 138,000 business readers in over 161 countries around the world and to over 650,000 Economic Bulletin Board users in 18 countries. Fees vary with the size of the listing. Many U.S. companies have had enormous success in locating buyers through this vehicle.

Participate in Catalog and Video/Catalog exhibitions

Catalog and Video/Catalog exhibitions are another low-cost means of advertising your product abroad. Your products are introduced to potential partners at major international trade shows—and you never have to leave the United States. For a small fee, the US&FCS officers in embassies show your catalogs or videos to interested agents, distributors and other potential buyers.

A number of private sector publications also offer U.S. companies the opportunity to display their products in catalogs sent abroad. A few include Johnston International's *Export Magazine, The Journal of Commerce* and the Thomas Publishing Company's *American Literature Review*.

Pursue Trade Leads

Rather than wait for potential foreign customers to contact you, another option is to search out foreign companies looking for the particular product you produce. Trade leads from international companies seeking to buy or represent U.S. products are gathered by US&FCS officers worldwide and are distributed on-line through the DOC's Economic Bulletin Board. There is a nominal annual fee and a connect-time charge. The leads also are published daily in *The Journal of Commerce* under the heading, "Trade Opportunities Program" and in other commercial news outlets.

Another source of trade leads is the World Trade Centers (WTC) *Network*, where you can advertise your product or service on an electronic bulletin board transmitted globally.

If your product is agricultural, the U.S. Department of Agriculture (USDA) Foreign Agricultural Service (FAS) disseminates trade leads collected by their 80 overseas offices. These leads may be accessed through the *AgExport* FAX polling system, the *AgExport Trade Leads Bulletin, The Journal of Commerce* or on several electronic bulletin boards.

Exhibit at Trade Shows

Trade shows also are another means of locating foreign buyers. DOC's **Foreign Buyer Program** certifies a certain number of U.S. trade shows each year. Foreign buyers are actively recruited by DOC commercial officers, and special services—such as meeting areas and translators—are provided to encourage and facilitate private business discussions.

International trade shows are another excellent way to market your product abroad. Many U.S. small businesses find that going to a foreign trade show once just is not enough.

Through a certification program DOC also supports about 80 international fairs and exhibitions held in markets worldwide. U.S. exhibitors receive pre- and post-event assistance. The USDA FAS sponsors about 15 major shows overseas each year.

Participate in Trade Missions

Participating in overseas trade missions is yet another way to meet foreign buyers. Public/private trade missions are often organized cooperatively by federal and state international trade agencies and trade associations. Arrangements are handled for you so that the process of meeting prospective partners or buyers is simplified.

Matchmaker Trade Delegations are DOC-sponsored trade missions to select foreign markets. Your company is matched carefully with potential agents and distributors interested in your product.

Being properly prepared for the kinds of inquiries you might encounter on overseas trade missions is important. The Small Business Administration offers pre-mission training sessions through some of its district offices, the Export Assistance Centers and the Service Corps of Retired Executives (SCORE) program.

Contact Multilateral Development Banks

In developing countries, large infrastructure projects are often funded by multilateral development banks such as the World Bank, the African, Asian,

Inter-American Development Banks and the European Bank for Reconstruction and Development. Multilateral development bank (MDB) projects often represent extensive opportunities for U.S. small businesses to compete for project work. Small businesses can be key beneficiaries for sub-contracting opportunities when larger U.S. firms win major project funding. DOC's Office of Multilateral Development Bank Operations (MDBO) estimates that MDB projects could amount to at least $15 billion dollars in export contracts for U.S. businesses.

The MDBO and its Multilateral Development Bank Counseling Center help U.S. business gain access to the many export opportunities created by project financing from the MDBs. The MDB Counseling Center provides U.S. business with commercial information on MDB opportunities, individual counseling and guidance, on-line access (through Internet or the Economic Bulletin Board) to the MDBs and business outreach around the United States. Additionally, the DOC's Office of Energy, Infrastructure, and Machinery, Infrastructure Division can assist in identifying contracting and subcontracting opportunities.

A list of MDBs is included in Part II, The Exporter's Directory.

QUALIFYING POTENTIAL BUYERS OR REPRESENTATIVES

Once you locate a potential foreign buyer or representative, the next step is to qualify them by reputation and financial position. First, obtain as much information as possible from the company itself. Here are a few sample questions you will want to ask:

- What is the company's history and what are the qualifications and backgrounds of the principal officers?
- Does the company have adequate trained personnel, facilities, resources to devote to your business?
- What is their current sales volume?
- What is the size of their inventory?
- How will they market your product (retail, wholesale or direct)?
- Which territories or areas of the country do they cover?
- Do they have other U.S. or foreign clients? Are any of these clients your competitors? It is important to obtain references from several current clients.
- What types of customers do they serve?
- Do you publish a catalogue?
- What is their sales force?

When you have this background information and are comfortable about proceeding, then obtain a credit report about their financial position. DOC's *World Trade Data Reports* (*WTDR*s), available from the nearest U.S. Export Assistance Center or your local District ITA Office, are compiled by US&FCS officers. A *WTDR* can usually provide an in-depth profile of the prospective company you are investigating.

There are also several commercial services for qualifying potential partners, such as Dun & Bradstreet's *Business Identification Service* and *Graydon* reports. U.S. banks and their correspondent banks or branches overseas, and foreign banks located in the United States can provide specific financial information.

Cultural Considerations

Keep in mind that cultural sensitivities will affect your market entry in any country outside the United States, including Canada. Do not assume that because the language of business is English, the way of doing business is American. Take the time to research cultural considerations along with market trends. A good overview of doing business with most nations is presented in *International Business Practices* or in *Culturegrams*. (*See* Exporter's Guide, Part II.)

In this chapter we have discussed methods of market entry, how to find potential foreign buyers and representatives and how to qualify whom you will be doing business with overseas. Advance market research and preparation is the best way for a small business to define a potential export market.

The next question that needs to be explored involves how to accomplish the business of exporting—that is, how the deal should be structured, the topic of Chapter 5, "The Export Transaction."

THE EXPORT TRANSACTION

PRICING

Pricing products to be competitive in international markets can be a challenge; pricing that works in one market may be totally uncompetitive in another. Although there is no one formula for establishing prices for exported products, there are a number of strategic and technical considerations that you can make in order to determine an appropriate pricing structure.

A pricing strategy is a key component of your export marketing plan and should be an integral part of your market penetration objectives. Your goals will vary depending on the target overseas market. Are you entering the market with a new or unique product? Are you selling excess or obsolete products? Can your product demand a higher price because of brand recognition or superior quality? Maybe you are willing to reduce profits to gain market share for long-term growth. Your pricing decisions will be affected by your company's goals.

It is important to obtain as much information as possible on local market prices as part of your market research. Pricing information can be collected in several ways. One source is overseas distributors and agents of similar products of equivalent quality. When feasible, traveling to the country where your products will be sold provides an excellent opportunity to gather pricing information. The U.S. Department of Commerce (DOC) can also assist in determining appropriate prices through its *Customized Sales Survey*.

To compile the *Customized Sales Survey*, DOC's United States & Foreign Commercial Service (US&FCS) research specialists in the target country interview importers, distributors, retailers, wholesalers, end-users and local producers of comparable products. They also inspect similar products on the market. Your customized report, available for a reasonable fee, is usually completed within 45 days.

Marketing Your Product

To successfully market a product in a domestic market, the manufacturer must take into consideration consumer preference, industry standards, correct labelling and other consumer-driven considerations.

When entering a foreign market, the manufacturer should consider the tastes and preferences in each market as part of marketing strategy. Frequently, only a small change may be required to market the product successfully. The color of the product, the design of the package, the size of the product all may need adjustment.

Consideration should be given to the product name (it may inadvertently have a negative connotation in the local language), cultural and/or religious connotations, appearance of container, compliance to standards (different electrical power, metric dimensions and local product regulations).

Another consideration when planning market strategy is understanding *ISO 9000*. Competitiveness in foreign countries—particularly on procurement bidding—is showing increased reliance on ISO 9000 compliance and designations. In many instances, subcontractors supplying parts or services for major overseas contractors are also required by the terms of foreign government contracts to be ISO 9000 qualified. *The International Standards Organization (ISO)* was founded in 1946 by 25 national standardization organizations including the American National Standards Institute (ANSI). Today some 100 countries have approved ISO certification for voluntary application.

In 1987, the ISO issued ISO 9000, a series of five documents (ISO 9000, 9001, 9002, 9003 and 9004) that provide guidance on the selection and implementation of an appropriate quality management program (system) for a supplier's operations, rather than the actual products. The purpose of the ISO 9000 series is to document, implement and demonstrate the quality assurance systems used by companies that supply goods and services internationally. ISO standards are required to be reviewed every five years. Revised standards were last published in mid-1994. Information on these revisions can be obtained from:

The American Society for Quality Control (ASQC)
611 East Wisconsin Avenue
Milwaukee, WI 53202
Phone: 414/272-8575 or 800/248-1946
FAX: 414/272-1734

There are three ways for a manufacturer to prove compliance with the requirements of one of the ISO 9000 standards: Manufacturers may evaluate their quality system and self-declare the conformance of the system to one of the ISO 9000 quality systems. Second-party evaluations occur when the buyer requires and conducts quality system evaluations of suppliers. These evaluations are mandatory only for companies wishing to become suppliers to that buyer. Third-party quality systems and evaluations and registrations may be voluntary or mandatory and are conducted by persons or organizations independent of both the supplier and the buyer. Interpretations of an ISO 9000 standard may not be consistent from one registrar to another.

The supplier's quality system is registered, not an individual product. Consequently, quality system registration does not imply product conformity to any given set of requirements. The demand for ISO 9000 registration in Europe and elsewhere seems to be coming primarily from the marketplace as a contractual rather than a regulatory requirement. As conformity to the ISO 9000 standards becomes recognized and required by foreign and domestic buyers and used by manufacturers as a competitive marketing tool, the demand for ISO 9000 compliance is expected to increase in non-regulated areas. It is therefore critical for manufacturers to determine what are their buyers' requirements regarding ISO 9000 compliance. Additional information on U.S., foreign and international voluntary standards, government regulations and rules of certification for nonagricultural products is available from:

National Center for Standards & Certification Information (NCSCI)
National Institute of Standards and Technology (NIST)
TRF Building, Room A163
Gaithersburg, MD 20899
Phone: 301/975-4040
FAX: 301/926-1559

For information on the EC 1992 Unified Market program, copies of Unified Market regulations, background information on the EC or assistance regarding specific EC trade opportunities or potential problems, contact:

The Office of EC Affairs
International Trade Administration, Room 3036
14th and Constitution Avenue, N.W.
Washington, D.C. 20230
Phone: 202/482-5823
FAX: 202/482-2155

Methods of International Pricing

The cost-plus method of international pricing is based on your domestic costs plus additional exporting costs such as international sales and promotional costs, product modification, etc. (Remember, costs associated with insuring or delivery are usually "pass through costs" that do not have a mark-up component in arriving at a selling price.) Any costs not applicable, such as domestic marketing costs, are subtracted from the overall cost prior to markup to your selling price. The cost-plus method allows you to maintain your domestic profit margin percentage, and thus to set a suitable price. This method does not, however, take into account local market conditions; your price may be too high to compete in a foreign market.

Different marketing costs and/or modifications to the product could change the cost basis dramatically, making the product either more or less costly for export. As a result, using the "marginal-cost" method provides a more realistic means of determining true cost of producing your product for export.

To use the marginal-cost method, first determine the *fixed costs*, if any, of producing an additional unit for export. Fixed costs are defined as costs which occur whether or not the company is selling anything; for example, mortgage payments on land or buildings. If a company is operating at a profit, and additional assets are not being employed, fixed costs have been covered. At this point, any additional costs of producing products are termed *variable costs*.

There may be instances where additional assets are not needed to meet international sales requirements. In this case, the company would generally only be concerned with variable costs, operating expenses, taxes and net profit in determining the product sales price.

A company may have to purchase new machinery to meet international sales demands. Obviously, there would be a fixed cost component to international production costs (fixed costs would include amortized payment of the equipment). In this case, a fixed-cost component must be included in the above example to reach the product sales price.

Some international expenses may include:

Packaging

Local regulations and customs may require special labelling, translated instructions or different packaging to appeal to local tastes. The selected mode of distribution may also require a particular kind of packaging.

Foreign Market Research

There may be fees for specialized services and publications used to gather market information.

Advertising and Marketing

Firms selling directly into new markets will most likely be responsible for the entire promotional effort. The firm can incur high initial outlays to establish product recognition in the new market. If an agent, distributor or trading company is employed, they can handle advertising and marketing as part of their contract.

Translation, Consulting and Legal Fees

Product instructions, sales agreements and other documentation typically will need to be translated into the local language. Be aware that idioms and words can differ greatly in regions using the same language. Expert translation of product labeling and instructions will enhance local marketing. Although many sales agreements are standard, it is advisable to have legal counsel to review all binding documents.

Foreign Agent/Distributor Product Information and Training

Agents and distributors may require special training to effectively market and service your products. This is true even if the agent sells products similar to your firm's products. Training will not only enable the agent to better represent your company's interests but gain a better understanding of your product.

After-Sales Service Costs

Product warranties and service contracts will enhance your product's image as a quality item. An appropriate after-sales service guarantee can support your sales efforts in the new market. Do not, however, promise service or warranties based on U.S. standards that you cannot deliver.

After taking these expenses into account, insurance, freight, duties and a profit margin can be added to arrive at a customer price. Depending on the market, currency fluctuations can significantly affect your locally based profit margin and the final price offered to the customer. *New-to-export companies should price products in U.S. dollars and request payment in dollars.* This is not an unusual request.

High-Price Option

This approach may be appropriate if your company is selling a new product, or if you are trying to position your product or service at the upper-end of the market. Selecting this option may attract competition and limit the market for your product while, at the same time, produce big profit margins.

Moderate-Price Option

This is a lower risk approach as contrasted to the high- or low-price option. Here you should be able to match competitors, build a market position and produce reasonable profit margins.

Low-Price Option

This approach may be relevant if you are trying to reduce inventory and do not have a long-term commitment to the market. You will impede competition but also produce low profit margins.

There may be no single strategy that is ideal for every company. Companies often draw upon a mix of options for each market or product.

Setting Terms of Sale

Price Quotations

The pro-forma invoice is the most commonly used document to give price quotations to potential customers. The quotation in a pro-forma invoice is usually considered binding, although prices may change prior to final sale. To prepare the invoice, you should give a detailed description of the product, an itemized list of charges and sale terms. Prices should be quoted in United States dollars to reduce foreign exchange risks. The invoice should also indicate the period during which the price quotation is valid.

You should be familiar with the common terms of sale used in international trade before preparing your pro-forma invoice. ***International Commercial Terms (INCOTERMS)*** are the universally recognized terms used in export and import contracts. These terms refer to the rights and obligations of each party: who pays what costs; when title to goods is transferred; and where the goods should be delivered. A complete list of INCOTERMS published in the book *Incoterms 1990* can be obtained from the International Chamber of Commerce and should be a permanent part of your business library (*see* Part II, The Exporter's Directory).

PRO-FORMA INVOICE*

SHIPPER:
   SMITH AND JONES CO.
   5555 RAILROAD AVE.
   NEW YORK, N.Y. 10001
   212-555-1234

Reference No. RB20693
DATE: JULY 18, 1993

CUSTOMER P.O. NO.

TERMS OF PAYMENT:
ESTIMATED DATE OF SHIPMENT

SOLD TO:
   GRUPO ESTEVEZ, S.A. DE C.V.
   TAMALES NO. 1 PISO 2
   12345 CD. POLANCO MEXICO

SHIP TO:
JUAREZ INDUSTRIALE
454 BLVD. CORTEZ
11115 MEXICO D.F. MEXICO

VIA: AERO CORTEZ

ITEM	*QUANTITY*	*DESCRIPTION*	*UNIT PRICE*	*TOTAL PRICE*
	100	COMPUTER MOTHERBOARDS	US $50.00	US $5,000.00
			FOB FACTORY	5,000.00
			INLAND FREIGHT FORWARDER FEES	100.00
			AIR FREIGHT	1,200.00
		FIVE (5) SEALED CARTONS	INSURANCE	20.00
		GROSS WEIGHT: 10 LBS.	C.I.F. MEXICO	6,320.00

_____
Authorized signature/Title

The above offering is based on current prices and is valid __60__ days from invoice date.

NOTE: This pro-forma invoice is only a sample. It is advisable to contact a freight forwarder in advance of shipping.

NEGOTIATING SALES AND DISTRIBUTOR AGREEMENTS

Sales Contracts

Knowing how to include INCOTERMS in a contract is important, but this represents only one aspect of the sales agreement. Legal rights and obligations of the parties should be spelled out in a single document, which can be incorporated into the final invoice. Frequently, the terms and conditions are contained on the back of the invoice.

Some of the terms and conditions necessary in a written sales agreement include:

Delivery Terms—Risk of Loss

A *force majeure* clause is standard in most agreements. This clause excuses the exporter from responsibility where a default in performance is caused by events beyond the exporter's control, such as war, acts of God or labor problems.

Payment and Finance Terms

In addition to defining the terms of payment, provisions should be included for late payments, partial payments and remedies for non-payment. The terms of payment should consider the use of letters of credit.

Warranties

Sales contracts generally describe the goods and their qualities, workmanship and durability. In some cases, the exporter is obligated by the law in the country of import. The importer will require the exporter to warrant that the goods meet certain standards of construction and performance.

Acceptance of Goods

Frequently, the importer will insist upon the right to inspect the goods upon delivery; if found defective, the importer can reject them and refuse to pay. However, the importer is still liable for country-of-importation duties and other taxes. The export documents should reflect any such requirements. It is advisable to stipulate in the contract the terms of buyer acceptance and preferable for any inspections to be done by a qualified third party.

Intellectual Property Rights

Protection of the exporter's patents, trademarks or copyrights should be assured in the agreement. However, protection under the laws of the foreign country are not automatic, and you should not assume that your product is protected.

Taxes
The obligations of the parties for payment of taxes other than customs duties should be defined in writing.

Dispute Settlement
It is advisable to specify how and where any disputes will be resolved, as well as which nation's law would be applied. Bear in mind that different countries have varying arbitration laws and systems which may apply.

AGENT AND DISTRIBUTOR AGREEMENTS

If you choose to use an agent or distributor, it will be necessary to develop a formal contractual agreement. Agent and distributor agreements spell out in more detail the issues mentioned above and define other aspects of the relationship between the parties to the agreement.

In the contract it is important to:
- specify the goods and/or services covered;
- describe the agent or distributor's sales territory, and whether they will have exclusive or non-exclusive sales rights;
- set the length of the term for which the agreement is applicable and agree upon specified minimum sales volumes and objectives;
- outline protection of intellectual property;
- describe other types of obligations imposed on the parties, violations of which would justify termination of the contract; and
- list specific intellectual property rights granted to the agent or distributor.

When negotiating and drafting contractual agreements, it is recommended that you consult an attorney with experience in international trade and exporting. Your company's business lawyer may be able to handle your questions or refer you to an "export-oriented" attorney. Your local bar association may provide referral services, as well.

Under agreement with the Federal Bar Association and the U.S. Department of Commerce, the Small Business Administration sponsors the **Export Legal Assistance Network (ELAN)**. ELAN is a group of attorneys throughout the United States who specialize in international trade. Your local SBA office or **U.S. Export Assistance Center (USEAC)** can assist in locating an ELAN attorney who will provide a free, initial legal consultation to discuss your export-related questions.

As an initial introduction, however, you may want to review the information contained in *International Business Practices*, which covers the legal aspects of doing business in over 100 countries. Copies are available from United States & Foreign Commercial Service (US&FCS) offices, USEACs or from the Government Printing Office.

Terms for financing export sales should be discussed during contract negotiations. While the U.S. seller will want to be paid as soon as possible, the foreign buyer will want to delay payment as long as possible, preferably until after the goods are resold. These two conflicting objectives will factor into any negotiations on export financing.

In addition to reaching a compromise on the method of payment, the U.S. exporter must also be able to offer the foreign buyer favorable financing terms—otherwise the sale could be lost to a foreign competitor with an equivalent product but better payment terms.

The final step in completing the export transaction is arranging for payment, the subject of Chapter 6, "Export Financing."

Export Financing

Financing Your Export Sales and Getting Paid

Few would disagree that small businesses should look overseas for profit opportunities in the 1990s. However, to succeed in the international marketplace, small firms must offer their customers competitive payment methods. This chapter will discuss how to choose the most appropriate international payment method, how to obtain export financing and—most important—how to get paid.

International Payment Methods

A small business exporter's principal concern should be to ensure that he or she gets paid in full and on time for each export sale. It does little good to make a sale if the buyer delays payment so long that the financing cost eats up your profit. Foreign buyers have concerns as well, such as ensuring that their orders arrive on time and as requested. Therefore, it is important that the *terms of payment be negotiated carefully to meet the needs of both the buyer and seller.*

The payment method used can significantly affect the financial risk of the buyer and seller in an export sale. In general, the more generous the sales terms are to a foreign buyer, the greater the risk to the exporter. As shown below, the primary methods of payment for international transactions, ranked in order of most secure to least secure for the exporter, include:

- payment in advance
- letters of credit
- documentary collections (drafts)
- consignment
- open account

Payment in advance

Requiring payment in advance as a term of sale is not uncommon, but in many cases it is too expensive and too risky for foreign buyers. Requiring full payment in advance can result in lost sales because a foreign (or even another domestic) competitor may be willing to offer more attractive terms. Before negotiating payment terms, find out whether your buyer can obtain a comparable product or service elsewhere and what kind of terms your competitors are offering. In some cases, such as when the buyer's credit worthiness is unknown or if your manufacturing process is specialized, lengthy or capital-intensive, it may be reasonable to insist upon progress payments or full or partial payment in advance.

Letters of Credit

Letters of credit (LC) are one of the most common and safest of payment methods available. An export letter of credit is an internationally recognized instrument issued by a bank on behalf of its client, the buyer. Of course, the buyer pays its bank a fee to render this service, so some buyers will resist LC terms if the competition is offering more lenient or less expensive terms. Keep in mind that the various payment methods can be used as marketing tools and therefore should be negotiated carefully by you and the buyer.

An LC is useful if you are unsure of a prospective buyer's credit worthiness but are satisfied with the credit worthiness of the buyer's bank. Sometimes it is difficult to obtain reliable credit information about a foreign buyer, but it may be less difficult to do so for the seller's bank. Moreover, this vehicle can be structured to protect the purchaser because no payment obligation arises until the goods have been satisfactorily delivered as promised.

The conditions of the LC are spelled out on the LC itself. When the conditions of delivery have been satisfied (usually by the documented, satisfactory and timely delivery of the goods), the purchaser's bank makes the required payment directly to the seller's bank in accordance with the terms of payment (in 15, 30, 60 or 90 days, whichever is specified).

The greatest degree of protection is afforded to the seller when the LC has been issued by the buyer's bank and confirmed by a major bank. LCs may be utilized for one-time transactions, or they can cover multi-shipments, depending upon what is agreed between the parties. Also, make sure you can deliver within the terms of the LC. It is suggested that you review the details of such documentation with a bank that has LC experience.

Letters of credit can take many forms, but a typical transaction might involve these steps:

- The exporter, upon receiving an order for a specified quantity of goods, sends the buyer (importer) a pro forma invoice defining all conditions of the transaction.
- The importer takes the pro forma invoice to the bank and applies for an LC.
- After verifying the terms and reaching the appropriate credit decisions,

the importer's bank opens the LC and sends it to the exporter's bank.

- The exporter's bank authenticates the LC, verifying that it was issued by a viable bank, and mails it to the exporter.
- The exporter compares the LC with the original pro forma invoice to ensure that the exporter can ship before expiration and that all conditions were incorporated as intended.
- The exporter prepares, generally with the help of a freight forwarder, an invoice and a packing list. These documents must be completed exactly as specified in the LC. The exporter also prepares a shipper's letter of instruction or SLI and any other specialized documents required, e.g., export license and certificate of origin. (Check with a customs broker to determine what documents are required in your case.)
- The freight forwarder receives the goods along with the completed paperwork in accordance with the terms of the LC.
- After the goods are shipped, the forwarder or exporter submits the LC and documents to the exporter's bank.
- The exporter's bank verifies that all required documents are in compliance with the letter of credit and forwards the documents package with a draft to the importer's bank with wiring (payment) instructions.
- The importer's bank reviews all documentation and, if the documents meet all requirements, credits the exporter's bank.
- The importer's bank simultaneously debits its customer's account.
- The exporter's bank credits the exporter's account.
- At the same time, the importer's bank releases documents to its customer. With documents in hand, the importer picks up the shipment.

Your banker and freight forwarder will become important resources during a letter-of-credit transaction. They will help to guide you through these steps.

Documentary Collections

Documentary collections involve the use of a draft, drawn by the seller on the buyer, requiring the buyer to pay the face amount either on sight (sight draft) or on a specified date in the future (time draft). The draft is an unconditional order to make such payment in accordance with its terms. Instructions that accompany the draft specify the documents needed before title to the goods will be passed from seller to buyer.

Because title to the goods does not pass until the draft is paid or accepted, to some degree both the buyer and seller are protected. However, if the buyer defaults on payment of the draft, the seller may have to pursue payment through the courts (or possibly, through arbitration, if such had been agreed upon between the parties). The use of drafts involves a certain level of risk; but drafts are less expensive for the purchaser than letters of credit.

DOCUMENTARY COLLECTIONS

BUYER	**SELLER**
• Agrees to buy products	• Agrees to be paid via documentary collection
	• Ships goods and submits shipping documents to bank for collection or acceptance
• Documents released to buyer against payment or acceptance	• Seller receives payment at sight or upon acceptance

Consignment

When goods are sold subject to consignment, no money is received by the exporter until after the goods have been sold by the purchaser. Title to the goods remains with the exporter until such time as all the purchase conditions are satisfied. As a practical matter, consignment is very risky. There is generally no way to predict how long it might take to sell the goods; moreover, if they are never sold, the exporter would have to pay the costs of recovering them from the foreign consignee.

Open account

An open account transaction means that the goods are manufactured and delivered before payment is required (for example, payment could be due 30, 60 or 90 days following shipment or delivery). In the United States, sales are likely to be made on an open-account basis if the manufacturer has been dealing with the buyer over a long period of time and has established a trusting relationship. In international business transactions, this method of payment should not be used unless the buyer is credit worthy and the country of destination is politically and economically stable, or unless the receivables are covered by export credit insurance. In certain instances it is possible to discount accounts receivable with a factoring company or other financial institution, referred to below.

The following diagram assesses the relative strengths and weaknesses of each payment method:

METHOD	USUAL TIME OF PAYMENT	GOODS AVAILABLE TO BUYER	RISK TO EXPORTER	RISK TO IMPORTER
Cash in Advance	Before shipment	After payment	None	Relies upon exporter to ship goods
Letter of Credit	After shipment, when documents complying with LC are presented	After payment	Very little or none depending on LC terms	Relies on exporter to ship goods
Documentary Collection Sight Draft	On presentation of draft to buyer	After payment	If draft unpaid, must dispose of goods	Relies on exporter to ship goods
Documentary Collection Time Draft	On maturity of draft	Before payment	Relies on buyer to pay draft; no control of goods	Almost none
Consignment	After sale	Before payment	High	Low
Open Account	After shipment, as agreed	Before payment	Relies on buyer to pay his account	None

EXPORT FINANCING

In the United States, small businesses typically turn to their local banks for working capital financing. However, most smaller banks do not retain staff with expertise in international trade. This is not to say, however, that such help is unavailable—only that small businesses must be persistent and tenacious in their efforts to find it. For example, if your bank's loan officer will not work with his or her bank's international staff (or the bank is unwilling to work with a correspondent), you should consider establishing a second banking relationship or, if necessary, moving all your accounts to a more aggressive lender with international banking expertise. So do not be afraid to shop around.

Given the difficulty most small businesses encounter when looking for export financing, *it is imperative that the financial arrangements be made well in advance.* To find a lender willing to consider your request, you must ensure that the purpose of the loan makes sense for the business, that the request is for a reasonable amount, and that you can demonstrate clearly how the loan will be repaid. Prospective borrowers also should understand some key distinctions before beginning discussions with a lender.

Venture Capital

Before approaching a bank for financial assistance, you should understand the distinction between venture capitalists and lenders. Venture capitalists invest in a business with the expectation that as the business grows, their equity in the business will grow exponentially. On the other hand, lenders are not in the venture capital business—they make their money on the difference between the rate at which they borrow money and the rate at which they lend to their customers.

International Trade Services

Small exporters also should understand the distinction between international trade *services* and *lending* for export transactions. Although many banks offer international trade services, such as advising, negotiating and confirming letters of credit, many banks' international divisions are not authorized to lend. Other banks have the authority to make loans as well as provide related services. You should verify that the bank officer with whom you are dealing has the authority to lend for an export transaction or can work with the small business or commercial division of the bank to finance your export sales.

Working Capital Financing and Trade Financing

It is important also to be aware of the difference between permanent working capital and trade financing. Permanent working capital is the amount of money needed to pay short-term liabilities that remain steady over a period of several years, for example, the non-fluctuating level of accounts receivable that a business maintains. A firm's ability to qualify for permanent working capital financing depends on, among other things, its prospects for generating sufficient net profits over the life of a loan to repay it. Trade finance, on the other hand, generally refers to financing the fluctuating working capital needs of a business, including specific export transactions. Trade finance loans can be self-liquidating. If so, the lending bank will place a lien on the export inventory and accounts receivable of the exporter and require that all sales proceeds financed by the loan be applied to pay down the loan first before the remainder is credited to the account of the borrower.

The self-liquidating feature of trade finance is critical to many small, undercapitalized businesses. Lenders who may otherwise have reached their lending limits for such businesses may nevertheless finance individual export sales, if the lenders are assured that the loan proceeds will be used solely for pre-export production, and any export sale proceeds will first be collected by them before the balance is passed on to the exporter. Given the extent of control lenders can exercise over such transactions and the existence of guaranteed payment mechanisms unique to—or established for—international trade, trade finance can be less risky for lenders than general working capital loans.

Pre-export, Accounts Receivable and Market Development Financing

Exporters should understand the distinctions between the various types of trade finance. Most small businesses need *pre-export* financing to help with the expense of gearing up for a particular export sale. Loan proceeds are commonly used to pay for labor and materials or to acquire inventory for export sales. Others may be interested in foreign *accounts receivable* financing. In that case, exporters can borrow from their banks an amount based on the volume and quality of such accounts receivable. Although banks rarely lend 100 percent of the value of the accounts receivable, many will advance up to 80 percent of the value of qualified accounts. Foreign credit insurance (such as the U.S. Export-Import Bank's Export Credit Insurance Program) is often used to enhance the quality of such accounts.

Financing for *foreign market development* activities, such as participation in overseas trade missions or trade shows, is often difficult for small businesses to arrange. Most banks are reluctant to finance such activities because, for many small firms, their ability to repay such loans depends on their success in consummating sales while on a mission—prospects that in many cases are speculative. Although difficult for many small firms to do, the recommended source for financing such activities is through the working capital of the firm or, in certain cases, through the use of personal credit cards.

Finally, take time to make sure your banker understands your business and products. Have a detailed export plan ready and, most important, be able to clearly show how and when a loan will be repaid.

PRIVATE SECTOR EXPORT FINANCING RESOURCES

Commercial Banks

International trade transactions traditionally have been financed by commercial banks. Commercial banks can make loans for pre-export activities. They can also help process letters of credit, drafts and other methods of payment discussed in this chapter. Banks have also become increasingly involved in making export loans backed by U.S. government export loan guarantees.

Many larger banks have international departments which can help with your company's particular export finance needs. If your bank does not have an international department, it probably has a correspondent relationship with a larger bank that can assist you.

Private Export Finance Companies

Private trade finance companies are becoming increasingly more common-place. They utilize a variety of financing techniques in return for fees, commissions, participation in the transactions or combinations thereof. International trade associations, such as a District Export Council, can assist you in locating a private trade finance company in your area.

Export Trading and Management Companies

Both EMCs and ETCs provide varying ranges of export services, including international market research and overseas marketing, insurance, legal assistance, product design, transportation, foreign order processing, warehousing, overseas distribution, foreign exchange and even taking title to a supplier's goods. All of these services can leverage the limited resources of small businesses.

Factoring Houses

Factoring houses, also called factors, purchase export receivables on a discounted basis. Using factors can enable the exporter to receive immediate payment for goods while at the same time alleviating the delay associated with overseas collections.

Factors purchase export receivables for a percentage fee at 2–7 percent below invoice value, depending on the market and type of buyer. The percentage rate will depend on whether the factor purchases the receivables on a recourse or non-recourse basis. In the case of a non-recourse purchase, the exporter is not bound to repay the factoring house if the foreign buyer defaults or other collection problems arise. Therefore, the percentage charge will be greater with non-recourse purchases.

Forfaiting Houses

Similar to factoring, exporters relinquish their rights to future payment in return for immediate cash. Where a debt obligation exists between the parties, it is sold to a third party on a non-recourse basis, but is guaranteed by an intermediary bank.

One U.S. exporter which used forfaiting found the benefits substantial:

> *Ed Lamb, President of Custom Die and Insert of Lafayette, Louisiana, was able to sell a 180-day letter of credit through a forfaiting house and got paid 178 days sooner. Forfaiting enabled Custom Die and Insert to consummate a $2.3 million-dollar export order to the Middle East.*

GOVERNMENT EXPORT FINANCING RESOURCES

Because private sector financing providers will only assume limited risk regarding foreign transactions, the U.S. government provides export financing assistance.

U.S. government export financing assistance comes in the form of guarantees made to U.S. commercial banks which in turn make the loans to exporters. Federal agencies, as well as certain state governments, have their own particular programs as noted below:

U.S. Small Business Administration (SBA)

SBA provides financial and business development assistance to help small businesses sell overseas. SBA's export loans are available under SBA's guarantee program. As a prospective applicant, you can request that your lender seek SBA participation if the lender is unable or unwilling to make a direct loan.

The financing staff of each SBA district and branch office administers the financial assistance programs. You can contact the finance division of your nearest SBA office for a list of participating lenders. The economic development staff of each SBA district and branch office can provide counseling on how to request export finance assistance from a lender.

Borrowers can use different SBA loan programs and types of loan guarantees simultaneously, as long as the total SBA-guaranteed portion does not exceed the agency's $750,000 statutory loan guarantee limit to any one borrower.

Regular Business Loan Program

Small businesses that need money for fixed assets and for working capital may be eligible for the SBA's regular *7(a) business loan guarantee program*. Loan guarantees for fixed-asset acquisition have a maximum maturity of 25 years. Guarantees for general purpose working capital loans have a maximum maturity of seven years. Export trading companies (ETCs) and export management companies (EMCs) also may qualify for the SBA's business loan guarantee program.

To be eligible, the applicant's business generally must be operated for profit and fall within size standards set by SBA. The standards vary by industry and are determined by either the number of employees or the volume of annual receipts. Check with your local SBA district office to determine if your company falls within the small business size standards. Loans cannot be made to businesses engaged in speculation or investment in rental real estate.

The SBA can guarantee up to 90 percent of a bank loan up to $155,000. For larger loans, the maximum guaranty is 85 percent up to $500,000. The lender may charge a maximum interest rate of 2.75 percentage points above the New York prime interest rate, or 2.25 percentage points above New York prime if the maturity is less than seven years.

Export Working Capital Program

The Export Working Capital Program (EWCP) can support single transactions or multiple export sales. Under the program, SBA guarantees 90 percent (up to $750,000) of a private sector loan. Loan maturities are generally for 12 months, with two options to renew, for a total of 36 months. Guarantees can be extended for pre-shipment working capital, post-shipment exposure coverage or a combination of pre- and post-shipment financing.

Small businesses can use EWCP proceeds: 1) to finance labor and materials for manufacturing goods for export; 2) to purchase goods or services for export; or 3) to finance accounts receivable generated from export sales. Proceeds may not be used to establish operations overseas, acquire fixed assets or pay existing debt. A company must have been in business—not necessarily exporting—for at least 12 continuous months before filing an application.

> *Waste-Tech, Inc., of Libertyville, Ill., a wholesaler and manufacturer of hi-tech pollution control equipment to remove water from sludge deposits, reducing the original volume for easier disposal, has 30 employees and has been exporting for nearly three years, with its manufacturing, engineering and sourcing of components accomplished in the United States. The company was recently awarded a contract for nearly $1.27 million to supply an eight-tube Python Pinch Press system to Enirisorce, an Italian mining company.*
>
> *For this first venture by Waste-Tech into the Italian market, SBA guaranteed 90 percent of an $833,000 loan by First of America Bank. First of America issued a standby letter of credit to support progress payments to be made by Enirisorce to Waste-Tech. According to Robert Manwaring, president of Waste-Tech, "I couldn't have done it without SBA's support . . . the [Export Working Capital] Program promotes a can-do attitude."*

SBA considers several factors in reviewing an EWCP application:
- Is there a transaction and is it viable?
- How reliable is the repayment source?
- Can the exporter perform under the terms of the deal?

Interest rates are negotiable between the applicant and the lender. SBA charges a guarantee fee of one-quarter of one percent (.25%); other fees may apply.

Collateral may include export inventory, foreign receivables, assignments of contract and letter of credit proceeds and domestic receivables. Personal guarantees usually are required to support the credit.

The EWCP offers several advantages for both the exporter and the lender, including a simplified application form and a quicker turnaround time on SBA's review and commitment. Under the program, small businesses can apply directly to the SBA for a preliminary commitment for a guaranty. With SBA's preliminary commitment in hand, an exporter can then find a lender willing to extend the credit. The lender must apply to SBA for the final commitment.

To apply for a working capital guaranty, a lender—or the exporter if a preliminary commitment is sought—should submit to SBA a completed EWCP application, along with:

BACKGROUND
- Brief resume of principals and key employees;
- History of business and copy of business plan, if available;

TRANSACTION(S)
- Explanation of use of proceeds and benefits of the loan guaranty, including details of the underlying transaction(s) for which the loan is needed;
- Copy of letter of credit and copy of buyer's purchase order or contract;
- Foreign credit insurance-related material (policy, application, buyer credit limit), if applicable;
- Copy of validated export license, or copy of application for export license, if required;

FINANCIAL INFORMATION
- Business financial statements (Balance Sheet and Income Statement) for the last three years, if applicable;
- Current financial statement (interim) dated within 90 days of the date of application filing;

- Aging of accounts receivable and accounts payable, as of list balance sheet date;
- The most recent federal and state income tax returns for the business;
- Schedule of all principals officer/owner's compensation for the past three years and current year to date;
- Personal financial statement(s) of the major shareholder(s)/partner(s) of the company (over 20%) and their most recent federal income tax return; and
- Monthly cash flow projections for the term of the loan, highlighting the proposed export transaction.

SBA and the **Export-Import Bank of the United States (Ex-Im Bank)** have blended their working capital programs for exporters. The new programs offer a unified approach to the government's support of export financing. SBA and Ex-Im Bank have divided the market as follows: For loan requests of $833,333 or less, SBA will guarantee the loan; for loan requests over $833,333, Ex-Im Bank will guarantee the loan.

> *The dilemma that one Georgia poultry processor faces is the envy of most small businesses. Romar International Georgia, Inc., with 130 employees, has experienced dramatic growth in the volume and size of its export sales.*
>
> *The company's bank, SouthTrust Bank of Alabama, has always been able to meet Romar's export working capital needs. But when Romar recently received a series of orders from customers in the Middle and Far East, the company requested its largest-ever sum of working capital. SouthTrust turned to the U.S. Small Business Administration (SBA) for support. Romar received an SBA-guaranteed $600,000 line of credit under the new Export Working Capital Program (EWCP).*
>
> *EWCP is a coordinated federal effort. The Export-Import Bank (Ex-Im Bank) and SBA have blended their export finance programs and divided the market, with SBA handling loans under $833,333 and Ex-Im Bank handling all loans over that amount. Romar, which attributes 98 percent of its sales to exports, plans to continue growing its international business. As Romar's sales grow, the company's working capital needs will grow, too. Romar expects that its future export working capital needs will exceed SBA's guarantee cap, and the company will soon "graduate" to Ex-Im's level in this program.*

The International Trade Loan Program

The International Trade Loan Program provides long-term financing to small businesses engaged or preparing to engage in international trade. Proceeds may be used to purchase or upgrade facilities or equipment, and to make other improvements that will be used within the United States to produce goods or services.

While the combined loan amount cannot exceed $1.25 million, up to $1 million can be used to purchase or upgrade facilities and equipment and up to $750,000 for can be used for working capital. The SBA's guarantee cannot exceed 90 percent of the loan amount. Loan maturities cannot exceed 25 years, excluding the working capital portion of the financing.

No debt payment is allowed. Proceeds can be used to buy land and buildings; build new facilities; renovate, improve or expand existing facilities; and purchase or recondition machinery, equipment and fixtures. The working capital portion of the borrowing could be in the form of either an EWCP or a portion of the term loan.

Applicants must establish either of the following to meet eligibility requirements:

* Loan proceeds will significantly expand existing export markets develop new ones.
* The applicant's business is adversely affected by import competition.

Small Business Investment Company (SBIC) Financing

An *SBIC*, approved and licensed by the SBA, may also provide equity or working capital exceeding the agency's $750,000 statutory maximum. SBICs can invest in export trading companies in which banks have equity participation as long as other SBIC requirements are met.

Export-Import Bank of the United States

Ex-Im Bank is an independent U.S. government agency that helps finance the overseas sales of U.S. goods and services through a variety of insurance, loan and guarantee programs. Ex-Im Bank has undertaken a major effort to reach more small business exporters with better financing facilities and services, to increase the value of these facilities and services to the exporting community, and to increase the dollar amount of Ex-Im Bank's authorizations supporting small business exports.

Ex-Im Bank's export financing hotline provides information on the availability and use of export credit insurance, guarantees and direct loans extended to finance the sale of U.S. goods and service abroad.

Briefing programs are offered by Ex-Im Bank to the small business community. The program includes regular seminars, group briefings and individual discussions held both within the Bank and around the country.

Export Credit Insurance Programs

Export credit insurance programs reduce an exporter's risk and can be obtained through an insurance agent or broker or from *Ex-Im Bank's Insurance Division*. A wide range of policies is available to accommodate many different export credit insurance needs. Insurance coverage:

- protects the exporter against the failure of foreign buyers to pay their credit obligations for commercial or political reasons;
- encourages exporters to offer foreign buyers competitive terms of payment;
- supports an exporter's prudent penetration of higher risk foreign markets; and
- gives exporters and their banks greater financial flexibility in handling overseas accounts receivable.

The *Small Business Policy* offers short-term (up to 180 days) insurance geared to meet the particular credit requirements of smaller, less experienced exporters. Under the policy, Ex-Im Bank assumes 95 percent of the commercial and 100 percent of the political risk involved in extending credit to the exporter's overseas customers. This policy frees the smaller exporter from "first loss" commercial risk deductible provisions that are usually found in regular insurance policies. The special coverage is available to companies which are just beginning to export, or have an average annual export credit sales volume of less than $3,000,000 for the past two years and meet the SBA definition of a small business.

> *Ted Hughes, a small business owner from Deluth, GA, had no trouble getting export sales. His trouble was he couldn't convince his banker to provide sufficient working capital to complete the sales.*
>
> *The EWCP has solved Ted Hughes' working capital problems. Hughes, president of W. Ted Hughes, Inc., found a new lender familiar with SBA's programs and willing to extend more credit, with SBA's guarantee. SouthTrust Bank in Atlanta provided Hughes with a $500,000 line of credit. SBA guaranteed 90 percent of the loan under the EWCP. Hughes sells used and re-manufactured construction equipment. He has to pay his*

dealers cash up front for the equipment. Then he ships the goods back to Deluth and turns them around for export.

"Hughes uses Ex-Im Bank's program to insure his receivables. SBA's guarantee provides comfort during the two-to-three week window when Hughes is purchasing the equipment, bringing it to Atlanta and preparing it for export," says Bill Browning, vice-president—Trade Finance, SouthTrust Bank.

Hughes now attributes 60 percent of his total sales to exports and hopes to increase that percentage soon.

The **Umbrella Policy** also covers short-term receivables of companies with only limited experience in export trade. This policy is available to commercial lenders, state agencies, finance companies, export trading and management companies, insurance brokers and similar agencies to insure their clients' receivables. Exporters are eligible if they have average annual export credit sales of less than $3,000,000 for the past two years and meet the SBA definition of a small business.

Pre-Export Finance Program

The **Working Capital Guarantee Program** assists small and medium size businesses in obtaining crucial working capital to fund their export activities. The program guarantees 90 percent of the principal and interest on working capital loans extended by commercial lenders to eligible U.S. exporters. The loan may be used for pre-export activities such as the purchase of inventory, raw materials, or the manufacture of a product. Ex-Im Bank requires the working capital loan to be secured with inventory of exportable goods, foreign accounts receivable or by other appropriate collateral.

Direct Loans

Ex-Im Bank provides direct loans to foreign buyers of U.S. capital goods and related services. Both the loan and guarantee programs cover up to 85 percent of the U.S. export value, with repayment terms of one year or more.

Direct loans are offered at the lowest interest rate permitted under the **Organization for Economic Cooperation and Development (OECD)** arrangement for the market and term.

Guarantee Program

Guarantees by Ex-Im Bank provide repayment protection for private sector loans to creditworthy buyers of U.S. capital equipment and related services.

Most guarantees provide comprehensive coverage of both political and commercial risks but political-risks-only coverage is also available. The guarantee covers 100 percent of principal and interest on the financed portion.

Customary repayment terms for capital goods in international trade are:

Contract Value	*Maximum Term*
Less than $75,000	2 years
$75,000–$150,000	3 years
$150,000–$300,000	4 years
$300,000 or more	5–10 years, depending on the nature of the sale and the OECD classification of the buyers' country.

Loans for projects and large product acquisitions, such as aircraft and capital-intensive machinery, are eligible for longer terms while lower unit value items such as automobiles and appliances receive shorter terms.

Ex-Im Bank also offers a medium-term insurance policy similar to the Guarantee program.

State Export Financing Programs

A number of state-sponsored export financing and loan guarantee programs are available. Many cities and states have established cooperative programs with the Ex-Im Bank and can provide specialized export finance counseling. Details of these programs are available through each state department of commerce or trade office.

Arkansas, California, Florida, Georgia, Hawaii, Illinois, Indiana, Louisiana, Maine, Maryland, Massachusetts, Michigan, Minnesota, Nebraska, Nevada, New Hampshire, New Mexico, New York (Erie County only), Ohio, Oklahoma, Pennsylvania, Puerto Rico, South Dakota, Texas, Vermont, Virginia, Washington, West Virginia and Wisconsin all provide direct or indirect export financing assistance.

Commodity Credit Corporation (CCC)

The United States Department of Agriculture's *Commodity Credit Corporation (CCC)* operates *Export Credit Guarantee Programs* to provide United States agricultural exporters or financial institutions a guarantee that they will be repaid for short- and intermediate-term commercial export financing to foreign buyers. These programs protect against commercial or noncommercial risk if the importer's bank fails to make payment. Under one program, the CCC will guarantee credit terms of up to three years and under another, credit terms from three-to-ten years are guaranteed. (*See* Part II, The Exporter's Directory.)

Once an exporter determines the kind of export financing assistance to be used and which payment method, the next step is to arrange for delivery of the goods to the buyer's destination. It is important to assess the various transportation options available, the subject of Chapter 7, "Transporting Goods Internationally."

TRANSPORTING GOODS INTERNATIONALLY

Now that financing has been arranged, steps must be taken to ensure that the goods for export are packed and shipped properly to reach their destination. When transporting goods internationally, proper documentation and correct packaging are critical to the export process.

One of the main differences between selling domestically and exporting is the documentation required. Providing proper documentation with your shipments is essential, if the goods are to arrive safely and on time.

Although the paperwork involved in exporting may be more burdensome and costly than that required for domestic sales, it should not deter you.

THE ROLE OF THE FREIGHT FORWARDER

The international freight forwarder acts as an agent for the exporter in moving cargo to the overseas destination. These agents are familiar with the import/export rules and regulations of foreign countries, methods of shipping, U.S. government regulations and the documents connected with foreign trade.

Freight forwarders can assist with an order from the start by advising the exporter of the freight costs, port charges, consular fees, costs of special documentation and insurance costs as well as their handling fees—all of which help in preparing the pro-forma invoice and price quotations. Freight forwarders may also recommend the best type of packing for protecting the merchandise in transit; they can arrange to have the merchandise packed at the port or containerized. The cost for their services is a legitimate export cost that should be figured into the price charged to the customer.

When the order is ready to ship, freight forwarders should be able to review the letter of credit, commercial invoices and packing list to ensure that everything is in order. Freight forwarders can also reserve the necessary space on board an ocean vessel, if the exporter desires.

The exporter may ask the freight forwarder to make arrangements with the customs broker to ensure that the goods comply with customs export documentation regulations. In addition, they may have the goods delivered to the carrier in time for loading. Freight forwarders may also prepare a bill of lading and any special required documentation. After shipment, they can forward all documents directly to the customer or to the paying bank.

In preparing your goods for international transport, you must first determine what mode of transport you will use. When shipping to Mexico and Canada, land transportation may be the preferred method of transport. Other ways of shipping internationally are by sea and air.

Maritime shipping is almost always slower and less expensive than air. However, an exporter must factor in the additional costs of sea freight, such as surface transportation to the dock. Another factor is the time value of money: payment may not be made until the ship reaches its destination—ocean freight can be significantly longer than air freight. Your international freight forwarder can assist in weighing the pros and cons of different modes of transportation.

Once you have decided on the best mode of transporting your goods, you must begin to compile the necessary documents.

DOCUMENTATION

Export Documentation Checklist—Documents Prepared Before the Shipment

Commercial Invoice/Consular Invoice

After the pro-forma invoice is accepted, the exporter must prepare a commercial invoice. The commercial invoice is necessary for both the exporter and importer.

The exporter needs the commercial invoice to prove ownership and secure payment. The description of the goods on the commercial invoice must correspond *exactly* to the description in the letter of credit or other method of payment. There can be no exceptions.

The importer needs the commercial invoice since it is often used by Customs authorities to assess duties. For this reason, it is common practice to prepare a commercial invoice in English and in the language of the destination country. The freight forwarder can advise you when a translated copy is necessary.

Similar to a commercial invoice, a consular invoice is required by certain countries. The consular invoice must be prepared in the language of the destination country and can be obtained from the country's consulate, and often must be "consularized."

In some countries, the commercial invoice must be prepared on a special form known as a "customs invoice." Your importer may request this of you.

Export License

Export controls are based on the type of goods being shipped and their ultimate destination. Most exports do not require a license, but most are shipped under a "general" license which does not require an application.

Should your particular export be subject to export controls, then a "validated" license must be obtained. To determine whether your product needs an export license, you must have the ***Export Commodities Classification Number (ECCN)*** for your product. If your freight forwarder cannot provide you with the ECCN, you may look the number up in the *Code of Federal Regulations, Title XV, Section 799.1*, available at a public or university library. Once you have this number, check with the U.S. Department of Commerce's (DOC) ***Bureau of Export Administration (BXA)*** to determine if your product may be subject to export controls (*see* Part II, The Exporter's Directory).

In general, your export would require a "validated" license if export of the goods would: threaten U.S. national security; affect certain foreign policies of the United States; or create short supply in domestic markets.

Shipper's Export Declaration (SED)

The most common document used by exporters is the ***Shipper's Export Declaration (Form 7525-V)***, for mail shipments valued at more than $500, and required for other shipments valued at more than $2,500. In addition, a SED must be prepared for all shipments covered by an Individually Validated Export License (IVL), regardless of value. The SED enables the Bureau of the Census to monitor for statistical purposes the kinds of products being exported from the United States. The SED must be presented to the carrier before the shipment departs.

A sample SED follows:

U.S. DEPARTMENT OF COMMERCE — BUREAU OF THE CENSUS — INTERNATIONAL TRADE ADMINISTRATION

FORM **7525-V** (1-1-88)

SHIPPER'S EXPORT DECLARATION

OMB No. 0607-0018

1a. EXPORTER *(Name and address including ZIP code)*

ZIP CODE	2. DATE OF EXPORTATION	3. BILL OF LADING/AIR WAYBILL NO.

b. EXPORTER'S EIN (IRS) NO.

c. PARTIES TO TRANSACTION
☐ Related ☐ Non-related

4a. ULTIMATE CONSIGNEE

b. INTERMEDIATE CONSIGNEE

5. FORWARDING AGENT

6. POINT (STATE) OF ORIGIN OR FTZ NO. **7.** COUNTRY OF ULTIMATE DESTINATION

8. LOADING PIER *(Vessel only)*

9. MODE OF TRANSPORT *(Specify)*

10. EXPORTING CARRIER

11. PORT OF EXPORT

12. PORT OF UNLOADING *(Vessel and air only)*

13. CONTAINERIZED *(Vessel only)*
☐ Yes ☐ No

14. SCHEDULE B DESCRIPTION OF COMMODITIES, *(Use columns 17—19)*

15. MARKS, NOS., AND KINDS OF PACKAGES

D/F (16)	SCHEDULE B NUMBER (17)	CHECK DIGIT	QUANTITY — SCHEDULE B UNIT(S) (18)	SHIPPING WEIGHT *(Kilos)* (19)	VALUE (U.S. dollars, omit cents) *(Selling price or cost if not sold)* (20)

21. VALIDATED LICENSE NO./GENERAL LICENSE SYMBOL

22. ECCN *(When required)*

23. Duly authorized officer or employee
The exporter authorizes the forwarder named above to act as forwarding agent for export control and customs purposes.

24. I certify that all statements made and all information contained herein are true and correct and that I have read and understand the instructions for preparation of this document, set forth in the "**Correct Way to Fill Out the Shipper's Export Declaration.**" I understand that civil and criminal penalties, including forfeiture and sale, may be imposed for making false or fraudulent statements herein, failing to provide the requested information or for violation of U.S. laws on exportation (13 U.S.C. Sec. 305; 22 U.S.C. Sec. 401; 18 U.S.C. Sec. 1001; 50 U.S.C. App. 2410).

Signature

Confidential – For use solely for official purposes authorized by the Secretary of Commerce (13 U.S.C. 301 (g)).

Title

Export shipments are subject to inspection by U.S. Customs Service and/or Office of Export Enforcement.

Date

25. AUTHENTICATION *(When required)*

This form may be printed by private parties provided it conforms to the official form. For sale by the Superintendent of Documents, Government Printing Office, Washington, D.C. 20402, and local Customs District Directors. The "**Correct Way to Fill Out the Shipper's Export Declaration**" is available from the Bureau of the Census, Washington, D.C. 20233.

Three items appearing on the SED may cause confusion:

Item 14, "Schedule B Description of Commodities"

You will need to determine the official description of the commodity you are shipping by obtaining a copy of the U.S. government publication entitled, *Harmonized System/Schedule B Statistical Classification of Domestic and Foreign Commodities Exported from the United States* and then transfer the appropriate description onto the SED. This is available from the Government Printing Office and from most freight forwarders.

Item 21, "Validated License No./General License Symbol"

If your product for export is controlled, the "validated" license number is inserted in this space. If you are exporting under a "general license," one of eight possible "General License Symbols" must be noted. The three most commonly used symbols are:

- **G-Dest** (General Destination): authorizes the export of any items not requiring a validated license.
- **GLV** (General License Limited Value): authorizes the export of a single shipment of limited-value items.
- **GTE** (General License for Temporary Export): authorizes the export of items for trade shows, training or temporary use abroad.

Item 22, ECCN (Export Control Commodity Number)

Only necessary when a "validated" license is required, the ECCN is the number assigned to your commodity from the *Bureau of Export Administration's Commodity Control List*. This special number must be supplied on the SED.

Shipper's Export Declaration

SED forms can be obtained through international freight forwarders, the BXA, the Government Printing Office or local Customs district offices. The *"Exact Way to Fill Out the Shipper's Export Declaration"* is available from the Bureau of the Census, Washington, DC 20233.

Certificate of Origin

Although the commercial invoice may contain a statement of origin, some countries (particularly those subject to certain free trade treaties, such as Canada, Mexico or the Caribbean Basin) require Certificates of Origin. Certificates of Origin allow for preferential duty rates if the exporter's country has an agreement with the importer's country to allow entry of certain products at lower tariffs.

Export Packing List

Considerably more detailed and informative than a standard domestic packing list, an export packing list itemizes the material in each individual package and indicates the type of package: box, crate, drum, carton, etc. It shows the individual net, legal, tare and gross weights and measurements for each package (in both U.S. and metric systems). Package markings should be shown along with the shipper's and buyer's references. A copy of the packing list should be attached to the outside of a package in a waterproof envelope marked "packing list enclosed." The list is used by the shipper or forwarding agent to determine the total shipment weight and volume and whether the correct cargo is being shipped. In addition, customs officials (both U.S. and foreign) may use the list to check the cargo. The original packing list should be forwarded along with your other original documents in line with the conditions of sale.

Insurance Certificate

If the exporter is providing insurance, a certificate will be needed confirming the type and amount of coverage for the goods being shipped. Normal accepted practice for coverage is 110 percent of the CIF value. This certificate should be made in negotiable form and must be endorsed before submitting to the bank.

Inspection Certificate

Many foreign purchasers request that the seller certify that the goods being shipped meet certain specifications. This certification is usually performed by an independent inspection firm.

Documents Used During the Inland Movement of the Goods

Shipper's Instructions

As an exporter, you are responsible for providing your freight forwarder with the necessary information regarding your shipment. The more details you provide, the greater the chances your goods will move free of problems. Your freight forwarder can provide you with a commonly used form for noting instructions.

Inland Bill of Lading

Inland bills of lading document the transportation of goods between inland points and the port from where the export will emanate. Rail shipments use *waybills on rail*. Pro-forma bills of lading are used in trucking.

Delivery Instructions

This document is prepared by the freight forwarder giving instructions to the trucking or railroad company where the goods for export are to be delivered.

Dock Receipts

This document transfers shipping obligations from the domestic to the international carrier as the shipment reaches the terminal.

Bill of Lading/Air Waybill

Bills of lading and air waybills provide evidence to title of the goods and set forth the international carrier's responsibility to transport the goods to their named destination.

There are two types of ocean bills of lading used to transfer ownership:

- *Straight* (non-negotiable): provides for delivery of goods to the person named in the bill of lading. The bill must be marked "non-negotiable."
- *Shipper's Order* (negotiable): provides for delivery of goods to the person named in the bill of lading or anyone designated.

The shipper's order is used with draft or letter-of-credit shipments and enables the bank involved in the export transaction to take title to the goods if the buyer defaults. The bank does not release title to the goods to the buyer until payment is received. The bank does not release funds to the exporter until conditions of sale have been satisfied.

When using air freight, *air waybills* take the place of bills of lading. Air waybills are only issued in non-negotiable form, therefore the exporter and the bank lose title to the goods once the shipment commences. Most air waybills also contain a customs declaration form.

PACKAGING

Goods shipped for export require substantially greater handling than domestic shipments. The exporter must pack the goods to ensure that the weight and measurements are kept to a minimum, breakage is avoided, the container is theft proof, and that the goods do not suffer the stresses of ocean shipment, such as excess moisture.

In addition to proper packing, the exporter should be aware that certain markings are necessary on goods transported internationally. Some countries require that the country of origin be marked on the outside of the container, and even have regulations as to how the mark of origin should appear.

The second type of marking with which the exporter should be familiar is labelling. Food and drugs must often carry special labelling as determined by the laws of the country of destination.

Third, certain "shipping marks" must appear on the outside of the package. The weight and dimensions should be visible and any special instructions should be shown, and you may want to repeat these instructions in the language of the importer's country.

If your business is not equipped to package your goods for export, there are export packaging companies which can perform this service for you. Ask your international freight forwarder for a list of export packaging companies in your area.

A temporary export license may be needed if you are visiting a country to make a presentation or meet with a client to show your product. A temporary export license allows you to take products which require U.S. licensing to other countries for a short time. An *ATA Carnet* also may be necessary. An ATA Carnet is a special customs document which provides temporary duty-free admission into countries of commercial samples, scientific and education equipment and goods for exhibit. The DOC Bureau of Export Administration can advise you on the need for a temporary export license. The ATA Carnet is administered by the International Bureau of Chambers of Commerce (*see* The Exporter's Directory, Part II).

Many businesses, after achieving success in exporting, or as an alternative to exporting, contemplate joint ventures or licensing agreements with foreign companies to produce goods overseas. Some companies even set up their own off-shore operations. "Strategic Alliances and Foreign Investment Opportunities" are the topic of Chapter 8.

CHAPTER 8

Strategic Alliances and Foreign Investment Opportunities

If your company is interested in delving further into the international trade arena, licensing, joint ventures and off-shore operations should be explored. While direct exporting may be a profitable method of market entry for some businesses, licensing your company's manufacturing rights to a foreign company or setting up a foreign manufacturing joint venture may be viable alternatives.

In comparison, setting up off-shore manufacturing operations may be a more economical way of doing business. Firms choosing to set up operations in different countries should check for local incentives. Government agencies will usually assist foreign businesses to set up operations and will provide a wide range of grants and taxation incentives, both for the corporation and its expatriate employees.

This chapter will discuss the relative advantages and disadvantages of alternatives to direct exporting, how to find licensing and joint venture manufacturing partners and how to finance overseas investment.

Strategic Alliances

Licensing

Licensing involves a contractual arrangement whereby a company licenses the rights to certain technological know-how, design and intellectual property to a foreign company in return for royalties or other kinds of payment. This arrangement worked well for a small business exporter from Virginia:

> *"In Spain we licensed a Barcelona-based company the rights to manufacture our 'Peace Frogs' T-shirts for a time before and during the '92 Olympics because per capita income was lower, competition from domestic producers stronger and tariffs were high. We were able to keep the price of the T-shirts competitive and the results were excellent for our business,"* says Peace Frogs president Catesby Jones.

Licensing offers a small business many advantages, such as rapid entry into foreign markets and virtually no capital requirements to establish manufacturing operations abroad. Returns are usually realized more quickly than for manufacturing ventures.

The disadvantages of licensing are that control may be lost over manufacturing and marketing, and more important, that the licensee may become a competitor if too much knowledge and know-how is transferred. Take care to protect trademarks and intellectual property.

One way to help ensure that your intellectual property is protected is to secure proper patent and trademark registration. In the interim before your patent is filed, you may ask a potential licensee to sign a confidentiality and non-disclosure agreement barring the licensee from manufacturing the product itself, or having it manufactured through third parties. Make sure such agreements are not in violation of laws in the host country.

Patents should be filed with the appropriate foreign government within one year of U.S. filing, in order to obtain patent protection under the Paris Convention, the international agreement on patents. Patent rules vary from country to country, so it is important to consult a competent international patent and trademark attorney.

Licensing to a foreign company the rights to your product will require a carefully crafted licensing agreement. Consulting an attorney is critical since rules on licensing also vary from country to country. Be careful that the agreement does not violate host country antitrust laws. Under the antitrust laws of many countries, the licensee cannot set the price at which a product will be re-sold by the licensor.

Check with the United States Trade Representative's Office (USTR) for current information on intellectual property rights (IPR) protection in different foreign countries or refer to the Country Commercial Guides on the National Trade Data Bank. In certain countries, USTR has applied a *priority country label* because of IPR violations. You may want to avoid licensing your company's patents and trademarks to these countries.

Foreign Manufacturing Joint Ventures

In contrast to licensing arrangements, foreign manufacturing joint ventures allow for the U.S. company to have a stake and management role in the foreign operation. Joint ventures require more of a direct investment than licensing and require training, management assistance and technology transfer.

Joint ventures can be equity or non-equity partnerships. Equity joint ventures are contractual arrangements with equal partners. Non-equity ventures involve the host country partner in the arrangement with a greater percentage. In some countries, a joint venture is the only way for a foreign company to set up operations. Laws often require that a certain percentage of stock belong to a citizen of the host country.

Foreign manufacturing joint ventures are risky in that geographical and cultural factors may interfere with the smooth running of operations. You will have to deal with entirely new management, located in a different country, whose first language may not be English.

Despite the drawbacks, using a foreign partner can have many benefits: the partner will have intimate knowledge of the target market and may have business and political contacts to make market entry easier.

Partner Selection Issues

Finding a suitable partner is critical to the success of any licensing or manufacturing joint venture arrangement. However, the selection process can be time-consuming and difficult without proper assistance. The United States government has developed a number of special programs to assist U.S. companies to select overseas partners.

The SBA-supported **UNISPHERE** Institute's International Ventures Network partners U.S. high technology firms with firms throughout the world. Strong and stable firms are identified through UNISPHERE's network of public and private trade promotion and economic development organizations in Europe, Asia and the Americas, to facilitate cross-border, high-tech ventures. Once specific venture opportunities are identified, UNISPHERE brings prospective partners face-to-face to define the venture. UNISPHERE's International Ventures Network also operates through UNINET™ on the Internet (*see* Chapter 2).

The Department of Commerce (DOC) **Matchmaker Trade Delegations** are an excellent way to make joint venture and licensee contacts. Matchmakers provide one-on-one pre-screened business appointments, arranged by the **United States & Foreign Commercial Service (US&FCS)** overseas staff, for U.S. companies in a foreign country.

> *"We know we could not have accomplished the potential representative interviews without being in Mexico for months, perhaps years," says Judy Dorsey, president of Conway Engineering Inc., an Oakland, California telecommunica-*

> *tions engineering services company. "The Matchmaker pro-*
> *gram has definitely taken the mystery out of doing business*
> *in a foreign country."*

A number of Matchmaker Trade Delegations are held each year. For companies unable to take advantage of a specific Matchmaker, you may consider the DOC's **"Gold Key Service."** For U.S. firms planning to visit a country, US&FCS overseas staff will assist in developing a market strategy, setting up orientation briefings, making introductions to potential joint venture partners, providing interpreters for meetings and helping with follow-up planning. Fees vary from country to country.

Some steps involved in foreign partner selection are as follows:

- Contact your local DOC office or *U.S. Export Assistance Center (EAC)*. Discuss your target market and what kind of partner you are seeking. They can tell you whether a Matchmaker program fitting your needs is scheduled. If not, they will send your request to the appropriate FCS representative abroad.
- A list of potential partners will be forwarded to you. Contact each one with a letter of introduction.
- After responses from potential candidates are obtained, conduct a financial and business reference check on the most qualified candidates. If you are unable to do this in-house, use a credit reporting firm.
- Make a trip abroad, either with a Matchmaker Trade Delegation or on your own, to meet with potential licensees or joint venture partners.
- Having made your final selection, begin contract negotiations with the assistance of legal counsel.

Foreign Investment Opportunities

Many companies find that, as a result of exporting profitably and licensing or joint venturing the manufacture of their products abroad, it becomes a more viable method of market entry to set up off-shore production operations.

Off-shore manufacturing requires greater investment than licensing or joint venture manufacturing, but also affords the greatest amount of control over operations.

Additional factors that may induce a company to set up off-shore production include: high transportation costs, prohibitive tariffs or duties on imports, lower production costs and foreign government investment incentives, such as tax holidays.

If you are seriously considering setting up an off-shore manufacturing plant, you will need to assess whether to acquire an existing facility or to construct a new one. The key factors in this decision-making process are the legal and tax ramifications, where to set up operations and how to finance the foreign investment. An off-shore operation may offer certain tax benefits and other inducements for your company to make an investment in their country. For example, the Irish Industrial Development Authority and the Irish Trade Board offer foreign corporations such incentives; and the Port of Copenhagen provides a variety of free services to American companies wanting to establish operations in Denmark.

Legal and Tax Implications

Much of the decision-making surrounding joint venture or off-shore manufacturing involves legal and tax issues. Some countries actively encourage and promote foreign investment. Countries receptive to, or in need of, foreign investment may have relaxed laws on kinds and amounts of foreign investments allowed and may even offer certain tax benefits.

U.S. and host country attorneys and accountants should be an integral part of the team you assemble to assess whether and where joint venture or off-shore manufacturing would be profitable for your company.

Location, Partner Selection and Financial Assistance

Foreign investment requires a substantial commitment of a company's time and money and a certain amount of risk. To provide investment assistance and to address the risk insurance needs of U.S. companies, the U.S. government created a separate, business-oriented agency to support American investors entering the international marketplace.

Overseas Private Investment Corporation (OPIC)

OPIC is the lead agency assisting U.S. businesses interested in investment overseas.

OPIC programs are available if the project:
- is a new venture, or expansion of an existing business;
- is located in a developing country where OPIC operates (OPIC operates in 140 countries);
- will assist in the socio-economic development of the host country;
- is approved by the host government; and
- is consistent with the economic interests of the United States and will not have a significant adverse effect on the U.S. economy or U.S. employment.

If your potential overseas investment fits these criteria, OPIC can be an extremely useful resource. OPIC offers a variety of programs, including financing and political risk insurance to help protect your investment and several pre-investment services.

Pre-investment Assistance

OPIC sponsors investment missions to introduce U.S. businesses to key foreign private sector leaders, government officials and potential joint venture partners. Since its inception in 1975, investment missions to 45 countries have been organized.

In addition to pre-investment assistance, OPIC provides financing to assist in the setup of overseas operations and risk insurance to mitigate some of the problems associated with investment in developing countries.

Financing

Direct loans are available to ventures sponsored by, or significantly involving, U.S. small businesses or cooperatives. OPIC loans range from $500,000 to $6 million. Loan guarantees are also made to lending institutions in the range of $2 million to $25 million, but can be as large as $50 million.

OPIC has also underwritten a number of geographic venture funds, including the *Africa Growth Fund*, the *East European Environmental Fund* and the *Latin America Growth Fund*. If your project fits the criteria necessary to be eligible for access to these funds, you may consider applying to the specific fund for financing assistance.

Insurance

Private investors may be hesitant to undertake long-term investments abroad, given the political uncertainties of many developing nations. To alleviate these concerns, OPIC insures U.S. investments against three major types of political risks: inconvertibility, expropriation and political violence, including civil strife.

Foreign Governments

Foreign governments, particularly in developing countries, often sponsor special agencies to aid and facilitate foreign direct investment. Some examples include the *Mexican Investment Board (MIB)*, the *Portuguese Trade Commission* and the *Bahrain Marketing and Promotions Office*. These foreign investment promotion agencies can provide detailed market information, joint venture leads and make contacts with key officials. They often maintain offices in the United States.

Some countries may also have special funds or financing arrangements to spur foreign investment in particular sectors or geographical areas. Foreign investment promotion agencies can lead you to these sources. Contact the appropriate foreign embassy in the United States for the name of the agency which can assist you.

A FINAL WORD ON GOING GLOBAL

In Chapter 4, we discussed methods of market entry with an emphasis on exporting. In this concluding chapter, we focused on licensing, joint venture manufacturing and off-shore production as options to be considered along with, or in addition to, exporting.

How you decide to enter overseas markets will depend on a variety of factors unique to your own small business. Going global can be a challenging experience for a small business, but the rewards can be substantial. As Susan Corrales-Diaz, president of Systems Integrated of California says:

> *"We have an opportunity to make a quantum jump into foreign markets by learning to effectively compete through exporting!"*

Let this optimism and enthusiasm be your guide as you go global. The U.S. Small Business Administration, as well as numerous other government agencies at the state and federal level, support and encourage your entry into the international arena. There are a multitude of programs and a worldwide staff to assist you.

PART 2
THE EXPORTER'S DIRECTORY

SECTION 1

U.S. Small Business Administration

U.S. Department of Commerce

U.S. SMALL BUSINESS ADMINISTRATION

Smaller firms seeking to participate in the international realm are faced with challenges such as finding overseas markets, dealing with the initial complexities of exporting and financing export sales. The U.S. Small Business Administration (SBA) offers aid to current and potential small or minority exporters through two major programs: 1) business development assistance and 2) financial assistance. These programs are directed by the SBA's Office of International Trade in Washington, DC, and administered through the SBA's network of field offices around the country.

Office of International Trade
U.S. Small Business Administration
409 Third Street, S.W.
Washington, D.C. 20416
Phone: 202/205-6720
Fax: 202/205-7272

U.S. Export Assistance Centers (EACs) offer, under one roof, the services and programs of SBA, the U.S. Department of Commerce and the Export-Import Bank of the United States, as well as other public/private trade partners. Four initial EAC sites opened in winter 1994; eleven more are scheduled to be opened in 1995—Seattle, Dallas, Denver, Boston, New York, Cleveland, St. Louis, New Orleans, Detroit, Philadelphia and Atlanta.

BALTIMORE
U.S. Export Assistance Center
World Trade Center
401 East Pratt Street, Suite 2432
Baltimore, MD 21202
Phone: 410/962-4539

LOS ANGELES
U.S. Export Assistance Center
One World Trade Center
Suite 1670
Long Beach, CA 90831
Phone: 310/980-4550

CHICAGO
U.S. Export Assistance Center
Xerox Center
55 West Monroe Street, Suite 2440
Chicago, IL 60603
Phone: 312/353-8040

MIAMI
U.S. Export Assistance Center
Trade Port Building
5600 Northwest 36th Street
6th Floor
Miami, FL 33166
Phone: 305/526-7425

SBA District Offices

ALABAMA
U.S. Small Business Administration
2121 Eighth Avenue North, Suite 200
Birmingham, AL 35203-2398
Phone: 205/731-1344
Fax: 205/731-1404

ALASKA
U.S. Small Business Administration
222 West Eighth Avenue, #67
Anchorage, AK 99513-7559
Phone: 907/271-4022 or
1/800/755-7034
Fax: 907/271-4545 or 907/271-4945

ARIZONA
U.S. Small Business Administration
2828 North Central Avenue, Suite 800
Phoenix, AZ 85004-1093
Phone: 602/640-2316
Fax: 602/640-2360

U.S. Small Business Administration
300 West Congress Street, Room 7-H
Tucson, AZ 85701-1319
Phone: 602/670-4739
Fax: 602/670-4752

ARKANSAS
U.S. Small Business Administration
2120 Riverfront Drive, Suite 100
Little Rock, AR 72202-1747
Phone: 501/324-5871
Fax: 501/324-5199

CALIFORNIA
REGION IX OFFICE
U.S. Small Business Administration
71 Stevenson Street, 20th Floor
San Francisco CA 94105-2939
Phone: 415/744-6402
Fax: 415/744-6435

U.S. Small Business Administration
2719 North Air Fresno Drive
Suite 107
Fresno, CA 93727-1547
Phone: 209/487-5189
Fax: 209/487-5636

U.S. Small Business Administration
330 North Brand Boulevard,
Suite 1200
Glendale, CA 91203-2304
Phone: 818/552-3210
Fax: 818/552-3260

U.S. Small Business Administration
660 J Street, Suite 215
Sacramento, CA 95814-2413
Phone: 916/498-6410
Fax: 916/498-6420

U.S. Small Business Administration
880 Front Street, Suite 4237
San Diego, CA 92101
Phone: 619/557-7250
Fax: 619/557-5894

U.S. Small Business Administration
211 Main Street, Fourth Floor
San Francisco, CA 94105-1988
Phone: 415/744-6820
Fax: 415/744-6812

U.S. Small Business Administration
200 West Santa Ana Boulevard,
Suite 700
Santa Ana, CA 92701
Phone: 714/550-7420
Fax: 714/550-0191

U.S. Small Business Administration
6477 Telephone Road, Building C-1,
Suite 10
Ventura, CA 93003-4459
Phone: 805/642-1866
Fax: 805/642-9538

COLORADO
REGION VIII OFFICE
U.S. Small Business Administration
633 17th Street
7th Floor
Denver, CO 80202-2395
Phone: 303/294-7021
Fax: 303/294-7153

U.S. Small Business Administration
721 19th Street, Suite 426
Denver, CO 80202-2559
Phone: 303/844-3984
Fax: 303/844-6490

CONNECTICUT
U.S. Small Business Administration
330 Main Street, Second Floor
Hartford, CT 06106
Phone: 203/240-4700
Fax: 203/240-4659

DELAWARE
U.S. Small Business Administration
One Rodney Square
920 North King Street, Suite 412
Wilmington, DE 19801
Phone: 302/573-6295
Fax: 302/573-6060

DISTRICT OF COLUMBIA
U.S. Small Business Administration
1110 Vermont Avenue, N.W.,
Ninth Floor
P.O. Box 34500
Washington, D.C. 20043-4500
Phone: 202/606-4000
Fax: 202/606-4225

FLORIDA
U.S. Small Business Administration
1320 South Dixie Highway, Suite 501
Coral Gables, FL 33146-2911
Phone: 305/536-5521
Fax: 305/536-5058

U.S. Small Business Administration
7825 Baymeadows Way, Suite 100B
Jacksonville, FL 32256-7504
Phone: 904/443-1900
Fax: 904/443-1980

U.S. Small Business Administration
501 East Polk Street, Suite 104
Tampa, FL 33602-3945
Phone: 813/228-2594
Fax: 813/228-2111

GEORGIA
REGION IV OFFICE
U.S. Small Business Administration
1375 Peachtree Street, N.E.,
Fifth Floor
Atlanta, GA 30367-8102
Phone: 404/347-2797
Fax: 404/347-2355

U.S. Small Business Administration
1720 Peachtree Road N.W.,
Suite 6000
Atlanta, GA 30309
Phone: 404/347-2441
Fax: 404/347-4745

GUAM
U.S. Small Business Administration
238 Archbishop F.C. Flores Street,
Room 508
Agana, GU 96910
Phone: 671/472-7277
Fax: 200/550-7365

HAWAII
U.S. Small Business Administration
300 Ala Moana Boulevard,
Room 2314
P.O. Box 50207 Honolulu,
HI 96850-4981
Phone: 808/541-2973
Fax: 808/541-2976

IDAHO
U.S. Small Business Administration
1020 Main Street, Suite 290
Boise, ID 83702-5745
Phone: 208/334-1696
Fax: 208/334-9353

ILLINOIS
REGION V OFFICE
U.S. Small Business Administration
300 South Riverside Plaza, Suite 1975
Chicago, IL 60606-6617
Phone: 312/353-5000
Fax: 312/353-3426

U.S. Small Business Administration
500 West Madison Street, Suite 1250
Chicago, IL 60661-2511
Phone: 312/353-4528
Fax: 312/886-5688

U.S. Small Business Administration
511 West Capitol Street, Suite 302
Springfield, IL 62704
Phone: 217/492-4416
Fax: 217/492-4867

INDIANA
U.S. Small Business Administration
429 North Pennsylvania Street,
Suite 100
Indianapolis, IN 46204-1873
Phone: 317/226-7272
Fax: 317/226-7259

IOWA
U.S. Small Business Administration
215 4th Avenue, S.E., Suite 200
Cedar Rapids, IA 52401-1806
Phone: 319/362-6405
Fax: 319/362-7861

U.S. Small Business Administration
210 Walnut Street, Room 749
Des Moines, IA 50309
Phone: 515/284-4422
Fax: 515/284-4572

KANSAS
U.S. Small Business Administration
100 East English Street, Suite 510
Wichita, KS 67202
Phone: 316/269-6616
Fax: 316/269-6499

KENTUCKY
U.S. Small Business Administration
600 Dr. Martin Luther King Jr. Place,
Room 188
Louisville, KY 40202
Phone: 502/582-5971
Fax: 502/582-5009

LOUISIANA
U.S. Small Business Administration
1 Canal Place
365 Canal Street, Room 3100
New Orleans, LA 70130
Phone: 504/589-6685
Fax: 504/589-2339

U.S. Small Business Administration
500 Fannin Street, Room 8A-08
Shreveport, LA 71101
Phone: 318/676-3196
Fax: 318/676-3214

MAINE
U.S. Small Business Administration
40 Western Avenue, Room 512
Augusta, ME 04330
Phone: 207/622-8242
Fax: 207/622-8277

MARYLAND
U.S. Small Business Administration
10 South Howard Street, Suite 6220
Baltimore, MD 21201
Phone: 410/962-4392
Fax: 410/962-1805

MASSACHUSETTS
REGION I OFFICE
U.S. Small Business Administration
155 Federal Street, Ninth Floor
Boston, MA 02110
Phone: 617/451-2023
Fax: 617/424-5485

U.S. Small Business Administration
10 Causeway Street, Room 265
Boston, MA 02222-1093
Phone: 617/565-5590
Fax: 617/565-5598

U.S. Small Business Administration
1550 Main Street, Room 212
Springfield, MA 01103
Phone: 413/785-0268
Fax: 413/785-0267

MICHIGAN
U.S. Small Business Administration
477 Michigan Avenue, Room 515
Detroit, MI 48226-2573
Phone: 313/226-6075
Fax: 313/226-4769

U.S. Small Business Administration
228 West Washington, Suite 11
Marquette, MI 49885
Phone: 906/225-1108
Fax: 906/225-1109

MINNESOTA
U.S. Small Business Administration
100 North Sixth Street, Suite 610
Minneapolis, MN 55403-1563
Phone: 612/370-2324
Fax: 612/370-2303

MISSISSIPPI
U.S. Small Business Administration
One Hancock Plaza, Suite 1001
Fourteenth Street
Gulfport, MS 39501-7758
Phone: 601/863-4449
Fax: 601/864-0179

U.S. Small Business Administration
101 West Capital Street, Suite 400
Jackson, MS 39201
Phone: 601/965-4378
Fax: 601/965-4294

MISSOURI
REGION VII OFFICE
U.S. Small Business Administration
911 Walnut Street, 13th Floor
Kansas City, MO 64106
Phone: 816/426-3608
Fax: 816/426-5559

U.S. Small Business Administration
Lucas Place
323 West 8th Street, Suite 501
Kansas City, MO 64105
Phone: 816/374-6708
Fax: 816/374-6759

U.S. Small Business Administration
815 Olive Street, Room 242
St. Louis, MO 63101
Phone: 314/539-6600
Fax: 314/539-3785

U.S. Small Business Administration
620 South Glenstone Street, Suite 110
Springfield, MO 65802-3200
Phone: 417/864-7670
Fax: 417/864-4108

MONTANA
U.S. Small Business Administration
301 South Park, Room 334
Helena, MT 59626-0054
Phone: 406/449-5381
Fax: 406/449-5474

NEBRASKA
U.S. Small Business Administration
11145 Mill Valley Road
Omaha, NE 68154
Phone: 402/221-4691
Fax: 402/221-3680

NEVADA
U.S. Small Business Administration
301 East Stewart Street, Room 301
Las Vegas, NV 89125-2527
Phone: 702/388-6611
Fax: 702/388-6469

U.S. Small Business Administration
50 South Virginia Street, Room 238
Reno, NV 89505-3216
Phone: 702/784-5268
Fax: 702/784-5069

NEW HAMPSHIRE
U.S. Small Business Administration
Stewart Nelson Building
143 North Main Street, Suite 202
P.O. Box 1257
Concord, NH 03302-1257
Phone: 603/225-1400
Fax: 603/225-1409

NEW JERSEY
U.S. Small Business Administration
60 Park Place, 4th floor
Newark, NJ 07102
Phone: 201/645-2434
Fax: 210/645-6265

U.S. Small Business Administration
2600 Mt. Ephraim Avenue
Camden, NJ 08104
Phone: 609/757-5183
Fax: 609/757-5335

NEW MEXICO
U.S. Small Business Administration
625 Silver Avenue, S.W.
Albuquerque, NM 87102
Phone: 505/766-1870
Fax: 505/766-1057

NEW YORK
REGION II OFFICE
U.S. Small Business Administration
26 Federal Plaza, Suite 31-08
New York, NY 10278
Phone: 212/264-1450
Fax: 212/264-0900

U.S. Small Business Administration
Leo W. O'Brian Federal Building,
Suite 815
Albany, NY 12207
Phone: 518/431-4261
Fax: 518/431-4265

U.S. Small Business Administration
111 West Huron Street, Room 1311
Buffalo, NY 14202
Phone: 716/846-4301
Fax: 716/846-4418

U.S. Small Business Administration
333 East Water Street, Fourth Floor
Elmira, NY 14901
Phone: 607/734-8130
Fax: 607/733-4656

U.S. Small Business Administration
35 Pinelawn Road, Suite 207W
Melville, NY 11747
Phone: 516/454-0750
Fax: 516/454-0769

U.S. Small Business Administration
100 State Street, Suite 410
Rochester, NY 14614
Phone: 716/263-6700
Fax: 716/263-3146

U.S. Small Business Administration
100 South Clinton Street, Suite 1071
Syracuse, NY 13261-7317
Phone: 315/448-0423
Fax: 315/448-0410

NORTH CAROLINA
U.S. Small Business Administration
200 North College Street, Suite A2015
Charlotte, NC 28202-2137
Phone: 704/344-6563
Fax: 704/344-6769

NORTH DAKOTA
U.S. Small Business Administration
657 Second Avenue North, Room 219
Fargo, ND 58102
Phone: 701/239-5131
Fax: 701/239-5645

OHIO
U.S. Small Business Administration
525 Vine Street, Suite 870
Cincinnati, OH 45202
Phone: 513/684-2814
Fax: 513/684-3251

U.S. Small Business Administration
1111 Superior Avenue, Suite 630
Cleveland, OH 44114-2507
Phone: 216/522-4180
Fax: 216/522-2038

U.S. Small Business Administration
2 Nationwide Plaza, Suite 1400
Columbus, OH 43215-2592
Phone: 614/469-6860
Fax: 614/469-2391

OKLAHOMA
U.S. Small Business Administration
200 North West Fifth Street, Suite 670
Oklahoma City, OK 73102
Phone: 405/231-5521
Fax: 405/231-4876

OREGON
U.S. Small Business Administration
222 S.W. Columbia Street, Suite 500
Portland, OR 97201-6695
Phone: 503/326-2682
Fax: 503/326-2808

PENNSYLVANIA
REGION III OFFICE
U.S. Small Business Administration
475 Allendale Road, Suite 201
King of Prussia, PA 19406
Phone: 610/962-3700
Fax: 610/962-3743

U.S. Small Business Administration
100 Chestnut Street, Room 309
Harrisburg, PA 17101
Phone: 717/782-3840
Fax: 717/782-4839

U.S. Small Business Administration
960 Penn Avenue, Fifth Floor
Pittsburgh, PA 15222
Phone: 412/644-2780
Fax: 412/644-5446

U.S. Small Business Administration
Penn Place
20 North Pennsylvania Avenue,
Room 2327
Wilkes-Barre, PA 18701-3589
Phone: 717/826-6497
Fax: 717/826-6287

PUERTO RICO
U.S. Small Business Administration
Carlos Chardon Avenue, Suite 691
Hato Rey, PR 00918
Phone: 809/766-5002
Fax: 809/766-5309

RHODE ISLAND
U.S. Small Business Administration
380 Westminster Mall, Fifth Floor
Providence, RI 02903
Phone: 401/528-4561
Fax: 401/528-4539

SOUTH CAROLINA
U.S. Small Business Administration
1835 Assembly Street, Room 358
Columbia, SC 29201
Phone: 803/765-5376
Fax: 803/765-5962

SOUTH DAKOTA
U.S. Small Business Administration
110 South Phillips Avenue, Suite 200
Sioux Falls, SD 57102-1109
Phone: 605/330-4231
Fax: 605/330-4215

TENNESSEE
U.S. Small Business Administration
50 Vantage Way, Suite 201
Nashville, TN 37228-1500
Phone: 615/736-5881
Fax: 615/736-7232

TEXAS
REGION VI OFFICE
U.S. Small Business Administration
8625 King George Drive, Building C
Dallas, TX 75235-3391
Phone: 214/767-7633
Fax: 214/767-7870

U.S. Small Business Administration
300 East Eighth Street, Suite 520
Austin, TX 78701
Phone: 512/482-5288
Fax: 512/482-5290

U.S. Small Business Administration
606 North Carancahua, Suite 1200
Corpus Christi, TX 78476
Phone: 512/888-3331
Fax: 512/888-3418

U.S. Small Business Administration
10737 Gateway West, Suite 320
El Paso, TX 79935
Phone: 915/540-5586
Fax: 915/540-5636

U.S. Small Business Administration
4300 Amon Carter Boulevard,
Suite 114
Ft. Worth, TX 76155
Phone: 817/885-6500
Fax: 817/885-6516

U.S. Small Business Administration
222 East Van Buren, Room 500
Harlingen, TX 78550
Phone: 210/427-8533
Fax: 210/427-8537

U.S. Small Business Administration
9301 Southwest Freeway, Suite 550
Houston, TX 77074-1591
Phone: 713/773-6500
Fax: 713/773-6550

U.S. Small Business Administration
1611 Tenth Street, Suite 200
Lubbock, TX 79401
Phone: 806/743-7462
Fax: 806/743-7487

U.S. Small Business Administration
505 East Travis, Room 112
Marshall, TX 75670
Phone: 903/935-5257
Fax: 903/935-1248

U.S. Small Business Administration
727 East Durango Boulevard,
Room A-527
San Antonio, TX 78206-1204
Phone: 210/229-5900
Fax: 210/229-5937

UTAH

U.S. Small Business Administration
125 South State Street, Room 2237
Salt Lake City, UT 84138-1195
Phone: 801/524-3209
Fax: 801/524-4160

VERMONT

U.S. Small Business Administration
87 State Street, Room 205
P.O. Box 605
Montpelier, VT 05601-4422
Phone: 802/828-4422
Fax: 802/828-4485

VIRGIN ISLANDS

U.S. Small Business Administration
3013 Golden Rock
Christiansted
St. Croix, VI 00820-4487
Phone: 809/778-5380
Fax: 809/778-1102

U.S. Small Business Administration
V.I. Maritime Building
3800 Crown Bay
St. Thomas, VI 00802
Phone: 809/774-8530
Fax: 809/774-2312

VIRGINIA

U.S. Small Business Administration
1504 Santa Rosa Road
Dale Building, Suite 200
Richmond, VA 23229
Phone: 804/771-2400
Fax: 804/771-8018

WASHINGTON
REGION X OFFICE
U.S. Small Business Administration
2601 Fourth Avenue, Room 440
Seattle, WA 98121-1273
Phone: 206/553-5676
Fax: 206/553-4155

U.S. Small Business Administration
915 Second Avenue, Room 1792
Seattle, WA 98174-1088
Phone: 206/220-6520
Fax: 206/220-6570

U.S. Small Business Administration
West 601 First Avenue
Tenth Floor East
Spokane, WA 99204-0317
Phone: 509/353-2800
Fax: 509/353-2829

WEST VIRGINIA
U.S. Small Business Administration
168 West Main St., Fifth Floor
P.O. Box 1608
Clarksburg, WV 26302-5631
Phone: 304/623-5631
Fax: 304/623-0023

U.S. Small Business Administration
550 Eagan Street, Room 309
Charleston, WV 25301
Phone: 304/347-5220
Fax: 304/347-5350

WISCONSIN
U.S. Small Business Administration
212 East Washington Avenue,
Room 213
Madison, WI 53703
Phone: 608/264-5261
Fax: 608/264-5541

U.S. Small Business Administration
310 West Wisconsin Avenue,
Suite 400
Milwaukee, WI 53203
Phone: 414/297-3941
Fax: 414/297-1377

WYOMING
U.S. Small Business Administration
100 East B Street, Room 4001
P.O. Box 2839
Casper, WY 82602-2839
Phone: 307/261-5761
Fax: 307/261-5499

U.S. DEPARTMENT OF COMMERCE

The U.S. Department of Commerce (DOC) encourages, serves and promotes the nation's international trade, economic growth and technological advancement. Within DOC, the International Trade Administration (ITA) promotes world trade and is the official U.S. government organization that coordinates all issues concerning trade development, international economic policy and programs and trade administration.

ITA units include: 1) country experts, 2) industry experts and 3) domestic and overseas commercial officers.

INTERNATIONAL TRADE ADMINISTRATION
U.S. Department of Commerce
14th & Constitution Avenue, N.W. Room 3850
Washington, D.C. 20230
Phone: 202/482-2867
Fax: 202/482-5933

Trade Information Center

The Trade Information Center (TIC) is a comprehensive resource for information on export assistance programs Government-wide. Center staff: 1) advise exporters on how to locate and use government programs, 2) guide businesses through the export process, 3) provide information on market research, trade leads, trade events, export financing and export licensing. The Trade Information Center also produces a brochure called *Export Programs: A Business Directory of U.S. Government Services*, which can be obtained by calling the Center.

The Trade Information Center can be reached through a nationwide toll-free number: 1-800-USA-TRADE (1/800/872-8723). Deaf and hearing impaired callers can use a toll-free telecommunications device: 1-800-TDD-TRADE (1/800/833-8723). The Center is open from 8:30 a.m. to 5:30 p.m., Monday through Friday, Eastern Time. A fax retrieval system is also available 24 hours a day through 1-800-USA-TRADE.

COUNTRY DESK OFFICERS

Country	Desk Officer	Phone/202
A		
Afghanistan	Timothy Gilman	482-2954
Albania	EEBIC	482-2645
Algeria	Christopher Cerone/	482-1860
	Claude Clement	482-5545
Angola	Finn Holm-Olsen	482-4228
Anguilla	Michelle Brooks	482-1658
Antigua/		
Barbuda	Michelle Brooks	482-1658
Argentina	Randolph Mye	482-1744
Armenia	BISNIS	482-4655
Aruba	Michelle Brooks	482-1658
ASEAN	Karen Goddin	482-3877
Australia	Gary Bouck	482-4958
Austria	John Larsen	482-2841
Azerbaijan	BISNIS	482-4655
B		
Bahamas	Mark Siegelman	482-0704
Bahrain	Claude Clement/	482-5545
	Christopher Cerone	482-1860
Balkan		
States	EEBIC	482-2645
(the former Yugoslavia)		
Bangladesh	John Simmons	482-2954
Barbados	Michelle Brooks	482-1658
Belarus	BISNIS	482-4655
Belgium	Simon Bensimon	482-5401
Belize	Michelle Brooks	482-1658
Benin	Debra Henke	482-5149
Bermuda	Michelle Brooks	482-1658
Bhutan	Timothy Gilman	482-2954
Bolivia	Tom Welch	482-0475
Botswana	Finn Holm-Olsen	482-4228
Brazil	Ted Johnson	482-3872

Country	Desk Officer	Phone/202
Brunei	Edward Oliver/	482-4958
	Raphael Cung	482-3894
Bulgaria	EEBIC	482-2645
Burkina		
Faso	Philip Michelini	482-4388
Burma	Gary Bouck/	482-4958
(Myanmar)	Raphael Cung	482-3894
Burundi	Philip Michelini	482-4388
C		
Cambodia	Hong-Phong B. Pho	482-3877
Cameroon	Debra Henke	482-5149
Canada	Office of Canada	482-0305
Cape Verde	Philip Michelini	482-4388
Caribbean		
Basin	Mark Siegelman	482-0704
Cayman		
Islands	Michelle Brooks	482-1658
Central African		
Republic	Philip Michelini	482-4388
Chad	Philip Michelini	482-4388
Chile	Roger Turner	482-0703
Colombia	Helen Lee	482-0057
Comoros	Chandra Watkins	482-4564
Congo	Debra Henke	482-5149
Costa Rica	Mark Siegelman	482-0704
Cote d'		
Ivoire	Philip Michelini	482-4388
Cuba	Mark Siegelman	482-0704
Cyprus	Ann Corro	482-3945
Czech		
Republic	EEBIC	482-2645
D		
Denmark	John Larsen	482-2841
Djibouti	Chandra Watkins	482-4564

Country	Desk Officer	Phone/202
Dominica	Michelle Brooks	482-1658
Dominican Rep.	Mark Siegelman	482-0704
E		
East Caribbean	Michelle Brooks	482-1658
Ecuador	Helen Lee	482-0057
Egypt	Paul Thanos/	482-1860
	Corey Wright	482-5506
El Salvador	Michelle Brooks	482-1658
Equatorial Guinea	Philip Michelini	482-4388
Eritrea	Chandra Watkins	482-4564
Estonia	EEBIC	482-2645
Ethiopia	Chandra Watkins	482-4564
European	Office of the EC	482-2905
Community	Fax Number	482-2155
F		
Finland	James Devlin	482-3254
France	Elena Mikalis	482-6008
G		
Gabon	Debra Henke	482-5149
Gambia	Philip Michelini	482-4388
Georgia	BISNIS	482-4655
Germany	Brenda Fisher/	482-2435
	John Larsen	482-2434
Ghana	Debra Henke	482-5149
Greece	Boyce Fitzpatrick	482-2177
Grenada	Michelle Brooks	482-1658
Guadeloupe	Michelle Brooks	482-1658
Guatemala	Helen Lee	482-0057
Guinea	Philip Michelini	483-4388
Guinea-Bissau	Philip Michelini	482-4388
Guyana	Michelle Brooks	482-1658

Country	Desk Officer	Phone/202
H		
Haiti	Mark Siegelman	482-0704
Honduras	Helen Lee	482-0057
Hong Kong	Sheila Baker	482-4681
Hungary	EEBIC	482-2645
I		
Iceland	Phillip Combs	482-2920
India	John Crown/	
	John Simmons/	482-2954
	Timothy Gilman	
Indonesia	Edward Oliver/	482-4958
	Gary Bouck	
Iran	Paul Thanos/	482-1860
	Claude Clement	482-5545
Iraq	Thomas Sams/	482-1860
	Corey Wright	482-5506
Ireland	Robert McLaughlin	482-3748
Israel	Paul Thanos/	482-1860
	Corey Wright	482-5506
Italy	Office of the EU	482-2920
Ivory Coast	Philip Michelini	482-4388
J		
Jamaica	Mark Siegelman	482-0704
Japan	Edward Leslie/	482-2425
	Eric Kennedy/	
	Cynthia Campbell/	
	Allan Christian	
Jordan	Corey Wright/	482-5506
	Paul Thanos	482-1860
K		
Kazakhstan	BISNIS	482-4655
Kenya	Chandra Watkins	482-4564
Korea	William Golike/	
	Dan Duvall/	482-4390
	Jeffrey Donius	

Country	Desk Officer	Phone/202	Country	Desk Officer	Phone/202
Kuwait	Corey Wright/	482-5506	Neth. Antilles	Michelle Brooks	482-1658
	Thomas Sams	482-1860	New Zealand	Gary Bouck	482-4958
Kyrgsztan	BISNIS	482-4655	Nicaragua	Mark Siegelman	482-0704
L			Niger	Philip Michelini	482-4388
Laos	Hong-Phong B.Pho	482-3877	Nigeria	Debra Henke	482-5149
Latvia	EEBIC	482-2645	Norway	James Devlin	482-4414
Lebanon	Corey Wright/	482-5506	**O**		
	Thomas Sams	482-1860	Oman	Claude Clement/	482-5545
Lesotho	Finn Holm-Olsen	482-4228		Christopher	
Liberia	Philip Michelini	482-4388		Cerone	482-1860
Libya	Claude Clement/	482-5545	**P**		
	Christopher Cerone	482-1860	Pacific	George Paine/	482-4958
Lithuania	EEBIC	482-2645	Islands	Gary Bouck	
Luxembourg	Simon Bensimon	482-5401	Pakistan	Timothy Gilman	482-2954
M			Panama	Mark Siegelman	482-0704
Macau	Sheila Baker	482-4681	Paraguay	Randolph Mye	482-1744
Madagascar	Chandra Watkins	482-4564	People's Rep.	Cheryl McQueen/	482-3932
Malawi	Finn Holm-Olsen	482-4228	of China	Laura McCall	482-3583
Malaysia	Edward Oliver/	482-2522	Peru	Tom Welch	482-0475
	Raphael Cung	482-3894	Philippines	Edward Oliver/	482-4958
Maldives	John Simmons	482-2954		Jean Kelly	
Mali	Philip Michelini	482-4388	Poland	EEBIC	482-2645
Malta	Ann Corro	482-3945	Portugal	Ann Corro	482-3945
Martinique	Michelle Brooks	482-1658	Puerto Rico	Mark Siegelman	482-0704
Mauritania	Philip Michelini	482-4388	**Q**		
Mauritius	Chandra Watkins	482-4564	Qatar	Claude Clement/	482-5545
Mexico	Office of Mexico	482-0305		Christopher Cerone	482-1860
Moldova	BISNIS	482-4655	**R**		
Mongolia	Sheila Baker	482-4681	Romania	EEBIC	482-2645
Montserrat	Michelle Brooks	482-1658	Russia	BISNIS	482-4655
Morocco	Claude Clement/	482-5545	Rwanda	Philip Michelini	482-4388
	Christopher Cerone	482-1860	**S**		
Mozambique	Finn Holm-Olen	482-4228	Sao Tome &		
N			Principe	Philip Michelini	482-4388
Namibia	Finn Holm-Olsen	482-4228	Saudi Arabia	Christopher Cerone/	482-1860
Nepal	Timothy Gilman	482-2954		Claude Clement	482-5545
Netherlands	Simon Bensimon	482-5401	Senegal	Philip Michelini	482-4388

Country	Desk Officer	Phone/202	Country	Desk Officer	Phone/202
Seychelles	Chandra Watkins	482-4564	Tunisia	Corey Wright/	482-5506
Sierra Leone	Philip Michelini	482-4388		Thomas Sams	482-1860
Singapore	Edward Oliver	482-4958	Turkey	Boyce Fitzpatrick	482-2177
	Raphael Cung	482-3894	Turkmenistan	BISNIS	482-4655
Slovak			Turks/		
Republic	EEBIC	482-2645	Caicos Islands	Mark Siegelman	482-0704
Somalia	Chandra Watkins	482-4564	**U**		
South Africa	Vicky Eicher	482-5148	Uganda	Chandra Watkins	482-4564
Spain	Ann Corro	482-3945	Ukraine	BISNIS	482-4655
Sri Lanka	John Simmons	482-2954	United Arab	Claude Clement/	482-5545
St.			Emirates	Christopher Cerone	482-1860
Barthelemy	Michelle Brooks	482-1658	United		
St.			Kingdom	Robert McLaughlin	482-3748
Kitts-Nevis	Michelle Brooks	482-1658			
St. Lucia	Michelle Brooks	482-1658	Uruguay	Roger Turner	482-0703
St. Martin	Michelle Brooks	482-1658	**V, W**		
St. Vincent-			Venezuela	Tom Welch	482-0475
Grenadines	Michelle Brooks	482-1658	Vietnam	Gary Bouck/	482-4958
Sudan	Chandra Watkins	482-4564		Hong-Phong B. Pho	482-3877
Suriname	Michelle Brooks	482-1658	Virgin Is.		
Swaziland	Finn Holm-Olsen	482-4228	(UK)	Michelle Brooks	482-1658
Sweden	James Devlin	482-4414	Virgin Is.		
Switzerland	Philip Combs	482-2920	(US)	Mark Siegelman	482-0704
Syria	Corey Wright/	482-5506	**X, Y**		
	Thomas Sams	482-1860	Yemen,	Christopher Cerone/	482-1860
T			Rep. of	Claude Clement	482-5545
Taiwan	Robert Chu/	482-4390	Yugoslav		
	Dan Duvall		Republics	EEBIC	482-2645
Tajikistan	BISNIS	482-4655	(former)		
Tanzania	Finn Holm-Olsen	482-4228	**Z**		
Thailand	Edward Oliver/	482-4958	Zaire	Philip Michelini	482-4388
	Jean Kelly		Zambia	Finn Holm-Olsen	482-4228
Togo	Debra Henke	482-5149	Zimbabwe	Finn Holm-Olsen	482-4228
Trinidad &					
Tobago	Michelle Brooks	482-1658			

Fax Retrieval Systems

A number of offices now offer documents on demand, delivered directly to your fax machine 24 hours a day. These automated systems each have a menu of available documents which can be sent to a fax machine by dialing from a touch-tone phone and following the instructions.

Uruguay Round Hotline—1/800/872-8723. The Uruguay Round Hotline fax retrieval system, located at the Trade Information Center, has information on the GATT agreement. Document #1000 is the menu of available information packets.

Eastern Europe Business Information Center (EEBIC)—202/482-5745. The EEBIC fax system has five main menus. Menu document #1000 has export and financing information. Document #2000 has a menu of documents relating to export and investment opportunities and upcoming trade events. A listing of documents with Eastern European country information is contained on menu document #3000. Document menus #4000 and #5000 have information on the *Eastern Europe Business Bulletin* and the *Eastern Europe Looks For Partners* publications respectively.

Business Information Service for the Newly Independent States (BIS-NIS)—202/482-3145. BISNIS has three document menus. Menu number 1, document #0001, has trade and investment opportunities and trade promotion information. Menu number 2, document #0002, has industry and country specific information, and financing alternatives. Menu number 3, document #0003, has information on BISNIS publications.

Japan Export Information Center—202/482-4565. The Japan Export Promotion Hotline provides information on the Japanese market. The main menu for this system is document #0101.

Office of NAFTA, Office of Latin America and the Caribbean—202/482-1495. Option #1 of Amerifax provides information on Canada and Mexico and the NAFTA agreement. The main menu is document #0101. Document #5000 contains information on making the NAFTA Rules of Origin Determination. Document #6000 has information on the Mexican tariff schedule, and the Canadian tariff menu is document #7000. Option #2 of Amerifax provides information on Latin America and the Caribbean. For a listing of documents on this region, request document #0100.

Asia Business Center—202/482-2522. *Flash Facts*—202/482-3875. The menu for the Pacific Basin system is document #1000. A listing of documents regarding Vietnam is available by requesting document #8600.

Office of Africa, Near East, and South Asia—202/482-1064. A list of documents covering the nations of the Near East is document #0100. The Office of Africa's menu is available as document #3000. Information on documents regarding South Asian countries is listed on menu document #4000.

Overseas Private Investment Corporation—202/336-8700. The system has information on OPIC project finance and political risk insurance programs.

Trade Information Center—1/800/872-8723. The main menu for the Trade Information Center is document #7000. This Hotline has information on the locations of National Trade Data Bank libraries, the most recent version of the Export Programs Directory, a directory of international trade contacts listed by state, and other trade information designed to help exporters.

U.S. AND FOREIGN COMMERCIAL SERVICE

DISTRICT OFFICE DIRECTORY

ALABAMA
Birmingham
Medical Forum Building , 7th Floor
950 22nd Street North, 35203
Phone: 205/731-0076
Fax: 205/731-0076

ALASKA
Anchorage
World Trade Center Alaska, Suite 300
421 West First Avenue, 99501-1635
Phone: 907/271-6237
Fax: 907/271-6242

ARIZONA
Phoenix
Phoenix Plaza, Suite 970
2901 North Central Avenue, 85012
Phone: 602/640-2513
Fax: 602/640-2518

ARKANSAS
Little Rock
TCBY Tower Building, Suite 700
425 West Capitol Avenue, 72201
Phone: 501/324-5794
Fax: 501/324-7380

CALIFORNIA
Los Angeles
Room 9200,
11000 Wilshire Boulevard, 90024
Phone: 310/235-7104
Fax: 310/235-7220

Long Beach
Suite 1670
One World Trade Center, 90831
Phone: 310/980-4550
Fax: 310/980-4561

Newport Beach
Suite 305
3300 Irvine Avenue, 92660
Phone: 714/660-1688
Fax: 714/660-8039

San Diego
Suite 230
6363 Greenwich Drive, 92122
Phone: 619/557-5395
Fax: 619/557-6176

San Francisco
14th Floor
250 Montgomery Street, 94104
Phone: 415/705-2300
Fax: 415/705-2297

Santa Clara
Techmart Building, Suite 456
5201 Great American Parkway, 95054
Phone: 408/970-4610
Fax: 408/970-4618

COLORADO
Denver
Suite 680
1625 Broadway, 80202
Phone: 303/844-6622
Fax: 303/844-5651

CONNECTICUT
Hartford
Federal Building, Room 610-B
450 Main Street, 06103
Phone: 203/240-3530
Fax: 203/240-3473

DELAWARE
Served by Philadelphia,
Pennsylvania, District Office

DISTRICT OF COLUMBIA
Served by Baltimore, Maryland, U.S.
Export Assistance Center

FLORIDA
Miami
Trade Port Building, 6th Floor
5600 Northwest 36th Street, 33166
Phone: 305/526-7425
Fax: 305/526-7434
Mailing address:
P.O. Box 590570
Miami, FL 33159-0570

Clearwater
128 North Osceola Avenue, 34615
Phone: 813/461-0011
Fax: 813/449-2889

Orlando
Eola Park Center, Suite 695
200 East Robinson Street, 32801
Phone: 407/648-6235
Fax: 407/648-6756

Tallahassee
Collins Building, Room 366G
107 West Gaines Street, 32399-2000
Phone: 904/488-6469
Fax: 904/487-1407

GEORGIA
Atlanta
Plaza Square North, Suite 310
4360 Chamblee-Dunwoody Road,
30341
Phone: 404/452-9101
Fax: 404/452-9105

Savannah
Room A-107
120 Barnard Street, 31401
Phone: 912/652-4204
Fax: 912/652-4241

HAWAII
Honolulu
P.O. Box 50026
Room 4106
300 Ala Moana Boulevard, 96850
Phone: 808/541-1782
Fax: 808/541-3435

IDAHO
Boise (Served by Portland, Oregon, District Office)
Joe R. Williams Building, 2nd Floor
700 West State Street, 83720-0093
Phone: 208/334-3857
Fax: 208/334-2783

ILLINOIS
Chicago
Xerox Center, Suite 2440
55 West Monroe, 60603
Phone: 312/353-8040
Fax: 312/353-8098

Wheaton
Illinois Institute of Technology,
Rice Campus
201 East Loop Road, 60187
Phone: 312/353-4332
Fax: 312/353-4336

Rockford
P.O. Box 1747
515 North Court Street, 61110-0247
Phone: 815/987-4347
Fax: 815/963-7943

INDIANA
Indianapolis
Penwood One, Suite 106
11405 North Pennsylvania Street
Carmel, IN 46032
Phone: 317/582-2300
Fax: 317/582-2301

IOWA
Des Moines
Federal Building, Room 817
210 Walnut Street, 50309
Phone: 515/284-4222
Fax: 515/284-4021

KANSAS
Wichita (Served by Kansas City, Missouri, District Office)
151 North Volutsia, 67214-4695
Phone: 316/269-6160
Fax: 316/683-7326

KENTUCKY
Louisville
601 West Broadway, Room 634B, 40202
Phone: 502/582-5066
Fax: 502/582-6573

LOUISIANA
New Orleans
Hale Boggs Federal Building,
Room 1043,
501 Magazine Street, 70130
Phone: 504/589-6546
Fax: 504/589-2337

MAINE
Augusta (Served by Boston, Massachusetts, District Office)
Suite 5068
40 Western Avenue, 04333
Phone: 207/622-8249
Fax: 207/626-9156

MARYLAND
Baltimore
World Trade Center, Suite 2432
401 East Pratt Street, 21202
Phone: 410/962-4539
Fax: 410/962-4529

MASSACHUSETTS
Boston
World Trade Center, Suite 307
164 Northern Avenue, 02210
Phone: 617/424-5990
Fax: 617/424-5992

MICHIGAN
Detroit
1140 McNamara Building
477 Michigan Avenue, 48226
Phone: 313/226-3650
Fax: 313/226-3657

*Grand Rapids
Room 406 City Hall
300 Monroe N.W., 49503
Phone: 616/456-2411
Fax: 616/456-2695

MINNESOTA
Minneapolis
108 Federal Building
110 South 4th Street, 55401
Phone: 612/348-1638
Fax: 612/348-1650

MISSISSIPPI
Jackson
Suite 310
201 West Capitol Street, 39201-2005
Phone: 601/965-4388
Fax: 601/965-5386

MISSOURI
St. Louis
Suite 303
8182 Maryland Avenue, 63105
Phone: 314/425-3302
Fax: 314/425-3381

Kansas City
Room 635
601 East 12th Street, 64106
Phone: 816/426-3141
Fax: 816/426-3140

MONTANA
Served by Boise, Idaho, Branch Office

NEBRASKA
*Omaha (Served by Des Moines,
Iowa, District Office)
11135 "O" Street, 68137
Phone: 402/221-3664
Fax: 402/221-3668

NEVADA
Reno
Suite 152
1755 East Plumb Lane, 89502
Phone: 702/784-5203
Fax: 702/784-5343

NEW HAMPSHIRE
*Portsmouth (Served by Boston,
Massachusetts, District Office)
Suite 29
601 Spaulding Turnpike, 03801-2840
Phone: 603/334-6074
Fax: 603/334-6110

NEW JERSEY
Trenton
Building #6, Suite 100
3131 Princeton Pike, 08648
Phone: 609/989-2100
Fax: 609/989-2395

NEW MEXICO
Santa Fe (Served by Dallas, Texas, District Office)
c/o New Mexico Department of
Economic Development
1100 St. Francis Drive, 87503
Phone: 505/827-0350
Fax: 505/827-0263

NEW YORK
Buffalo
1304 Federal Building
111 West Huron Street, 14202
Phone: 716/846-4191
Fax: 716/846-5290

Rochester
Suite 220
111 East Avenue, 14604
Phone: 716/263-6480
Fax: 716/325-6505

New York
Room 3718
26 Federal Plaza, 10278
Phone: 212/264-0634
Fax: 212/264-1356

NORTH CAROLINA
Greensboro
Room 400
400 West Market Street, 27401
Phone: 910/333-5345
Fax: 910/333-5158

NORTH DAKOTA
Served by Minneapolis, Minnesota, District Office

OHIO
Cincinnati
9504 Federal Building
550 Main Street, 45202
Phone: 513/684-2944
Fax: 513/684-3200

Cleveland
Bank One Center, Suite 700
600 Superior Avenue East, 44114-2650
Phone: 216/522-4750
Fax: 216/522-2235

OKLAHOMA
Oklahoma City
Room 200
6601 Broadway Extension, 73116
Phone: 405/231-5302
Fax: 405/231-4211

Tulsa
440 South Houston Street, 74127
Phone: 918/581-7650
Fax: 918/581-2844

OREGON
Portland
One World Trade Center, Suite 242
121 S.W. Salmon, 97204
Phone: 503/326-3001
Fax: 503/326-6351

PENNSYLVANIA
Philadelphia
660 American Avenue, Suite 201
King of Prussia, PA, 19406
Phone: 610/962-4980
Fax: 610/962-4989

Pittsburgh
2002 Federal Building
1000 Liberty Avenue, 15222
Phone: 412/644-2850
Fax: 412/644-4875

PUERTO RICO
San Juan (Hato Rey)
Federal Building, Room G-55
Chardon Avenue, 00918
Phone: 809/766-5555
Fax: 809/766-5692

RHODE ISLAND
Providence (Served by Hartford, Connecticut, District Office)
7 Jackson Walkway, 02903
Phone: 401/528-5104
Fax: 401/528-5067

SOUTH CAROLINA
Columbia
Strom Thurmond Federal Bldg.,
Suite 172
1835 Assembly Street, 29201
Phone: 803/765-5345
Fax: 803/253-3614

Charleston
c/o Trident Technical Chamber
of Commerce
P.O.Box 975, 29402
81 Mary Street, 29403
Phone: 803/727-4051
Fax: 803/727-4052

SOUTH DAKOTA
Sioux Falls (Served by Omaha, Nebraska, District Office)
200 N. Phillips Avenue,
Commerce Center
Suite 302, 57102
Phone: 605/330-4264
Fax: 605/330-4266

TENNESSEE
Nashville
Parkway Towers, Suite 114
404 James Robertson Parkway,
37219-1505
Phone: 615/736-5161
Fax: 615/736-2454

Memphis
The Falls Building, Suite 200
22 North Front Street, 38103
Phone: 901/544-4137
Fax: 901/575-3510

*Knoxville
301 East Church Avenue, 37915
Phone: 615/545-4637
Fax: 615/545-4435

TEXAS
Dallas
Suite 170
2050 North Stemmons Freeway
P.O. Box 58130, 75258
Phone: 214/767-0542
Fax: 214/767-8240

*Austin
1700 Congress Avenue, Second Floor
P.O. Box 12728, 78711
Phone: 512/482-5939
Fax: 512/482-5940

Houston
Suite 1160
#1 Allen Center,
500 Dallas, 77002
Phone: 713/229-2578
Fax: 713/229-2203

UTAH
Salt Lake City
Suite 105
324 South State Street, 84111
Phone: 801/524-5116
Fax: 801/524-5886

VERMONT
**Montpelier (Served by Boston,
Massachusetts, District Office)*
4th Floor
109 State Street, 05609
Phone: 802/828-4508
Fax: 802/828-3258

VIRGINIA
Richmond
700 Center, Suite 550
704 East Franklin Street, 23219
Phone: 804/771-2246
Fax: 804/771-2390

WASHINGTON
Seattle
Suite 290
3131 Elliott Avenue, 98121
Phone: 206/553-5615
Fax: 206/553-7253

*Tri Cities
Suite 350
320 North Johnson Street,
Kennewick, WA 99336
Phone: 509/735-2751
Fax: 509/783-9385

WEST VIRGINIA
Charleston
Suite 807
405 Capitol Street, 25301
Phone: 304/347-5123
Fax: 304/347-5408

WISCONSIN
Milwaukee
Room 596
517 East Wisconsin Avenue, 53202
Phone: 414/297-3473
Fax: 414/297-3470

WYOMING
*Served by Denver, Colorado, District
Office*

*** Denotes Trade Specialist at a
Branch Office**

SECTION 2

Small Business Development Centers

International Trade Programs

SBDC International Trade Programs

Small Business Development Centers (SBDCs) provide a wide range of business assistance including export counseling. There are over 900 SBDCs throughout the United States. Over twenty SBDCs have designated International Trade Centers; all SBDCs provide some trade counseling/referral.

Designated SBDC International Trade Centers

ALABAMA
University of Alabama in
Birmingham
1717 Eleventh Avenue South,
Suite 419
Birmingham, AL 35294-4410
Phone: 205/934-7260
FAX: 205/934-7645

Alabama International Trade Center
University of Alabama
201 Bidgood Hall
Tuscaloosa, AL 35487-0396
Phone: 205/348-7621
FAX: 205/348-6974

CALIFORNIA
California Department of Commerce
801 K Street, Suite 1700
Sacramento, CA 95814
Phone: 916/324-5068
FAX:916/322-5084

Export Small Business Development
Center of Southern California
110 East Ninth Street, Suite A-669
Los Angeles, CA 90079
Phone: 213/892-1111
FAX: 213/892-8232

FLORIDA
Trade Expansion Center
University of West Florida, Building 8
Pensacola, FL 32514
Phone: 904/474-2908
FAX: 904/474-2126

Florida Atlantic University
777 Glades Road, Building T-9
P.O. Box 3091
Boca Raton, FL 33431-0991
Phone: 407/362-5620
FAX: 407/362-5623

GEORGIA
University of Georgia
Chicopee Complex
1180 East Broad Street
Athens, GA 30602
Phone: 706/542-7436
FAX: 706/542-6776

ILLINOIS
Illinois Department of Commerce
and Community Affairs
620 East Adams Street
Springfield, IL 62701
Phone: 217/524-5856
FAX: 217/785-6328

College of Dupage
22nd & Lambert Road
Glen Ellyn, IL 60137-6599
Phone: 708/858-2800, Ext. 2771
FAX: 708/790-1197

Bradley University
141 North Jobst Hall, First Floor
Peoria, IL 61625
Phone: 309/677-2992
FAX: 309/677-3386

Small Business Development Center
Southern Illinois University,
Edwardsville
Campus Box 1107
Edwardsville, IL 62026
Phone: 618/692-2929
FAX: 618/692-2647

LOUISIANA

Northeast Louisiana University
College of Business Administration
700 University Avenue
Monroe, LA 71209
Phone: 318/342-5506
FAX: 318/342-5510

University of New Orleans
1600 Canal Street, Suite 620
New Orleans, LA 70112
Phone: 504/539-9292
FAX: 504/539-9295

MICHIGAN

Wayne State University
2727 Second Avenue, Room 107
Detroit, MI 48201
Phone: 313/964-1798
FAX: 313/964-4164

Center for International Business
Development
Michigan State University
7 Eppley Center
East Lansing, MI 48824-1121
Phone: 517/353-4336
FAX: 517/432-1009

MISSISSIPPI

University of Mississippi
Old Chemistry Building, Suite 216
University, MS 38677
Phone: 601/232-5001
FAX: 601/232-5650

International Trade Center
Hinds Community College
P.O. Box 1170
Raymond, MS 39154
Phone: 601/857-3536
FAX: 601/857-3535

OREGON

Lane Community College
Oregon Small Business Network
44 West Broadway, Suite 501
Eugene, OR 97401
Phone: 503/726-2250
FAX: 503/345-6006

Portland Community College
Open Campus
International Trade Program
121 SW Salmon Street, Suite 210
Portland, OR 97204
Phone: 503/274-7482
FAX: 503/228-6350

PENNSYLVANIA
University of Pennsylvania
The Wharton School
423 Vance Hall
Philadelphia, PA 19104
Phone: 215/898-1219
FAX: 215/573-2135

Wharton Export Network
3733 Spruce Street, Suite 413
Philadelphia, PA 19104
Phone: 215/898-4861
FAX: 215/898-1299

Lehigh Small Business
Development Center
The Rauch Business Center
621 Taylor Street
Bethlehem, PA 18015
Phone: 610/758-3980
FAX: 610/758-5205

Kutztown University
Small Business Development Center
2986 North Second Street
Harrisburg, PA 17110
Phone: 717/720-4230
FAX: 717/233-3181

TENNESSEE
Small Business Development Center
University of Memphis
Memphis, TN 38152
Phone: 901/678-2500
FAX: 901/678-4072

TEXAS
North Texas Small Business
Development Center
Dallas Community College
1402 Corinth
Dallas, TX 75215
Phone: 214/565-5833
FAX: 214/565-5813

Small Business Development Center
P.O. Box 580299
2050 Stemmons Freeway
World Trade Center, Suite 150
Dallas, TX 75258
Phone: 214/747-1300, Code 68
FAX: 214/748-5774

University of Houston
Small Business Development Center
1100 Louisiana, Suite 500
Houston, TX 77002
Phone: 713/752-8404
FAX: 713/756-1500

South Texas Border
Small Business Development Center
University of Texas at San Antonio
1222 North Main, Suite 450
San Antonio, TX 78212
Phone: 210/558-2460
FAX: 210/558-2464

WASHINGTON
Washington State University
College of Business and Economics
245 Todd Hall
Pullman, WA 99164-4727
Phone: 509/335-1576
FAX: 509/335-0949

International Trade Institute
North Seattle Community College
9600 College Way North
Seattle, WA 98103
Phone: 206/527-3732
FAX: 206/527-3734

OTHER SBDCs ACTIVE IN INTERNATIONAL TRADE

ARIZONA
Arizona Small Business Development
Center Network
2411 West 14th Street
Tempe, AZ 85281
Phone: 602/731-8720
FAX: 602/731-8729

COLORADO
Colorado Office of Business
Development
1625 Broadway, Suite 1710
Denver, CO 80202
Phone: 303/892-3840
FAX: 303/892-3848

Front Range Community College
Small Business Development Center
3645 West 112th Avenue
Westminster, CO 80030
Phone: 303/460-1032
FAX: 303/469-7143

IDAHO
Boise State University
College of Business
1910 University Drive
Boise, ID 83725
Phone: 208/385-1640
FAX: 208/385-3877

International Trade Coordinator
Lewis Clark State College
500 Eighth Avenue
Lewiston, ID 83501
Phone: 208/799-2465
FAX: 208/799-2831

INDIANA
Indiana Economic Development
Council
One North Capital, Suite 425
Indianapolis, IN 46204-2248
Phone: 317/631-0871
FAX: 317/231-7067

IOWA

Iowa State University
Small Business Development Center
137 Lynn Avenue
Ames, IA 50014
Phone: 515/292-6351
FAX: 515/292-0020

Northeast Iowa Small Business
Development Center
Dubuque Area Chamber of
Commerce
770 Town Clock Plaza
Dubuque, IA 52001
Phone: 319/588-3350
FAX: 319/557-1591

Eastern Iowa Small Business
Development Center
304 West Second Street
Davenport, IA 52801
Phone: 319/322-4499
FAX: 319/322-8241

MASSACHUSETTS

University of Massachusetts
School of Management, Room 205
Amherst, MA 01003
Phone: 413/545-6301
FAX: 413/545-1273

MISSOURI

University of Missouri, Columbia
300 University Place
Columbia, MO 65211
Phone: 314/882-0344
FAX: 314/884-4297

Central Missouri State University
Small Business Development Center
Grinstead 75
Warrensburg, MO 64093-5087
Phone: 816/543-4402
FAX: 816/543-8159

Missouri Southern State College
Small Business Development Center
107 Matthews Hall
3950 Newman Road
Joplin, MO 64801
Phone: 417/625-9313
FAX: 417/625-9782

Southwest Missouri State University
Small Business Development Center
901 South National
Box 88
Springfield, MO 65804
Phone: 417/836-5685
FAX: 417/836-7666

MONTANA

Montana Department of Commerce
SBDC
1424 Ninth Avenue
Helena, MT 59620
Phone: 406/444-4780
FAX: 406/444-1872

NEBRASKA

University of Nebraska, Omaha
60th & Dodge Streets, CBA
Room 407
Omaha, NE 68182
Phone: 402/554-2521
FAX: 402/554-3747

University of Nebraska, Omaha
1313 Farnam, Room 132
Omaha, NE 68182
Phone: 402/595-2381
FAX: 402/595-2385

NEVADA
University of Nevada SBDC
Mail Stop 032
Reno, NV 89557-0100
Phone: 702/784-1717
FAX: 702/784-4337

NEW HAMPSHIRE
University of New Hampshire
108 McConnell Hall
Durham, NH 03824
Phone: 603/862-2200
FAX: 603/862-4876

International Trade Resource Center
601 Spaulding Turnpike, Suite 29
Portsmouth, NH 03801-2840
Phone: 603/334-6074
FAX: 603/334-6110

NEW JERSEY
Rutgers University
Ackerson Hall, Third Floor
180 University Avenue
Newark, NJ 07102
Phone: 201/648-5950
FAX: 201/648-1110

NEW YORK
State University of New York
SUNY Plaza, S-523
Albany, NY 12246
Phone: 518/443-5398
FAX: 518/465-4992

International Trade Coordinator
Small Business Development Center
State University College, Buffalo
1300 Elmwood Avenue, Ba-117
Buffalo, NY 14222
Phone: 716/878-4030
FAX: 716/878-4067

Small Business Development Center
Rockland Community College
145 College Road
Suffern, NY 10901
Phone: 914/356-0370
FAX: 914/356-0381

NORTH CAROLINA
University of North Carolina
4509 Creedmoor Road, Suite 201
Raleigh, NC 27612
Phone: 919/571-4154
FAX: 919/571-4161

OHIO
Ohio Department of Development
77 South High Street
P.O. Box 1001
Columbus, OH 43216-0101
Phone: 614/466-2711
FAX: 614/466-0829

Southeast Ohio Small Business
Development Center
Ohio University at Athens
Innovation Center
20 East Circle Drive, Suite 190
Athens, OH 45701
Phone: 614/593-1797
FAX: 614/593-1795

Toledo Small Business
Development Center
300 Madison Avenue. Suite 270
Toledo, OH 43604
Phone: 419/252-2700
FAX: 419/252-2724

Lake County Small Business
Development Center
Lake County Economic
Development Center
Lakeland Community College
7750 Clock Tower Drive
Kirtland, OH 44094
Phone: 216/951-1290
FAX: 216/951-7736

Marietta College SBDC
Marietta College
Marietta, OH 45750
Phone: 614/376-4832
FAX: 614/376-4901

RHODE ISLAND
Bryant College
1150 Douglas Pike
Smithfield, RI 02917
Phone: 401/232-6111
FAX: 401/232-6416

SOUTH CAROLINA
University of South Carolina
College of Business Administration
1710 College Street
Columbia, SC 29208
Phone: 803/777-4907
FAX: 803/777-4403

VIRGINIA
Virginia Department of Economic
Development
P.O. Box 798
Richmond, VA 23206-0798
Phone: 804/371-8253
FAX: 804/225-3384

Northern Virginia
Small Business Development Center
4260 Chainbridge Road, Suite A-1
Fairfax, VA 22030
Phone: 703/993-2131
FAX: 703/993-2126

Longwood Small Business
Development Center
Longwood College
515 Main Street
Farmville, VA 23909
Phone: 804/395-2086
FAX: 804/395-2359

James Madison University
Small Business Development Center
College of Business
Zane Showker Hall, Room 527
Harrisonburg, VA 22807
Phone: 703/568-3227
FAX: 703/568-3299

Small Business Development Center
of Hampton Roads
420 Bank Street, P.O. Box 327
Norfolk, VA 23501
Phone: 804/622-6414 or
804/825-2957
FAX: 804/622-5563 or 804/825-3552

WASHINGTON, D.C.
Howard University
Small Business Development Center
2600 Sixth Street, N.W.
Room 128
Washington, D.C. 20059
Phone: 202/806-1550
FAX: 202/806-1777

SECTION 3

OTHER FEDERAL AGENCIES

U.S. DEPARTMENT OF STATE

U.S. Department of State commercial and economic staffs provide political and economic briefings and advice on the business culture and practices of the host country to U.S. firms traveling overseas. State Department Foreign Service officers are responsible for commercial work in 96 embassies and 36 consulates not covered by the U.S. and Foreign Commercial Service (US&FCS), and they work closely with their US&FCS colleagues worldwide.

Contact: State Department operator (202) 647-4000

The Bureau of Economic and Business Affairs in the U.S. Department of State formulates and implements policies regarding foreign economic matters and international trade promotion and business services. The Office of the Coordinator for Business Affairs in the Bureau of Economic and Business Affairs ensures that the Department of State and its overseas missions provide consistent and effective support to U.S. business. The coordinator for business affairs is the primary point of contact for business concerns within the Department of State.

Contact: Office of the Coordinator for Business Affairs
             U.S. Department of State
             Telephone: 202/736-4167
             FAX: 202/647-5957

Country Desk Officers in regional bureaus maintain regular contact with overseas diplomatic missions and provide country specific economic and political analysis for U.S. companies. There are the bureaus of African, Inter-American, European, Near East, South Asian, and East Asian and Pacific Affairs. Each bureau has a commercial coordinator to assist U.S. businesses.

This section lists State Department Country Desk Officers and Passport Offices throughout the United States.

State Department Country Desk Officers

Country	Phone (202)	Country	Phone (202)
Afghanistan	647-9552	Cape Verde	647-1596
Albania	647-3747	Cen. African Rep.	647-1707
Algeria	647-4680	Chad	647-1707
Andorra	647-1412	Chile	647-2575
Angola	647-8434	China	647-6300
Antigua and Barbuda	647-2130	Colombia	647-4173
Argentina	647-3402	Comoros	647-6473
Armenia	647-6758	Congo	647-3139
Australia	647-9691	Cook Islands	647-3546
Austria	647-2005	Costa Rica	647-3518
Azerbaijan	647-6048	Cote d'Ivoire	647-1540
Bahamas	647-2621	Council of Europe	647-2469
Bahrain	647-6571	Croatia	647-7361
Bangladesh	647-9552	CSCE	647-7299
Barbados	647-2130	Cuba	647-7480
Belarus	647-8671	Cyprus	647-6113
Belgium	647-6592	Czech Republic	647-1457
Belize	647-3330	Denmark	647-6582
Benin	647-1540	Diego Garcia	647-6453
Bermuda	647-8027	Djibouti	647-5684
Bhutan	647-2141	Dominica	647-2130
Bolivia	647-4193	Dominican Republic	647-2620
Bosnia-Herzegovina	647-7679	Ecuador	647-4176
Botswana	647-8433	Egypt	647-2365
Brazil	647-9407	El Salvador	647-3681
British IO Territory	647-5684	Equatorial Guinea	647-1707
Brunei	647-3276	Eritrea	647-9742
Bulgaria	647-0310	Estonia	647-8908
Burkina Faso	647-2791	Ethiopia	647-6485
Burma	647-7108	European Community	647-3928
Burundi	647-3139	Fiji	647-3546
Cambodia	647-3133	Finland	647-9980
Cameroon	647-1707	France	647-1412
Canada	647-2170	French Antilles	647-2130

Country	Phone (202)	Country	Phone (202)
French Polynesia	647-3546	Kyrgyzstan	647-8956
Gabon	647-3139	Laos	647-3133
Gambia	647-4567	Latvia	647-8908
GCC Affairs	647-6562	Lebanon	647-1038
Georgia	647-6795	Lesotho	647-8433
Germany	647-2155	Liberia	647-1658
Ghana	647-1596	Libya	647-4674
Gibraltar	647-8027	Liechtenstein	647-2005
Greece	647-6113	Lithuania	647-8908
Greenland	647-5669	Luxembourg	647-6557
Grenada	647-2130	Macau	647-6300
Guadeloupe	647-2130	Macedonia	647-0757
Guatemala	647-3559	Madagascar	647-6473
Guinea	647-3407	Malawi	647-8432
Guinea-Bissau	647-1596	Malaysia	647-3276
Guyana	647-2621	Maldives	647-2351
Haiti	647-5088	Mali	647-2791
Honduras	647-0087	Malta	647-3746
Hong Kong	647-6300	Marshall Islands	647-0108
Hungary	647-3238	Martinique	647-2130
Iceland	647-5669	Mauritania	647-3407
India	647-2141	Mauritius	647-6473
Indonesia	647-3276	Mexico	647-8186
Iran	647-6111	Micronesia	647-0108
Iraq	647-5692	Moldova	647-6764
Ireland	647-8027	Monaco	647-1412
Israel	647-3672	Mongolia	647-6300
Italy	647-3746	Morocco	647-4675
Jamaica	647-2621	Mozambique	647-8433
Japan	647-3152	Namibia	647-9429
Jordan	647-1022	NATO	647-7299
Kazakhstan	647-6859	Nauru	647-3546
Kenya	647-6479	Nepal	647-1450
Kiribati	647-3546	Netherlands	647-6557
Korea	647-7717	Netherlands Antilles	647-2621
Kuwait	647-6562	New Caledonia	647-3546

Country	Phone (202)	Country	Phone (202)
Newly Indep. States	647-1152	Spain	647-1412
New Zealand	647-9691	Sri Lanka	647-2351
Nicaragua	647-1510	Sudan	647-6475
Niger	647-2791	Suriname	647-2621
Nigeria	647-1597	Swaziland	647-8433
Norway	647-5669	Sweden	647-5669
OECD	647-2469	Switzerland	647-2005
Oman	647-6571	Syria	647-1131
Pacific Islands	647-3546	Taiwan Coor.	647-7711
Pakistan	647-9823	Tajikistan	647-8956
Palau	647-0108	Tanzania	647-6473
Panama	647-4986	Thailand	647-7108
Papua New Guinea	647-3546	Togo	647-1540
Paraguay	647-1551	Tonga	647-3546
Peru	647-3360	Trinidad & Tobago	647-2130
Philippines	647-1221	Tunisia	647-3614
Poland	647-4139	Turkey	647-6114
Portugal	647-1412	Turkmenistan	647-8956
Qatar	647-6558	Tuvalu	647-3546
Romania	647-4272	Uganda	647-6479
Russia	647-6739	Ukraine	647-6799
Rwanda	647-3139	United Arab Emirates	647-6558
San Marino	647-2453	United Kingdom	647-8027
Såo Tomé & Príncipe	647-3139	Uruguay	647-1551
Saudi Arabia	647-7550	Uzbekistan	647-8956
Senegal	647-2865	Vanuatu	647-3546
Serbia-Montenegro	647-2452	Vatican	647-3746
Seychelles	647-6473	Venezuela	647-4216
Sierra Leone	647-4567	Vietnam	647-3132
Singapore	647-3278	Western Samoa	647-3546
Slovakia	647-3191	Yemen	647-6562
Slovenia	647-7152	Zaire	647-2080
Solomon Islands	647-3546	Zambia	647-8432
Somalia	647-6453	Zimbabwe	647-9429
South Africa	647-8252		
South Pacific Com.	647-3546		

U.S. DEPARTMENT OF STATE PASSPORT AGENCIES

CALIFORNIA
Los Angeles Passport Agency
11000 Wilshire Boulevard,
Room 13100
Los Angeles, CA 90024-3615
Phone: 310/235-7070

San Francisco Passport Agency
525 Market Street, Suite 200
San Francisco, CA 94105-2773
Phone: 415/744-4444

CONNECTICUT
Stamford Passport Agency
One Landmark Square
Broad and Atlantic Streets
Stamford, CT 06901-2767
Phone: 203/325-3530 or
203/325-3538

DISTRICT OF COLUMBIA
Washington Passport Agency
1111 19th Street, N.W.
Washington, D.C. 20522-1705
Phone: 202/647-0518 or
202/955-0351

FLORIDA
Miami Passport Agency
Federal Office Building, Third Floor
51 Southwest First Avenue
Miami, FL 33130-1680
Phone: 305/536-4681

HAWAII
Honolulu Passport Agency
First Hawaiian Tower, Suite 500
1132 Bishop Street
Honolulu, HI 96813-2809
Phone: 808/522-8283 or
808/522-8286

ILLINOIS
Chicago Passport Agency
Kluczynski Federal Building,
Suite 380
230 South Dearborn Street
Chicago, IL 60604-1564
Phone: 312/353-7155

LOUISIANA
New Orleans Passport Agency
Postal Services Building
Room T-12005
701 Loyola Avenue
New Orleans, LA 70113
Phone: 504/589-6161 or
504/589-6163

MASSACHUSETTS
Boston Passport Agency
Thomas P. O'Neill Federal Building
Room 247
10 Causeway Street
Boston, MA 02222
Phone: 617/565-6990

NEW HAMPSHIRE
National Passport Center
31 Rochester Avenue
Portsmouth, NH 03810
Phone: 603/334-0500

NEW YORK
New York Passport Agency
Rockefeller Center, Room 270
630 Fifth Avenue-0031
New York, NY 10111
Phone: 212/399-5290

PENNSYLVANIA
Philadelphia Passport Agency
U.S. Customs House, Room 103
2nd and Chestnut Streets
Philadelphia, PA 19106-1684
Phone: 215/597-7480

TEXAS
Houston Passport Agency
Mickey Leland Federal Building
1919 Smith Street, Suite 1100
Houston, TX 77022
Phone: 713/653-3153

WASHINGTON
Seattle Passport Agency
Henry M. Jackson Federal Building
915 Second Avenue, Room 992
Seattle, WA 98174-1091
Phone: 206/220-7788

Export-Import Bank of the United States

The Export-Import Bank (Ex-Im Bank) of the United States is the U.S. government agency that facilitates the export financing of U.S. goods and services. Ex-Im Bank offers four major export finance support programs: loans, guarantees, working capital guarantees and export credit insurance.

Ex-Im Bank's export credit insurance program provides insurance policies to give exporters protection against the commercial and political risks of default when they find that they must offer credit to compete for or expand foreign sales. The program includes a Small Business Insurance Policy that offers special assistance to small businesses in their exporting efforts.

Export-Import Bank U.S. Toll-Free Number: 1/800/565-EXIM or 202/565-3946

Business Development Group
811 Vermont Avenue, N.W.
Washington, D.C. 20571
Phone: 202/565-3900
FAX: 202/565-3931

Electronic Bulletin Board
202/565-3835

REGIONAL OFFICES

MIDWEST
U.S. Export Assistance Center
55 W. Monroe Street, Suite 2440
Chicago, IL 60603
Phone: 312/353-8081
FAX: 312/353-8098

SOUTHWEST
Ashford Crossing II
1880 South Dairy Ashford, Suite 585
Houston, TX 77077
Phone: 713/589-8182
FAX: 713/589-8184

WEST
222 N. Sepulveda Blvd., Suite 1515
El Segundo, CA 90245
Phone: 310/322-1152
FAX: 310/322-2041

SOUTHEAST
U.S. Export Assistance Center
5600 N.W. 36th Street, Suite 617
Miami, FL 33159-0570
Phone: 305/526-7425
FAX: 305/526-7435

NORTHEAST
6 World Trade Center, Suite 238
New York, NY 10048
Phone: 212/466-2950
FAX: 212/466-2959

Overseas Private Investment Corporation

Overseas Private Investment Corporation (OPIC) encourages and assists U.S. private investments in lesser developed nations. OPIC insurance and financing are available in 140 countries around the world. OPIC provides for political risk insurance for overseas investment and direct loans of up to $6 million for small businesses.

For information about what OPIC can do, call 202/336-8799 or FAX: 202/833-3375.

> Overseas Private Investment Corporation
> 1100 New York Avenue, N.W.
> Washington, D.C. 20527
> Phone: 202/336-8799
> FAX: 202/789-2566

U.S. Trade Representative

The Office of the U.S. Trade Representative (USTR) is an agency of the Executive Office of the President responsible for developing and coordinating U.S. international trade and commodity and trade-related investment policy.

The agency provides trade policy leadership and negotiating expertise in major areas of responsibility including the following:

- All matters within the General Agreement on Tariffs and Trade (GATT);
- Trade, commodity and trade-related investment matters dealt with by international institutions such as the Organization for Economic Cooperation and Development (OECD) and the United Nations Conference on Trade and Development (UNCTAD);
- Other trade and trade-related investment issues including intellectual property protection issues and import policy; and
- Enforcement and implementation of U.S. trade laws.

United States Trade Representative
Office of Public Affairs and Private
Sector Liaison
600 17th Street, N.W., Room 103
Washington, D.C. 20506
Phone: 202/395-3350
FAX: 202/395-7226

Office of the General Counsel
United States Trade Representative
600 17th Street, N.W., Room 223
Washington, D.C. 20506
Phone: 202/395-3432
FAX: 202/395-3911

Office of Agriculture
United States Trade Representative
600 17th Street, N.W., Room 423
Washington, D.C. 20506
Phone: 202/395-5006
FAX: 202/395-3911

Office of Industry
United States Trade Representative
600 17th Street, N.W., Room 420
Washington, D.C. 20506
Phone: 202/395-5656
FAX: 202/395-3911

Office of Environment and
Intellectual Property
United States Trade Representative
600 17th Street, N.W., Room 409
Washington, D.C. 20506
Phone: 202/395-7320
FAX: 202/395-3911

Office of Services, Investment
& Science
United States Trade Representative
600 17th Street, N.W., Room 409
Washington, D.C. 20506
Phone: 202/395-3606
FAX: 202/395-3911

Office of Textiles
United States Trade Representative
600 17th Street, N.W., Room 300
Washington, D.C. 20506
Phone: 202/395-3026
FAX: 202/395-3911

U.S. Department of the Treasury-Customs Service

The U.S. Customs Service, an agency within the Department of the Treasury, is responsible for enforcing the laws of the United States at the country's borders with respect to goods entering or leaving the country. Headquartered in Washington, D.C., the U.S. Customs Service divides its offices among seven regions.

U.S. Customs Service Offices

Headquarters Office
U.S. Customs Service
1201 Constitution Avenue, N.W.
Washington, D.C. 20229
Phone: 202/927-6724

NAFTA Hotline
U.S. Customs
202/927-0066

Northeast Regional Offices

MASSACHUSETTS
10 Causeway Street
Boston, MA 02222-1056
Phone: 617/565-6240

NEW YORK
6 World Trade Center
New York, NY 10048
Phone: 212/466-4487

Northeast District Offices

MAINE
312 Fore Street
P.O. Box 4688
Portland, ME 04112
Phone: 207/780-3326

MARYLAND
200 St. Paul Place
Baltimore, MD 21202
Phone: 410/962-2666

NEW JERSEY
Hemisphere Center
Newark, NJ 07114
Phone: 201/645-3760

NEW YORK
Kennedy Airport Area
Building 77, Room 228, 2nd Floor
Jamaica, NY 11430
Phone: 718/553-1542

111 West Huron Street, Room 603
Buffalo, NY 14202
Phone: 716/846-4373

127 North Water Street
Ogdensburg, NY 13669
Phone: 315/393-0660

PENNSYLVANIA

Second and Chestnut Streets,
Room 102
Philadelphia, PA 19106
Phone: 215/597-4605

RHODE ISLAND

49 Pavilion Avenue
Providence, RI 02905
Phone: 401/528-5080

VERMONT

Main & Stebbins Streets
P.O. Box 1490
St. Albans, VT 05478
Phone: 802/524-6527

SOUTHEAST REGIONAL OFFICE

FLORIDA

909 Southeast First Avenue
Miami, FL 33130
Phone: 305/536-5952

SOUTHEAST DISTRICT OFFICES

FLORIDA

P.O. Box 025280
Miami, FL 33102-5280
Phone: 305/869-2800

4430 East Adamo Drive, Suite 301
Tampa, FL 33605
Phone: 813/228-2381

GEORGIA

One East Bay Street
Savannah, GA 31401
Phone: 912/652-4256

NORTH CAROLINA

One Virginia Avenue
Wilmington, NC 28401
Phone: 919/343-4601

PUERTO RICO

One La Puntilla
Old San Juan, PR 00901
Phone: 809/729-6950

SOUTH CAROLINA

200 East Bay Street
Charleston, SC 29401
Phone: 803/724-4312

VIRGIN ISLANDS

Main P.O. Sugar Estate
Charlotte Amalie
St. Thomas, VI 00801
Phone: 809/774-2510

VIRGINIA
101 East Main Street
Norfolk, VA 23510
Phone: 804/441-6546

WASHINGTON, D.C.
P.O. Box 17423
Washington, D.C. 20041
Phone: 703/318-5900

Southwest Regional Office

TEXAS
2323 South Shepherd, Ste. 200
Houston, TX 77019
Phone: 713/942-6840

Southwest District Offices

TEXAS
1215 Royal Lane
P.O. Box 619050
Fort Worth, TX 75261
Phone: 214/574-2170

9400 Viscount Street
P.O. Box 9516
El Paso, TX 79925
Phone: 915/540-5800

Lincoln Juarez Bridge
P.O. Box 3130
Laredo TX, 78044-3130
Phone: 210/726-2267

4550 75th Street
Port Arthur, TX 77642
Phone: 409/724-0087

ARIZONA
International & Terrace Streets
Nogales, AZ 85621
Phone: 602/761-2010

South Central Regional Office

LOUISIANA
423 Canal Street
New Orleans, LA 70130
Phone: 504/589-6476

South Central District Office

ALABAMA
150 North Royal Street
Mobile, AL 36602
Phone: 205/690-2106

North Central Regional Office

ILLINOIS
55 East Monroe Street
Chicago, IL 60603-5890
Phone: 312/353-9258

North Central District Offices

ILLINOIS
610 South Canal Street
Chicago, IL 60607
Phone: 312/353-6100

MICHIGAN
477 Michigan Avenue, Room 200
Detroit, MI 48226-2568
Phone: 313/226-3177

MINNESOTA
515 West First Street, Room 209
Duluth, MN 55802-1390
Phone: 218/720-5201

110 South Fourth Street
Minneapolis, MN 55401
Phone: 612/348-1690

MISSOURI
7911 Forsyth Boulevard, Suite 625
St. Louis, MO 63134
Phone: 314/428-2662

MONTANA
300 Second Avenue South
P.O. Box 789
Great Falls, MT 59405
Phone: 406/453-7631

NORTH DAKOTA
Federal Building
P.O. Box 610
Pembina, ND 58271
Phone: 701/825-6201

OHIO
Plaza Nine Building, 6th Floor
55 Erieview Plaza
Cleveland, OH 44114
Phone: 216/891-3800

WISCONSIN
6269 Ace Industrial Drive
P.O. Box 37260
Milwaukee, WI 53237-0260
Phone: 414/297-3925

Pacific Regional Office

CALIFORNIA
One World Trade Center, Suite 705
Long Beach, CA 90831
Phone: 310/980-3238

Pacific District Offices

ALASKA
605 West Fourth Avenue
Anchorage, AK 99501
Phone: 907/271-2675

CALIFORNIA
300 South Ferry Street
Terminal Island
San Pedro, CA 90731
Phone: 310/514-6001

880 Front Street, Suite 5-S-9
San Diego, CA 92101
Phone: 619/557-5360

P.O. Box 2450
San Francisco, CA 94105
Phone: 415/744-7700

HAWAII
335 Merchant Street
P.O. Box 1641
Honolulu, HI 96806
Phone: 808/541-1725

OREGON
511 Northwest Broadway
Portland, OR 97209
Phone: 503/326-2865

WASHINGTON
1000 Second Avenue, Suite 2200
Seattle, WA 98104
Phone: 206/553-0554

U.S. Department of Agriculture

The U.S. Department of Agriculture's Foreign Agricultural Service (FAS) represents U.S. agricultural interests through its network of agricultural counselors, attaches and trade officers stationed overseas and its backup team of analysts, marketing specialists, negotiators and related specialists in Washington, D.C.

Export services include trade leads, foreign buyers lists, export market profiles, trade negotiations, credit guarantees, food assistance, market development and efforts to counter unfair trade practices abroad. The Trade Assistance and Planning Office (TAPO) of the FAS is the main contact point for persons interested in participating in export programs carried out by FAS and the Commodity Credit Corporation.

Foreign Agricultural Service

TAPO
USDA/FAS, Room 4939
Washington, D.C. 20250
Phone: 202/690-0159
FAX: 202/690-4374

Grain and Feed
202/720-4168

Horticultural Products
202/720-7931

Oilseeds and Products
202/720-7037

Dairy, Livestock, Seafood and Poultry
202/720-3899

Tobacco, Cotton and Seeds
202/720-9516

Forest Products
202/720-0638

U.S. AGENCY FOR INTERNATIONAL DEVELOPMENT

The U.S. Agency for International Development (USAID) is the principal Federal agency that implements the U.S. Foreign Economic Assistance Program in nearly 100 countries throughout the developing world. Acting on behalf of the U.S. government, USAID commits a loan or awards a grant to an eligible USAID-recipient country. From these loans and grants flow technical assistance projects and commodity programs implemented through the provision of technical assistance services and/or commodities from U.S. suppliers.

USAID's Center for Trade & Investment Services (CTIS) promotes increased business activity between U.S. businesses and foreign entrepreneurs in Asia, the Near East, Africa, Latin America, Eastern Europe and the Newly Independent States of the former Soviet Union.

CTIS assists U.S. business by:
- Providing a central point of contact for all inquiries about business opportunities in USAID-assisted countries;
- Providing information about USAID-financed procurement opportunities;
- Providing information about USAID's private sector programs overseas;
- Sponsoring industry-specific transaction conferences; and
- Linking U.S. firms with entrepreneurs overseas.

> Center for Trade & Investment Services
> USAID, G/EG/CTIS
> SA-2, Room 100
> Washington, D.C. 20523-0229
> Phone: 800/872-4348 (outside of Washington, DC)
> Phone: 202/663-2660 (local)
> FAX: 202/663-2670
> INTERNET: CTIS@USAID.GOV (electronic mail only)

USAID's *Office of Small and Disadvantaged Business Utilization/ Minority Resource Center (OSDBU/MRC)* maintains the USAID *Consultant Registry Information System (ACRIS)*. ACRIS is an automated database that describes the capabilities of U.S. businesses, organizations and institutions that have expressed interest in participating in USAID-financed technical assistance projects. The Office also maintains the mailing list for the *A.I.D. Procurement Information Bulletin*, which announces intended procurement of USAID-financed commodities and publishes *The Guide to Doing Business with the Agency for International Development*. OSDBU/MRC is the advocate for U.S. small businesses and disadvantaged enterprises (including women-owned businesses). OSDBU/MRC ensures their consideration as sources for the procurement of goods and services financed through USAID development assistance activities. The office also coordinates the agency's implementation of the Disadvantaged Enterprises Program (formerly the Gray Amendment).

Office of Small and Disadvantaged Business
Utilization/Minority Resource Center
USAID/OSDBU/MRC
Washington, D.C. 20523-1414
Phone: 703/875-1551
FAX: 703/875-1862

Publications and information about USAID are available today through your Internet service provider's access to Internet at the following address:

gopher@info.usaid.gov

Information will be continuously updated to provide the public with new methods for doing business with USAID.

USAID MISSION DIRECTORY

AFRICA, EAST AND SOUTHERN
USAID/Nairobi, Kenya
Regional Economic Development
Services Office (REDSO/ESA)
Washington, DC 20521-8900

ALBANIA
American Embassy/Tirana
PSC 59, Box 100 (A)
APO AE 09624

ARMENIA
USAID/Yerevan
Washington, D.C. 20521-7020

BANGLADESH
USAID/Dhaka
Washington, D.C. 20521-6120

BARBADOS
American Embassy/USAID
APO AA 34055

BELIZE
(closing by September 30, 1996)
USAID/Belize City
Washington, D.C. 20521-3050

BENIN
USAID/Cotonou
Washington, D.C. 20521-2120

BOLIVIA
USAID/La Paz
American Embassy/USAID
Unit #3914
APO AE 34032

BOTSWANA
(closing by September 30, 1995)
USAID/Gaborone
Washington, D.C. 20521-2170

BRAZIL
USAID/Brasilia Unit #350
APO AA 34030

BULGARIA
USAID/Sofia
Washington, D.C. 20521-5740

BURKINA FASO
(closing by September 30, 1995)
USAID/Ouagadougou
Washington, D.C. 20521-2440

BURUNDI
USAID/Bujumbura
Washington, D.C. 20521-2100

CAMBODIA
American Embassy
Phnom Penh, Box P
APO AP 96546

CAMEROON
(closing by September 30, 1995)
USAID/Yaoundé
Washington, D.C. 20521-2520

CAPE VERDE
(closing by September 30, 1996)
USAID/Praia
Washington, D.C. 20521-2460

CHAD
(closing by September 30, 1995)
USAID/N'Djamena
Washington, D.C. 20521-2410

CHILE
(closing by September 30, 1996)
American Embassy Santiago
Unit #4128
APO AA 34033

COLOMBIA
American Embassy/USAID
APO AA 34038

COSTA RICA
(closing by September 30, 1996)
American Embassy Costa Rica
APO AA 34020

CROATIA/SLOVENIA
USAID/Zagreb
Unit #25402
APO AE 09213

CZECH REPUBLIC
American Embassy Prague
Unit #25402
APO AE 09213

DOMINICAN REPUBLIC
USAID/Santo Domingo
Unit #5541
APO AA 34041

ECUADOR
American Embassy
Unit #5330
APO AA 34039-3420

EGYPT
USAID/Cairo
Unit #64902
APO AE 09839-4902

EL SALVADOR
American Embassy
El Salvador
APO AA 34023

ESTONIA
American Embassy
Helsinki, (Box T)
APO AE 09723

ETHIOPIA
USAID/Addis Ababa
Washington, D.C. 20521-2030

GAMBIA
USAID/Banjul
Washington, D.C. 20521-2070

GHANA
USAID/Accra
Washington, D.C. 20521-2020

GUATEMALA
American Embassy Guatemala
Unit #3323
APO AA 34024

GUINEA
USAID/Conakry
Washington, D.C. 20521-2110

GUINEA-BISSAU
USAID/Bissau
Washington, D.C. 20521-2080

HAITI
USAID/Port au Prince
Washington, D.C. 20521-3400

HONDURAS
USAID/Tegucigalpa
Unit #2927
APO AA 34022

HUNGARY
American Embassy Budapest
Unit #25402
APO AE 09213-5270

INDIA
USAID/New Delhi
Washington, D.C. 20521-9000

INDONESIA
American Embassy/USAID
Box 4
APO AP 96520

JAMAICA
USAID/Kingston
Washington, D.C. 20521-3210

JORDAN
USAID/Amman
Unit #70206
APO AE 09892-0206

KAZAKHSTAN
USAID/Alma Ata
Washington, D.C. 20521-7030

KENYA
USAID/Nairobi
Washington, D.C. 20521-8900

LATVIA
American Embassy
Helsinki, (Box R)
APO AE 09723

LESOTHO
(closing by September 30, 1995)
USAID/Maseru
Washington, D.C. 20521-2340

LITHUANIA
American Embassy
Helsinki, (Box V)
APO AE 09723

MADAGASCAR
USAID/Antananarivo
Washington, D.C. 20521-2040

MALAWI
USAID/Lilongwe
Washington, D.C. 20521-2280

MALI
USAID/Bamako
Washington, D.C. 20521-2050

MONGOLIA
American Embassy Ulaanbaater
PSC 461, Box 300
FPO AP 96521-0002

MOROCCO
American Embassy Rabat
PSC 74, Box 22
APO AE 09718

MOZAMBIQUE
USAID/Maputo
Washington, D.C. 20521-2330

NAMIBIA
USAID/Windhoek
Washington, D.C. 20521-2540

NEPAL
USAID/Kathmandu
Washington, D.C. 20521-6190

NICARAGUA
American Embassy
USAID/Managua
Unit #2715, Box 9
APO AA 34021

NIGER
USAID/Niamey
Washington, D.C. 20521-2420

NIGERIA
USAID/Lagos
Washington, D.C. 20521-8300

OMAN
(closing by September 30, 1996)
USAID/Muscat
Washington, D.C. 20521-6220

PAKISTAN
(closing by September 30, 1995)
USAID Unit #62206
APO AE 09812-2206

PANAMA
USAID/Panama City
Unit #0949
APO AA 34002

PARAGUAY
USAID/Asunción
APO AE 34036

PERU
American Embassy/USAID
Unit #3760
APO AA 34031

PHILIPPINES
American Embassy/USAID
Unit #8115
APO AP 96440

POLAND
American Embassy Warsaw
Washington, D.C. 20521-5010

ROMANIA
American Embassy/USAID
Unit #25402
APO AE 09213-5260

RUSSIA
American Embassy
USAID/Moscow
PSC 77
APO AE 09721

RWANDA
USAID/Kigali
Washington, D.C. 20521-2210

SENEGAL
USAID/Dakar
Washington, D.C. 20521-2130

SLOVAKIA
USAID/Bratislava
Washington, D.C. 20521-5840

SOMALIA
USAID/Mogadishu
Washington, D.C. 20521-2360

REPUBLIC OF SOUTH AFRICA
USAID/Pretoria
Washington, D.C. 20521-9300

SRI LANKA
USAID/Colombo
Washington, D.C. 20521-6100

SUDAN
American Embassy
Khartoum
Unit #63900
APO AE 09829-3900

SWAZILAND
USAID/Mbabane
Washington, D.C. 20521-2350

TANZANIA
USAID/Dar es Salaam
Washington, D.C. 20521-2140

THAILAND
(closing by September 30, 1995)
USAID, Box 47
APO AD 96546-7200

TUNISIA
(closing by September 30, 1995)
USAID/Tunis
Washington, D.C. 20521-6360

UGANDA
USAID/Kampala
Washington, D.C. 20521-2190

UKRAINE
USAID/Kiev
Washington, D.C. 20521-5850

URUGUAY/ARGENTINA
(closing by September 30, 1995)
American Embassy Montevideo
Unit #4516
APO AA 34035

WEST BANK, GAZA
American Consulate Jerusalem
APO AE 09830

YEMEN ARAB REPUBLIC
USAID/Sana'a
Washington, D.C. 20521-6330

ZAMBIA
USAID/Lusaka
Washington, D.C. 20521-2310

SECTION 4

State Government

International Trade Resources

State Government International Trade Resources

State international trade offices offer trade information and leads, export seminars and a variety of other services.

ALABAMA
Alabama Office of International
Development
401 Adams Avenue, Suite 600
Montgomery, AL 36130
Phone: 205/242-0400
FAX: 205/242-0486

ALASKA
Alaska Department of Commerce and
Economic Development
Office of International Trade
3601 C Street, Suite 798
Anchorage, AK 99503
Phone: 907/561-5585
FAX: 907/561-4577

ARIZONA
Arizona Department of Commerce
International Trade and Investment
Division
3800 North Central, Suite 1500
Phoenix, AZ 85012
Phone: 602/280-1371
FAX: 602/280-1378

ARKANSAS
Arkansas Industrial Development
Commission
Office of International Marketing
One State Capitol Mall
Little Rock, AR 72201
Phone: 501/682-5275
FAX: 501/324-9856

CALIFORNIA
California International Trade
& Investment
801 K Street, Suite 1926
Sacramento, CA 95814
Phone: 916/324-5511
FAX: 916/324-5791

COLORADO
Colorado International Trade Office
1625 Broadway, Suite 680
Denver, CO 80202
Phone: 303/892-3850
FAX: 303/892-3820

CONNECTICUT
Connecticut Department of
Economic Development
International Division
865 Brook Street
Rocky Hill, CT 06067
Phone: 203/258-4200
FAX: 203/529-0535

DELAWARE
Delaware Division of Economic
Development
Office of Business Development
99 Kings Highway, Box 1401
Dover, DE 19903
Phone: 302/739-4271
FAX: 302/739-5749

DISTRICT OF COLUMBIA
District of Columbia Office of
International Business
717 14th Street, N.W.
Suite 11, Box 4
Washington, D.C. 20005
Phone: 202/727-1576
FAX: 202/727-1588

FLORIDA
Florida Department of Commerce
International Trade & Development
107 West Gaines Street, Suite 366
Tallahassee, FL 32399-2000
Phone: 904/487-1399
FAX: 904/487-1407

GEORGIA
Georgia Department of Industry,
Trade and Tourism
Division of Trade
P.O. Box 1776
Atlanta, GA 30301
Phone: 404/656-3556
FAX: 404/651-6505

HAWAII
Hawaii Department of Business,
Economic Development, and Tourism
P.O. Box 2359
Honolulu, HI 96804
Phone: 808/586-2423
FAX: 808/586-2452

IDAHO
Idaho Department of Commerce
International Business Development
700 West State Street
P.O.Box 83720
Boise, Idaho 83720-0093
Phone: 208/334-2470
FAX: 208/334-2783

ILLINOIS
Illinois Department of Commerce and
Community Affairs
International Business Division
100 West Randolph, Suite 3-400
Chicago, IL 60601
Phone: 312/814-7164
FAX: 312/814-6581

INDIANA
Indiana Department of Commerce
International Trade Division
One North Capitol, Suite 700
Indianapolis, IN 46204
Phone: 317/232-4949
FAX: 317/232-4146

IOWA
Iowa Department of Economic
Development
International Marketing Division
200 East Grand Avenue
Des Moines, IA 50309
Phone: 515/242-4713
FAX: 515/242-4918

KANSAS
Kansas Department of
Commerce & Housing
700 Southwest Harrison Street,
Suite 1300
Topeka, KS 66603-3712
Phone: 913/296-4027
FAX: 913/296-5263

KENTUCKY
Kentucky Commerce Cabinet
Office of International Trade
Capitol Plaza Tower
500 Mero, 34th Floor
Frankfort, KY 40601
Phone: 502/564-2170
FAX: 502/564-3256

LOUISIANA
Louisiana Department of Economic
Development
Office of International Trade,
Finance & Development
P.O. Box 94185
Baton Rouge, LA 70804
Phone: 504/342-5388
FAX: 504/342-5389

MAINE
Maine Department of Economic and
Community Development
State House Station 59
Augusta, ME 04333
Phone: 207/289-2656
FAX: 207/287-5701

MARYLAND
Maryland International Division
World Trade Center, 7th Floor
401 East Pratt Street
Baltimore, MD 21202
Phone: 410/333-4295
FAX: 410/333-8200

MASSACHUSETTS
Massachusetts Office of International
Trade & Investment
100 Cambridge Street, Suite 1302
Boston, MA 02202
Phone: 617/367-1830
FAX: 617/227-3488

MICHIGAN
Department of Commerce
Michigan International Trade
Authority
525 West Ottawa
P.O.Box 30105
Lansing, MI 48909
Phone: 517/335-1317
FAX: 517/335-2521

MINNESOTA
Minnesota Trade Office
1000 MN World Trade Center
30 East 7th Street
St. Paul, MN 55101
Phone: 612/297-4657
FAX: 612/296-3555

MISSISSIPPI
Mississippi Department of
Economic Development
Trade and Export Division
P.O. Box 849
Jackson, MS 39205
Phone: 601/359-3155
FAX: 601/359-3605

MISSOURI
Missouri Department of
Economic Development
International Trade and Development
P.O. Box 118
Jefferson City, MO 65102
Phone: 314/751-4855
FAX: 314/751-7384

MONTANA
Montana Department of Commerce
1424 Ninth Avenue
Helena, MT 59620
Phone: 406/444-3494
FAX: 406/444-2903

NEBRASKA
Nebraska Department of
Economic Development
International Trade Promotion
301 Centennial Mall South
P.O. Box 94666
Lincoln, NE 68509-4666
Phone: 402/471-3111
FAX: 402/471-3778

NEVADA
Nevada Commission on
Economic Development
International Office
5151 South Carson Street
Carson City, NV 89710
Phone: 702/687-4325
FAX: 702/687-4450

NEW HAMPSHIRE
New Hampshire Department of
Resources and Economic
Development
172 Pembroxe Road
P.O. Box 1856
Concord, NH 03302-1856
Phone: 603/271-2591
FAX: 603/271-2629

NEW JERSEY
New Jersey Department of
Commerce and Economic
Development
Division of International Trade
28 West State Street, 8th Floor
Trenton, NJ 08625
Phone: 609/633-3606
FAX: 609/633-3675

NEW MEXICO
New Mexico Office of
International Trade
Economic Development and
Tourism Department
1100 St. Francis Drive
Santa Fe, NM 87503
Phone: 505/827-0272
FAX: 505/827-0328

New Mexico Economic Development
& Tourism Department
1100 St. Francis Drive
Santa Fe, NM 87503
Phone: 1/800/374-3061
FAX: 505/827-0407

NEW YORK

New York State Department of
Economic Development
1515 Broadway, 51st Floor
New York, NY 10036
Phone: 212/827-6210
FAX: 212/827-6279 or 212/827-6152

XPORT Trading Company
Port Authority of New York and
New Jersey
1 World Trade Center—34N
New York, NY 10048
Phone: 212/435-3077
FAX: 212/432-0297

NORTH CAROLINA

North Carolina Department
of Commerce
430 North Salisbury Street,
Room 2056
Raleigh, NC 27611
Phone: 919/733-7193
FAX: 919/733-0110

NORTH DAKOTA

North Dakota Economic
Development Commission & Finance
1833 East Bismarck Expressway
Bismarck, ND 58504
Phone: 701/328-5300
FAX: 701/328-5320

OHIO

Ohio Department of Development
International Trade Division
77 South High Street, 29th Floor
P.O. Box 1001
Columbus, OH 43216-1001
Phone: 614/466-5017
FAX: 614/463-1540

OKLAHOMA

Oklahoma Department of Commerce
International Trade Division
P.O. Box 26980
Oklahoma City, OK 73126-0980
Phone: 405/843-9770
FAX: 405/841-5245

OREGON

Oregon Economic Development
Department
International Trade Division
One World Trade Center, Suite 300
121 S.W. Salmon Street
Portland, OR 97204
Phone: 503/229-5625
FAX: 503/222-5050

PENNSYLVANIA

Pennsylvania Department of
Commerce
Bureau of International Trade
464 Forum Building
Harrisburg, PA 17120
Phone: 717/787-7190
FAX: 717/234-4560

PUERTO RICO
Puerto Rico Department of
Agriculture
P.O. Box 10163
Santurce, PR 00908-1163
Phone: 809/722-0891
FAX: 809/923-9747

RHODE ISLAND
Rhode Island Department of
Economic Development
International Trade Division
7 Jackson Walkway
Providence, RI 02903
Phone: 401/277-2601
FAX: 401/277-2102

Rhode Island Department of
Agriculture
22 Hayes Street, Room 120
Providence, RI 02908-5025
Phone: 401/277-2781
FAX: 401/277-6047

SOUTH CAROLINA
South Carolina Department of
Commerce
P.O. Box 927
Columbia, SC 29202
Phone: 803/737-0400
FAX: 803/737-0418

SOUTH DAKOTA
South Dakota Office of Economic
Development
Export Trade Marketing Division
711 East Wells Avenue,
Capitol Lake Plaza
Pierre, SD 57501
Phone: 605/773-5032
FAX: 605/773-3256

TENNESSEE
Tennessee Department of Economic
and Community Development
320 Sixth Avenue, Seventh Floor
Nashville, TN 37243-0405
Phone: 615/741-5870
FAX: 615/741-5829

TEXAS
Texas Department of Commerce
P.O. Box 12728
Austin, TX 78711
Phone: 512/472-5059
FAX: 512/936-0303

UTAH
Utah Division of Business and
Economic Development
International Business Development
324 South State Street, Suite 500
Salt Lake City, UT 84111
Phone: 801/538-8737
FAX: 801/538-8889

VERMONT
Vermont Department of
Economic Development
Pavilion Office Building
109 State Street
Montpelier, VT 05609
Phone: 802/828-3221
FAX: 802/828-3258

VIRGINIA
Virginia Department of
Economic Development
International Marketing
P.O. Box 798
Richmond, VA 23206
Phone: 804/371-8106
FAX: 804/371-8860

WASHINGTON
Washington Department of Trade
and Development
Business & Market Development
2001 Sixth Avenue, Suite 2600
Seattle, WA 98121
Phone: 206/464-7143
FAX: 206/464-7222

WEST VIRGINIA
Governor's Office of Community
& Industrial Development
State Capitol, Room M-146
Charleston, WV 25305-0311
Phone: 304/558-0400
FAX: 304/558-4983

WISCONSIN
Wisconsin Bureau of
International Development
Department of Development
123 West Washington Avenue
P.O. Box 7970
Madison, WI 53707
Phone: 608/266-1480
FAX: 608/266-5551

WYOMING
Wyoming International Trade Office
Division of Economic and
Community Development
2301 Central Avenue
Cheyenne, WY 82002
Phone: 307/777-6412
FAX: 307/777-5840

State Trade Finance Programs

States with trade finance programs can assist you in putting together an export loan package or can work with the SBA in providing co-guaranteed loans for higher amounts than possible if done separately. The following states have worked with the SBA or are providing co-guarantees with the SBA Export Working Capital Program (EWCP)

CALIFORNIA

Director
California Export Finance Office
107 South Broadway, Suite 8039
Los Angeles, CA 90012
Phone: 213/897-0915
FAX: 213/897-0915

FLORIDA

Supervisor
Business Finance Section
Bureau of Business Assistance
Florida Department of Commerce
443 Collins Building
107 West Gaines Street
Tallahassee, FL 3239-2000
Phone: 904/487-0463

KANSAS

Director
Export Financing Program
Division of Trade Development
Kansas Department of Commerce
400 SW 8th street, 5th floor
Topeka, KS 66603-3957
Phone: 913/296-4027

MARYLAND

Executive Director
Maryland Small Business
Financing Authority
Redwood Towers, 22nd floor
217 East Redwood Street
Baltimore, MD 21202
Phone: 410/333-4270

NEW YORK

Director
Division of Small Business
New York State Dept of Economic
Development
1515 Broadway, 51st floor
New York, NY 10036
Phone: 212/827-6140

TEXAS

Director
Texas Exporters Loan
Guarantee Program
Texas Dept. of Commerce
Business Finance Div.
816 Congress Avenue
P.O. Box 12728
Austin, TX 78711
Phone: 512/320-9634

FOREIGN EMBASSIES IN THE UNITED STATES

FOREIGN EMBASSIES IN THE UNITED STATES

Foreign Embassies in the United States maintain a staff of commercial officers that can assist businesses in obtaining market access information and explain procedures for conducting business in their respective countries, such as regulatory and tariff guidelines.

Embassy of the Republic of
Afghanistan
2341 Wyoming Avenue, N.W.
Washington, D.C. 20008
Phone: 202/234-3770
FAX: 202/328-3516

Embassy of Algeria
2137 Wyoming Avenue, N.W.
Washington, D.C. 20008
Phone: 202/265-2800
FAX: 202/667-2174

Embassy of Argentina
Economics Division
1600 New Hampshire Avenue, N.W.
Washington, D.C. 20036
Phone: 202/939-6400
FAX: 202/775-4388

Embassy of Armenia
1660 L Street, N.W., 11th Floor
Washington, D.C. 20036
Phone: 202/628-5766
FAX: 202/628-5769

Embassy of Australia
1601 Massachusetts Avenue, N.W.
Washington, D.C. 20036
Phone: 202/797-3000
FAX: 202/797-3168

Embassy of Austria
3524 International Court, N.W.
Washington, D.C. 20008
Phone: 202/895-6700
FAX: 202/895-6750

Embassy of Bahamas
2220 Massachusetts Avenue, N.W.
Washington, D.C. 20008
Phone: 202/319-2660
FAX: 202/319-2668

Embassy of Bahrain
3502 International Drive, N.W.
Washington, D.C. 20008
Phone: 202/342-0741
FAX: 202/362-2192

Embassy of Bangladesh
2201 Wisconsin Avenue, N.W.,
Suite 300
Washington, D.C. 20007
Phone: 202/342-8372
FAX: 202/333-4971

Embassy of Belgium
3330 Garfield Street, N.W.
Washington, D.C. 20008
Phone: 202/333-6900
FAX: 202/333-6252

Embassy of Belize
2535 Massachusetts Avenue, N.W.
Washington, D.C. 20008
Phone: 202/332-9636
FAX: 202/332-6888

Embassy of Bolivia
3014 Massachusetts Avenue, N.W.
Washington, D.C. 20008-3603
Phone: 202/483-4410
FAX: 202/328-3712

Embassy of Botswana
3400 International Drive, Suite 7M
Washington, D.C. 20008
Phone: 202/244-4990
FAX: 202/244-4164

Embassy of Brazil
3006 Massachusetts Avenue, N.W.
Washington, D.C. 20008
Phone: 202/745-2700
FAX: 202/745-2827

Embassy of Brunei
2600 Virginia Avenue, N.W.,
Suite 300
Washington, D.C. 20037
Phone: 202/342-0159
FAX: 202/342-0158

Embassy of Bulgaria
1621 22nd Street, N.W.
Washington, D.C. 20008
Phone: 202/387-7969
FAX: 202/234-7973

Embassy of Burkina Faso
2340 Massachusetts Avenue, N.W.
Washington, D.C. 20008
Phone: 202/332-5577
FAX: 202/667-1882

Embassy of Burma
2300 S Street, N.W.
Washington, D.C. 20008
Phone: 202/332-9044
FAX: 202/332-9046

Embassy of Burundi
2233 Wisconsin Avenue, N.W.,
Suite 212
Washington, D.C. 20007
Phone: 202/342-2574
FAX: 202/342-2578

Embassy of Cameroon
2349 Massachusetts Avenue, N.W.
Washington, D.C. 20008
Phone: 202/265-8790
FAX: 202/387-3826

Embassy of Canada
501 Pennsylvania Avenue, N.W.
Washington, D.C. 20001
Phone: 202/682-1740
FAX: 202/682-7726

Embassy of Cape Verde
3415 Massachusetts Avenue, N.W.
Washington, D.C. 20007
Phone: 202/965-6820
FAX: 202/965-1207

Embassy of The Central African
Republic
1618 22nd Street, N.W.
Washington, D.C. 20008
Phone: 202/483-7800
FAX: 202/332-9893

Embassy of Chad
2002 R Street, N.W.
Washington, D.C. 20009
Phone: 202/462-4009
FAX: 202/265-1937

Embassy of Chile
1732 Massachusetts Avenue, N.W.
Washington, D.C. 20036
Phone: 202/785-1746
FAX: 202/887-5579

Embassy of China
2133 Wisconsin Avenue, N.W.
Washington, D.C. 20007
Phone: 202/625-3360
FAX: 202/337-5845

Embassy of Colombia
2118 Leroy Place, N.W.
Washington, D.C. 20008
Phone: 202/387-8338
FAX: 202/232-8643

Embassy of Costa Rica
2114 S Street, N.W.
Washington, D.C. 20008
Phone: 202/234-2945
FAX: 202/265-4795

Embassy of Cyprus
2211 R Street, N.W.
Washington, D.C. 20008
Phone: 202/462-5772
FAX: 202/483-6710

Embassy of Czech Republic
3900 Spring of Freedom Street, N.W.
Washington, D.C. 20008
Phone: 202/363-6307
FAX: 202/966-8540

Embassy of Denmark
3200 Whitehaven Street, N.W.
Washington, D.C. 20008
Phone: 202/234-4300
FAX: 202/328-1470

Embassy of Djibouti
1156 15th Street, N.W., Suite 515
Washington, D.C. 20005
Phone: 202/331-0270
FAX: 202/331-0302

Embassy of The Dominican Republic
1715 22nd Street, N.W.
Washington, D.C. 20008
Phone: 202/332-6280
FAX: 202/265-8057

Embassy of Ecuador
2535 15th Street, N.W.
Washington, D.C. 20009
Phone: 202/234-7200
FAX: 202/667-3482

Embassy of Egypt
3521 International Court, N.W.
Washington, D.C. 20008
Phone: 202/895-5400
FAX: 202/244-4319

Embassy of El Salvador
2308 California Street, N.W.
Washington, D.C. 20008
Phone: 202/265-9671
FAX: 202/328-0563

Embassy of Ethiopia
2134 Kalorama Road, N.W.
Washington, D.C. 20008
Phone: 202/234-2281
FAX: 202/328-7950

Embassy of Finland
3301 Massachusetts Avenue, N.W.
Washington, D.C. 20008
Phone: 202/298-5800
FAX: 202/298-6041

Embassy of France
4101 Reservoir Road, N.W.
Washington, D.C. 20007
Phone: 202/944-6000
FAX: 202/944-6336

Embassy of Gabon
2034 20th Street, N.W.
Washington, D.C. 20009
Phone: 202/797-1000
FAX: 202/332-0668

Embassy of Gambia
1155 15th Street, N.W., Suite 1000
Washington, D.C. 20005
Phone: 202/785-1399
FAX: 202/785-1430

Embassy of Germany
4645 Reservoir Road, N.W.
Washington, D.C. 20007-1998
Phone: 202/298-4000
FAX: 202/298-4249

Embassy of Ghana
3512 International Drive, N.W.
Washington, D.C. 20008
Phone: 202/686-4520
FAX: 202/686-4527

Embassy of Great Britain
3100 Massachusetts Avenue, N.W.
Washington, D.C. 20008
Phone: 202/462-1340
FAX: 202/898-4255

Embassy of Greece
2221 Massachusetts Avenue, N.W.
Washington, D.C. 20008
Phone: 202/667-3168
FAX: 202/939-5824

Embassy of Guatemala
Economic and Commercial Office
2220 R Street, N.W.
Washington, D.C. 20008
Phone: 202/745-4952
FAX: 202/745-1908

Embassy of Guinea
2112 Leroy Place, N.W.
Washington, D.C. 20008
Phone: 202/483-9420
FAX: 202/483-8688

Embassy of Guyana
2490 Tracy Place, N.W.
Washington, D.C. 20008
Phone: 202/265-6900
FAX: 202/232-1297

Embassy of Haiti
2311 Massachusetts Avenue, N.W.
Washington, D.C. 20008
Phone: 202/332-4090
FAX: 202/745-7215

Embassy of Honduras
3007 Tilden Street, N.W., Suite 4M
Washington, D.C. 20008
Phone: 202/966-7702
FAX: 202/966-9751

Embassy of the Republic of Hungary
3910 Shoemaker Street, N.W.
Washington, D.C. 20008
Phone: 202/362-6730
FAX: 202/966-8135

Embassy of Iceland
1156 15th Street, N.W.
Washington, D.C. 20005
Phone: 202/265-6653
FAX: 202/265-6656

Embassy of India
2107 Massachusetts Avenue, N.W.
Washington, D.C. 20008
Phone: 202/939-7000
FAX: 202/797-1347

Embassy of Indonesia
2020 Massachusetts Avenue, N.W.
Washington, D.C. 20036
Phone: 202/775-5200
FAX: 202/775-5365

Embassy of Iraq
1801 P Street, N.W.
Washington, D.C. 20009
Phone: 202/483-7500
FAX: 202/462-5066

Embassy of Ireland
2234 Massachusetts Avenue, N.W.
Washington, D.C. 20008
Phone: 202/462-3939
FAX: 202/232-5993

Embassy of Israel
3514 International Drive, N.W.
Washington, D.C. 20008
Phone: 202/364-5500
FAX: 202/364-5607

Embassy of Italy
1601 Fuller Street, N.W.
Washington, D.C. 20009
Phone: 202/328-5500
FAX: 202/238-5593

Embassy of the Ivory Coast
2424 Massachusetts Avenue, N.W.
Washington, D.C. 20008
Phone: 202/797-0300
FAX: 202/387-6381

Embassy of Jamaica
1520 New Hampshire Avenue, N.W.
Washington, D.C. 20036
Phone: 202/452-0660
FAX: 202/452-0081

Embassy of Japan
2520 Massachusetts Avenue, N.W.
Washington, D.C. 20008
Phone: 202/939-6700
FAX: 202/328-2184

Embassy of Jordan
3504 International Drive, N.W.
Washington, D.C. 20008
Phone: 202/966-2664
FAX: 202/966-3110

Embassy of Kenya
2249 R Street, N.W.
Washington, D.C. 20008
Phone: 202/387-6101
FAX: 202/462-3829

Embassy of Korea
2450 Massachusetts Avenue, N.W.
Washington, D.C. 20008
Phone: 202/939-5600
FAX: 202/797-0595

Embassy of Kuwait
3500 International Drive, N.W.
Washington, D.C. 20008
Phone: 202/364-2200
FAX: 202/364-2241

Embassy of Lebanon
2560 28th Street, N.W.
Washington, D.C. 20008
Phone: 202/939-6300
FAX: 202/939-6324

Embassy of Liberia
5303 Colorado Avenue, N.W.
Washington, D.C. 20011
Phone: 202/723-0437
FAX: 202/726-4913

Embassy of Luxembourg
2200 Massachusetts Avenue, N.W.
Washington, D.C. 20008
Phone: 202/265-4171
FAX: 202/328-8270

Embassy of Madagascar
2374 Massachusetts Avenue, N.W.
Washington, D.C. 20008
Phone: 202/265-5525
FAX: 202/265-3034

Embassy of Malaysia
2401 Massachusetts Avenue, N.W.
Washington, D.C. 20008
Phone: 202/328-2700
FAX: 202/332-8914

Embassy of Mali
2130 R Street, N.W.
Washington, D.C. 20008
Phone: 202/332-2249
FAX: 202/332-6603

Embassy of Malta
2017 Connecticut Avenue, N.W.
Washington, D.C. 20008
Phone: 202/462-3611
FAX: 202/387-5477

Embassy of Mexico
1911 Pennsylvania Avenue, N.W.
Washington, D.C. 20006
Phone: 202/728-1700
FAX: 202/728-1712

Embassy of Morocco
1601 21st Street, N.W.
Washington, D.C. 20009
Phone: 202/462-7979
FAX: 202/462-7643

Embassy of Nepal
2131 Leroy Place, N.W.
Washington, D.C. 20008
Phone: 202/667-4550
FAX: 202/667-5534

Embassy of the Netherlands
4200 Wisconsin Avenue, N.W.
Washington, D.C. 20016
Phone: 202/244-5300
FAX: 202/362-3430

Embassy of New Zealand
37 Observatory Circle, N.W.
Washington, D.C. 20008
Phone: 202/328-4800
FAX: 202/667-5227

Embassy of Nicaragua
1627 New Hampshire Avenue, N.W.
Washington, D.C. 20009
Phone: 202/939-6570
FAX: 202/939-6542

Embassy of Nigeria
2201 M Street, N.W.
Washington, D.C. 20037
Phone: 202/822-1500
FAX: 202/775-1385

Embassy of Norway
2720 34th Street, N.W.
Washington, D.C. 20008
Phone: 202/333-6000
FAX: 202/337-0870

Embassy of Oman
1717 Massachusetts Avenue, N.W.,
Suite 400
Washington, D.C. 20036
Phone: 202/387-2014
FAX: 202/797-1558

Embassy of Pakistan
2315 Massachusetts Avenue, N.W.
Washington, D.C. 20008
Phone: 202/939-6200
FAX: 202/387-0484

Embassy of Panama
2862 McGill Terrace, N.W.
Washington, D.C. 20008
Phone: 202/483-1407
FAX: 202/483-8413

Embassy of Paraguay
2400 Massachusetts Avenue, N.W.
Washington, D.C. 20008
Phone: 202/483-6960
FAX: 202/234-4508

Embassy of Peru
1700 Massachusetts Avenue, N.W.
Washington, D.C. 20036
Phone: 202/833-9860
FAX: 202/659-8124

Embassy of The Philippines
1600 Massachusetts Avenue, N.W.
Washington, D.C. 20036
Phone: 202/467-9300
FAX: 202/328-7614 or 202/467-9417

Embassy of Poland
2640 16th Street, N.W.
Washington, D.C. 20009
Phone: 202/234-3800
FAX: 202/328-6271

Embassy of Portugal
2125 Kalorama Road, N.W.
Washington, D.C. 20008
Phone: 202/328-8610
FAX: 202/462-3726

Embassy of Qatar
600 New Hampshire Avenue, N.W.,
Suite 1180
Washington, D.C. 20037
Phone: 202/338-0111
FAX: 202/337-2989

Embassy of Romania
1607 23rd Street, N.W.
Washington, D.C. 20008
Phone: 202/332-4846
FAX: 202/232-4748

Embassy of Russia
2650 Wisconsin Avenue, N.W.
Washington, D.C. 20007
Phone: 202/298-5700
FAX: 202/298-5735

Embassy of Saudi Arabia
601 New Hampshire Avenue, N.W.
Washington, D.C. 20037
Phone: 202/342-3800
FAX: 202/944-5983

Embassy of Senegal
2112 Wyoming Avenue, N.W.
Washington, D.C. 20008
Phone: 202/234-0540
FAX: 202/332-6315

Embassy of Singapore
3501 International Place, N.W.
Washington, D.C. 20008
Phone: 202/537-3100
FAX: 202/537-0876

Embassy of South Africa
3051 Massachusetts Avenue, N.W.
Washington, D.C. 20008
Phone: 202/232-4400
FAX: 202/265-1607

Embassy of Spain
2375 Pennsylvania Avenue, N.W.
Washington, D.C. 20037
Phone: 202/452-0100
FAX: 202/833-5670

Embassy of Sri Lanka
2148 Wyoming Avenue, N.W.
Washington, D.C. 20008
Phone: 202/483-4025
FAX: 202/232-7181

Embassy of Sudan
2210 Massachusetts Avenue, N.W.
Washington, D.C. 20008
Phone: 202/338-8565
FAX: 202/667-2406

Embassy of Sweden
1501 M Street, N.W.
Washington, D.C. 20005
Phone: 202/467-2600
FAX: 202/467-2699

Embassy of Switzerland
2900 Cathedral Avenue, N.W.
Washington, D.C. 20008
Phone: 202/745-7900
FAX: 202/387-2564

Embassy of Syria
2215 Wyoming Avenue, N.W.
Washington, D.C. 20008
Phone: 202/232-6313
FAX: 202/234-9548

Embassy of Thailand
1024 Wisconsin Avenue, N.W.
Washington, D.C. 20007
Phone: 202/944-3600
FAX: 202/944-3611

Embassy of Trinidad and Tobago
1708 Massachusetts Avenue, N.W.
Washington, D.C. 20036
Phone: 202/467-6490
FAX: 202/785-3130

Embassy of Tunisia
1515 Massachusetts Avenue, N.W.
Washington, D.C. 20005
Phone: 202/862-1850
FAX: 202/862-1858

Embassy of the Republic of Turkey
Office of the Chief Chancellor for
Economic and Foreign Affairs
2523 Massachusetts Avenue, N.W.
Washington, D.C. 20008
Phone: 202/483-5367
FAX: 202/328-6055

Embassy of the Ukraine
3350 M Street, NW
Washington, D.C. 20007
Phone: 202/333-0606
FAX: 202/333-0817

Embassy of the United Arab Emirates
3000 K Street, N.W., Suite 600
Washington, D.C. 20007
Phone: 202/338-6500
FAX: 202/337-7029

Embassy of Uruguay
1918 F Street, N.W.
Washington, D.C. 20006
Phone: 202/331-1313
FAX: 202/331-8142

Embassy of Uganda
5911 16th Street, N.W.
Washington, D.C. 20011
Phone: 202/726-7100
FAX: 202/726-1727

Embassy of Venezuela
1099 30th Street, N.W.
Washington, D.C. 20007
Phone: 202/342-2214
FAX: 202/342-6820

Embassy of Yugoslavia
2410 California Street, N.W.
Washington, D.C. 20008
Phone: 202/462-6566
FAX: 202/797-9663

Embassy of Zaire
1800 New Hampshire Avenue, N.W.
Washington, D.C. 20009
Phone: 202/234-7690

Embassy of Zambia
2419 Massachusetts Avenue, N.W.
Washington, D.C. 20008
Phone: 202/265-9717
FAX: 202/332-0826

Embassy of Zimbabwe
1608 New Hampshire Avenue, N.W.
Washington, D.C. 20009
Phone: 202/332-7100
FAX: 202/483-9326

SECTION 6

MULTILATERAL DEVELOPMENT ORGANIZATIONS

MULTILATERAL DEVELOPMENT ORGANIZATIONS

Multilateral development bank (MDB) organizations making loans to foreign nations can be a source of exporting opportunities for U.S. companies.

The Office of Multilateral Development Bank Operations (MDBO) in the U.S. Department of Commerce's U.S. & Foreign Commercial Service provides information and counseling on commercial opportunities through the multilateral development banks. The MDBO and its Multilateral Development Bank Counseling Center explain the workings of these institutions and how best to pursue procurement opportunities funded by the MDBs.

> Office of Multilateral Development Bank Operations
> U.S. Department of Commerce, Room 1107
> 14th and Constitution Avenues, N.W.
> Washington, DC 20230
> Phone: 202/482-3399
> FAX: 202/273-0927

U.S. executive directors at multilateral development organizations can help in providing procurement contracts resulting from loans or grants made by their respective institutions. The following is a list of contacts:

The World Bank is a lending agency which annually commits more than $20 billion for over 200 new projects in developing nations. Monthly business briefings are held by the World Bank Group to provide essential information about business opportunities arising from Bank supported projects. World Bank officials describe procedures that companies should follow to keep informed about projects; how to compete for upcoming contracts; and how to pursue foreign investment opportunities. The cost is $50.00.

Contact: Monthly Business Briefings
The World Bank
Room P-8042
1818 H Street, N.W.
Washington, DC 20433
Phone: 202/473-1819
FAX: 202/334-0003

Information: Phone: 202/458-0110

International Monetary Fund
700 19th Street, N.W., Room 13-320
Washington, DC 20431
Phone: 202/623-7759

Inter-American Development Bank
1300 New York Avenue, N.W.
Washington, DC 20577
Phone: 202/623-1000

The publication of the Inter-American Development Bank, The IDB, is available free of charge by faxing a request to 202/623-1419 or e-mail to CeciliaJ@IADB.ORG.

American Chambers of Commerce Abroad

Foreign Chambers of Commerce in the United States

International Trade Organizations

AMERICAN CHAMBERS OF COMMERCE ABROAD

American Chambers of Commerce Abroad (AmChams) are voluntary associations of business executives concerned with U.S. foreign trade and investment. AmChams assert U.S. business views in host countries by representing their members before governments, business communities and the general public. Typical AmCham services include:

- Export-import trade leads;
- Business and government contacts;
- Meetings featuring U.S. and foreign business leaders and officials;
- Periodic bulletins and publications;
- Clearinghouse of information on trade, investment and commerce;
- Information centers for customs duties, tariffs and regulations; and
- Library and reference facilities for member use.

ARGENTINA

American Chamber of Commerce
in Argentina
Avenue Leandro North Alem 1110,
Piso 13
1001 Buenos Aires, Argentina
Phone: 541-311-5420
FAX: 541-311-9076

AUSTRALIA

American Chamber of Commerce
in Australia—Sydney
Suite 4, Gloucester Walk
88 Cumberland Street
Sydney, N.S.W. 2000, Australia
Phone: 612-241-1907
FAX: 612-251-5220

American Chamber of Commerce
in Australia—South Australia
Level 1, 300 Flinders Street
Adelaide, S.A. 5000, Australia
Phone: 618-224-0761
FAX: 618-224-0628

American Chamber of Commerce
in Australia—Victoria
Level 21, 500 Collins Street
Melbourne, Victoria 3000, Australia
Phone: 613-614-7744
FAX: 613-614-8181

American Chamber of Commerce
in Australia—Queensland
Level 23, 68 Queen Street
Brisbane, N.S.W. 4000, Australia
Phone: 617-221-8542
FAX: 617-221-6313

American Chamber of Commerce
in Australia—West Australia
Level 6, 231 Adelaide Terrace
Perth, W.A. 6000, Australia
Phone: 619-325-9540
FAX: 619-221-3725

AUSTRIA
American Chamber of Commerce
in Austria
Porzellangasse 35
A-1090 Vienna, Austria
Phone: 43-1-319-5751
FAX: 43-1-319-5151

BELGIUM
American Chamber of Commerce
in Belgium
Avenue des Arts 50, Boite 5
B-1040 Brussels, Belgium
Phone: 32-2-513-67-70
FAX: 32-2-513-79-28

BOLIVIA
American Chamber of Commerce
of Bolivia
Casilla 8268
Avenida Arce 2071, Office 3
La Paz, Bolivia
Phone: 5912-342-523; 356-843
FAX: 5912-371-503

BRAZIL
American Chamber of Commerce
in Brazil—Rio de Janeiro
C.P. 916, Praca Pio X-15, Fifth Floor
20040 Rio de Janeiro, RJ—Brazil
Phone: 5521-203-2477
FAX: 5521-263-4477

American Chamber of Commerce
for Brazil—Salvador
Rua da Espanha, 2, Salas 604-606
40000 Salvador, Bahia, Brazil
Phone: 5571-242-0077; 242-5606
FAX: 5571-243-9986

American Chamber of Commerce
for Brazil—Sao Paulo
Rua Alexandre Dumas 1976
04717004 Sao Paulo, SP, Brazil
Phone: 5511-246-9199
FAX: 5511-246-9080

CHILE
Chilean-American Chamber
of Commerce
Avenida Américo Vespucio Sur 80,
9° Piso
82 Correo 34
Santiago, Chile
Phone: 562-208-4140
FAX: 562-206-0911

CHINA
American Chamber of Commerce
in the People's Republic of China—
Beijing
G/F Great Wall Sheraton Hotel
North Donghuan Road
Beijing, China
Phone: 861-500-5566
FAX: 861-508-8494; 508-8495

American Chamber of Commerce
in Shanghai
Shanghai Centre, 4th Floor, Suite 435
1376 Nanjing Xi Lu
Shanghai 200040, People's Republic
of China
Phone: 86-21-279-7119
FAX: 86-21-279-8802

COLOMBIA

Colombian-American Chamber
of Commerce
Transversial 19, #122, 63
Bogotá, Colombia
Phone: 571-215-8716
FAX: 571-213-7071

American Chamber of Commerce
in Colombia—Cali
Avenida 1 N, No.3N-97
Cali, Colombia 92
Phone: 572-667-2993; 661-0162
FAX: 572-667-2992

Colombian-American Chamber
of Commerce—Cartagena
3241 Santa Teresa Street
Cartagena, Colombia
Phone: 575-660-0793
FAX: 575-365-1704

Colombian-American Chamber of
Commerce—Medellín
Apartado Aéreo 66655
Medellín, Colombia
Phone: 574-268-7491
FAX: 574-268-3198

COSTA RICA

Costa Rican-American Chamber
of Commerce
c/o Aerocasillas, P.O. Box 025216
Department 1576
Miami, FL 33102-5216
Phone: 506-220-2200
FAX: 506-220-2300

CZECH & SLOVAK REPUBLICS

American Chamber of Commerce
in Czech and Slovak Republics
Karlovo Namesti 24
120 80 Prague 2, Czech Republic
Phone: 42-2-299-887
FAX: 42-2-291-481

DOMINICAN REPUBLIC

American Chamber of Commerce
in the Dominican Republic
Torre B.H.D., Piso 4
Av. Winston Churchill, P.O. Box 95-2
Santo Domingo, Dominican Republic
Phone: 1-809-544-2222
FAX: 1-809-544-0502

ECUADOR

Ecuadorian-American Chamber
of Commerce
Edificio Multicentro, 4° P,
Oficina 404
Avda. 6 de Diciembre y La Nina
Quito, Ecuador
Phone: 5932-507-450; 507-451
FAX: 5932-504-571

Ecuadorian-American Chamber
of Commerce
F. Cordova 812, Piso 3, Oficina 1
Edificio Torres de la Merced
Guayaquil, Ecuador
Phone: 5934-566-481; 563-177;
563-201; 563-305; 565-761
FAX: 5934-563-259

EGYPT

American Chamber of Commerce
in Egypt
Cairo Marriott Hotel, Suite 1541
P.O. Box 33 Zamalek
Cairo, Egypt
Phone: 20-2-340-8888
FAX: 20-2-340-9482

EL SALVADOR

American Chamber of Commerce
of El Salvador
87 Avenue North, #720
Apartment A, Col. Escalón
San Salvador, El Salvador
Phone: 503-223-3292
FAX: 503-224-6856

FRANCE

American Chamber of Commerce
in France
21 Avenue George V
F-75008 Paris, France
Phone: 33-1-47-23-70-28
FAX: 33-1-47-20-18-62

GERMANY

American Chamber of Commerce
in Germany
Rossmarkt 12, Postfach 100 162
D-60311 Frankfurt/Main 1, Germany
Phone: 49-69-929-1040
FAX: 49-69-929-10411

American Chamber of Commerce
in Germany—Berlin
Budapesterstrasse 29
D-10787 Berlin, Germany
Phone: 49-30-261-55-86
FAX: 49-30-262-26-00

GREECE

American—Hellenic Chamber
of Commerce
16 Kanari Street, 3rd Floor
Athens 106 74, Greece
Phone: 30-1-36-18-385; 36-23-231
FAX: 30-1-36-10-170; 36-20-995

GUAM

Guam Chamber of Commerce
102 Ada Plaza Center
P.O. Box 283
Agana, Guam 96910
Phone: 671-472 6311
FAX: 671-472-6202

GUATEMALA

American Chamber of Commerce
in Guatemala
10 Calle 4-63 Zona 10
Guatemala City, Guatemala
Phone: 5022-346-170
FAX: 5022-312-166

HONDURAS

Honduran-American Chamber
of Commerce
Hotel Honduras Maya,
Apdo. Pos. 1838
Tegucigalpa, Honduras
Phone: 504-32-70-43;
504-32-31-91 ext.7818
Specify that you want the Commerce
FAX: 504-32-20-31

Honduran-American Chamber of
Commerce—San Pedro Sula
Centro Bella Aurora, 6A 13-14C N.O.
San Pedro Sula, Honduras
Phone: 504-580-164; 165; 166
FAX: 504-522-401

HONG KONG

American Chamber of Commerce
in Hong Kong
1030 Swire House, Central G.P.O.
Box 355
Hong Kong
Phone: 852-2526-0165
FAX: 852-2810-1289

HUNGARY

American Chamber of Commerce
in Hungary
Dozsa Gyorgy ut. 84/A, Room 405
H-1068 Budapest, Hungary
Phone: 36-1-269-6016
FAX: 36-1-122-8890

INDIA

American Business Council—
New Delhi
Attn: Ms. Alka Kapur
Mohan Dev Building, 11th floor
13 Tolstoy Marg
New Delhi 110 001
Phone: 91-11-332-2723; 332-3021
FAX: 91-11-371-2827; 688-8714

INDONESIA

American Chamber of Commerce
in Indonesia
The Landmark Center, 22nd Floor,
Suite 2204
Jalan Jendral Sudirman I
Jakarta, Indonesia
Phone: 62-21-571-0800, Ext. 2222
FAX: 622-1-571-0656

IRELAND

American Chamber of Commerce
in Ireland
20 College Green
Dublin 2, Ireland
Phone: 353-1-679-3733
FAX: 353-1-679-3402

ISRAEL

Israel-American Chamber of
Commerce and Industry
35 Shaul Hamelech Boulevard
P.O. Box 33174
Tel Aviv, Israel 61333
Phone: 972-3-6952341; 6967628
FAX: 972-3-6951272

ITALY
American Chamber of Commerce
in Italy
Via Cantu 1
20123 Milan, Italy
Phone: 39-2-86-90-661
FAX: 39-2-80-57-737

IVORY COAST
American Chamber of Commerce,
Ivory Coast
01 BP 3394
Abidjan 01, Ivory Coast
Phone: 225-21-67-66; 44-68-48
FAX: 225-21-68-17

JAMAICA
American Chamber of Commerce of
Jamaica
The Wyndham Kingston Hotel,
Suite 3112
77 Knutsford Boulevard
Kingston 5, Jamaica
Phone: 1-809-929-7866; 929-7867;
968-2089; 968-2090
FAX: 1-809-929-8597

JAPAN
American Chamber of Commerce in
Japan—Tokyo
Bridgeston Toranomon Building, 5F
3-25-2, Toranomon
Minato-ku, Tokyo 105, Japan
Phone: 813-3433-5381
FAX: 813-3436-1446

American Chamber of Commerce
in Okinawa
P.O. Box 235
Okinawa City 904
Okinawa, Japan
Phone: 81-98933-5146
FAX: 81-98933-7695

KOREA
American Chamber of Commerce
in Korea
Chosun Hotel, Room 307
Seoul, Korea
Phone: 8862-752-3061
FAX: 822-755-6577

MALAYSIA
American-Malaysian Chamber
of Commerce
11.03 Lev 11, Amoda/22 Jalan Imbi
55100 Kuala Lumpur, Malaysia
Phone: 603-248-2407; 248-2540
FAX: 603-242-8540

MEXICO
American Chamber of Commerce
in Mexico—Mexico City
Mailing address in the U.S.
P.O. Box 60326, Apdo. 113
Houston, Texas 77205-1794
Phone: 525-724-3800
FAX: 525-703-3908; 2911

American Chamber of Commerce
in Mexico—Guadalajara
Avda. Montezuma #442
Col. Jardines del Sol
45050 Zapopan, Jalisco, Mexico
Phone: 5236-34-6606
FAX: 5236-34-7374

American Chamber of Commerce
of Mexico, A.C.
Rio Orinoco 307 Ote
Del Valle
Garza Garcia, N.L. 66220 Mexico
Phone: 528-335-6237; 335-6238;
335-6239; 335-6240; 335-6210
FAX: 528-335-6211

MOROCCO
American Chamber of Commerce
in Morocco
18, Rue Colbert
Casablanca 01, Morocco
Phone: 212-2-31-14-48
FAX: 212-2-31-66-07

THE NETHERLANDS
The American Chamber of
Commerce in the Netherlands
Van Karnebeklaan, 14
2585 BB The Hague, The
Netherlands
Phone: 31-70-3-65-98-08
FAX: 31-70-3-64-69-92

NEW ZEALAND
The American Chamber of
Commerce in New Zealand
P.O. Box 106002
Downtown
Auckland 1001
Phone: 64-9-309-9140
FAX: 64-9-309-1090

NICARAGUA
American Chamber of Commerce
of Nicaragua
P.O. Box 2720
Managua, Nicaragua
Phone: 5052-67-30-99
FAX: 5052-67-30-98

PAKISTAN
American Chamber of Commerce
of Pakistan
NIC Building, Sixth Floor Abbasi
Shaheed Road
GPO Box 1322
Karachi 74400 Pakistan
Phone: 92-21-526-436
FAX: 92-21-568-3935

PANAMA
American Chamber of Commerce
& Industry of Panama
Apartado 168, Balboa
Panama 1, Republic of Panama
Phone: 507-69-3881
FAX: 507-23-3508

PARAGUAY
Paraguayan-American Chamber
of Commerce
General Diaz 521
Edif. El Faro Internacional P° 4
Asunción, Paraguay
Phone: 59521-442-135; 442-136
FAX: 59521-442-135

PERU
American Chamber of Commerce
in Peru
Avenida Ricardo Palma 836
Lima 18, Perú
Phone: 5114-47-9349
FAX: 5114-47-9352

THE PHILIPPINES
American Chamber of Commerce
in the Philippines
Corinthian Plaza, 2nd floor
P.O. Box 1578 Paseo de Roxas
Makati, Metro Manila, Philippines
Phone: 632-818-7911
FAX: 632-816-6359

POLAND
American Chamber of Commerce
in Poland
Plac Powstancow Warszawy 1
00-950 Warsaw, Poland
Phone: 4822-26-39-60
FAX: 4822-26-51-31

PORTUGAL
American Chamber of Commerce
in Portugal
Rua de D. Estafania 155, 5th Floor
Left
Lisbon 1000, Portugal
Phone: 351-1-57-25-61
FAX: 351-1-57-25-80

SAUDI ARABIA
American Business Association—
Eastern Province
P.O. Box 88
Dhahran Airport
Dhahran 31932, Saudi Arabia
Phone: 966-3-857-0595
FAX: 966-3-857-8130

American Businessmen's Group
of Riyadh
P.O. Box 34992
Riyadh 11478, Saudi Arabia
Phone: 966-1-477-7341
FAX: 966-1-411-2729

SINGAPORE
The American Chamber of
Commerce in Singapore
Scotts Road, #16-07 Shaw Center
Singapore 0922
Phone: 65-235-0077
FAX: 65-732-5917

SOUTH AFRICA
American Chamber of Commerce
in South Africa
P.O. Box 1132
Houghron 2041 South Africa
Phone: 27-11-788-0265; 0266
FAX: 27-11-880-1632

SPAIN
American Chamber of Commerce
in Spain
Avenida Diagonal 477
08036 Barcelona, Spain
Phone: 34-3-405-12-66
FAX: 34-3-405-31-24

American Chamber of Commerce
in Spain—Madrid
Hotel Euro Building
Padre Damian 23
28036 Madrid, Spain
Phone: 34-1-359-65-59
FAX: 34-1-359-65-20

SRI LANKA
American Chamber of Commerce
of Sri Lanka
c/o U.S. Embassy
210 Galle Road
Colombo 3, Sri Lanka
Phone: 941-448-007
FAX: 941-437-345

SWEDEN
American Chamber of Commerce
in Sweden
Box 5512
114 85 Stockholm, Sweden
Phone: 46-08-783-5300
FAX: 46-08-662-88-84

SWITZERLAND
Swiss American Chamber
of Commerce
Talacker 41
8001 Zurich, Switzerland
Phone: 41-1-211-24-54
FAX: 41-1-211-95-72

TAIWAN
American Chamber of Commerce—
Kaohsiung
1/F, 123-7 Ta Pei Road
Niao Sung Hsiang
Kaohsiung County 83305, Taiwan
Phone: 886-07-731-3712
FAX: 886-07-731-3712

American Chamber of Commerce
in Taipei
Room 1012-Chia Hsin
Building Annex
96 Chung Shan North Road,
Section 2
P.O. Box 17-277
Taipei 104, Taiwan
Phone: 866-2-581-7809
FAX: 886-2-542-3376

THAILAND
American Chamber of Commerce
in Thailand
P.O. Box 11-1095
140 Wireless Road, Seventh Floor
Kian Gwan Building
Bangkok, Thailand
Phone: 662-251-9266
FAX: 662-255-2454

TURKEY
Turkish-American Businessmen's
Association
Mr. Bulent Senver, Chairman
Fahri Gizdem Sokak 22/5
80280 Gayrettepe
Istanbul, Turkey
Phone: 212-274-28-24;
212-288-62-12
FAX: 212-275-93-16

Turkish-American Businessmen's
Association
Hilton, Tahran Cad.
06700 Ankara, Turkey
Phone: 90-312-426-77-38
FAX: 90-312-426-77-38

Turkish-American Businessmen's
Association
Mr. Reha Akin, Chairman
Organize Sanayi Bolgesi
16400 Inegol, Bursa, Turkey
Phone: 90-224-714-90-54
FAX: 90-224-714-80-51

Turkish-American Businessmen's
Association
Mr. Talip Dagdelen, Chairman
Inonu Cad. No: 40
Gazlantep, Turkey
Phone: 90-342-231-12-38
FAX: 90-342-231-57-26

Turkish-American Businessmen's
Association of Izmir
Mr. Turgut Koyuncuoglu, Chairman
Altay Is Merkezi 601
Sair Esref Bulvari #18
Izmir, 35250, Turkey
Phone: 90-232-441-10-68; 90-232-
441-40-70
FAX: 90-232-441-40-69

UNITED ARAB EMIRATES
American Business Council of
Dubai/Northern Emirates
World Trade Center, Suite 1610
P.O. Box 9281
Dubai, United Arab Emirates
Phone: 971-4-314-735
FAX: 971-4-314-227

UNITED KINGDOM
American Chamber of Commerce
in the United Kingdom
75 Brook Street
London W1Y 2EB, England
Phone: 44-71-493-03-81
FAX: 44-71-493-23-94

URUGUAY
Chamber of Commerce Uruguay-
U.S.A.
Calle Bartólome Mitre 1337/108
Casilla de Correo 809
11000 Montevideo, Uruguay
Phone: 5982-959048
FAX: 5982-959059

VENEZUELA
Venezuelan-American Chamber of
Commerce and Industry
Torre Credival, Piso 10
2da. Avenida de Campo Alegre,
Apartado 5181
Caracas 1010A, Venezuela
Phone: 582-263-0833
FAX: 582-263-1829; 2060

FOREIGN CHAMBERS OF COMMERCE IN THE UNITED STATES

Foreign Chambers of Commerce in the United States serve to promote and encourage international trade and can be an excellent source of information and contacts.

ARGENTINA

Argentina-American Chamber
of Commerce
10 Rockefeller Plaza, Tenth Floor
New York, NY 10020
Phone: 212/698-2238
FAX: 212/698-2239

AUSTRALIA

Australian American Chamber of
Commerce, Inc.
611 Larchmont Blvd., 2nd floor
Los Angeles, CA 90004
Phone: 213/469-4300
FAX: 213/469-6419

AUSTRIA

U.S.-Austrian Chamber of
Commerce, Inc.
165 West 46th Street, Suite 1112
New York, NY 10036
Phone: 212/819-0117; 819-0158
FAX: 212/819-0117

BELGIUM

Belgian-American Chamber of
Commerce in the United States
350 Fifth Avenue, Suite 1322
New York, NY 10118
Phone: 212/967-9898
FAX: 212/629-0349

BRAZIL

Brazilian-American Chamber of
Commerce in the United States
22 West 48th Street, Room 404
New York, NY 10036
Phone: 212/575-9030
FAX: 212/921-1078

Brazilian-American Chamber
of Commerce
80 Southwest Eighth Street,
Suite 1800
Miami, FL 33130
Phone: 305/579-9030
FAX: 305/579-9756

CHINA

U.S. Office of China Chamber of
International Commerce
4301 Connecticut Avenue, N.W.,
Suite 136
Washington, DC 20008
Phone: 202/244-3244
FAX: 202/244-0478

COLOMBIA

Colombian-American Association, Inc.
150 Nassau, Suite 2015
New York, NY 10038
Phone: 212/233-7776
FAX: 212/233-7779

DENMARK

Danish-American Chamber
of Commerce
885 Second Avenue, 18th floor
New York, NY 10017
Phone: 212/980-6240
FAX: 212/754-1904

ECUADOR

Ecuadorean-American
Association, Inc.
150 Nassau, Suite 2015
New York, NY 10038
Phone: 212/233-7776
FAX: 212/233-7779

EGYPT

U.S.-Egypt Chamber of Commerce
330 East 39th Street, #32L
New York, NY 10016
Phone: 212/867-2323
FAX: 212/697-0465

FINLAND

Finnish-American Chamber
of Commerce
866 UN Plaza, Suite 249
New York, NY 10017
Phone: 212/821-0225
FAX: 212/750-4417

FRANCE

French-American Chamber of
Commerce in the United States
509 Madison Avenue, Suite 1900
New York, NY 10022
Phone: 212/371-4466
FAX: 212/371-5623

GERMANY

German-American Chamber
of Commerce
40 West 57th Street, 31st Floor
New York, NY 10019-4092
Phone: 212/974-8830
FAX: 212/974-8867

German-American Chamber
of Commerce
104 South Michigan Avenue,
Suite 600
Chicago, IL 60603-5978
Phone: 312/782-8557
FAX: 312/782-3892

German-American Chamber
of Commerce
5220 Pacific Concourse Dr.,
Suite 280
Los Angeles, CA 90045
Phone: 310/297-7979
FAX: 310/297-7966

German-American Chamber
of Commerce
465 California Street, Suite 910
San Francisco, CA 94104
Phone: 415/392-2262
FAX: 415/392-1314

Representative for German Industry
and Trade
1627 I Street N.W., Suite 550
Washington, DC 20006
Phone: 202/659-4777
FAX: 202/659-4779

Representative for German
Industry and Trade
5555 San Felipe, Suite 1030
Houston, TX 77056
Phone: 713/877-1114
FAX: 713/877-1602

Representative for German
Industry and Trade
3475 Lenox Road, N.E., Suite 620
Atlanta, GA 30326
Phone: 404/239-9494
FAX: 404/264-1761

GUATEMALA
Guatemala-U.S. Trade Association
300 Sevilla Ave., 210A
Coral Gables, FL 33134
Phone: 305/443-0343
FAX: 305/443-0699

GREECE
Hellenic-American Chamber of
Commerce
960 Avenue of the Americas,
Suite 1204
New York, NY 10001
Phone: 212/629-6380
FAX: 212/564-9281

INDIA
India-America Chamber of
Commerce of America
P.O. Box 873
Grand Central Station
New York, NY 10163-0873
Phone: 212/755-7181; 424-8256
FAX: 212/424-8500

IRELAND
Ireland Chamber of Commerce
in the United States
1305 Post Rd., Suite 205
Fairfield, CT 06430
Phone: 212/248-0008
FAX: 203/255-6752

ISRAEL
American-lsrael Chamber of
Commerce
350 Fifth Avenue, Suite 1919
New York, NY 10118-1988
Phone: 212/971-0310
FAX: 212/971-0331

American-Israel Chamber of
Commerce
180 North Michigan Avenue,
Suite 911
Chicago, IL 60601
Phone: 312/641-2937
FAX: 312/641-2941

ITALY
Italy-American Chamber of
Commerce, Inc.
730 Fifth Avenue, Suite 600
New York, NY 10019
Phone: 212/459-0044
FAX: 212/459-0090

JAPAN
Honolulu-Japanese Chamber
of Commerce
2454 South Beretania Street
Honolulu, HI 96826
Phone: 808/949-5531
FAX: 808/949-3020

Japanese Business Association of
Southern California
550 South Hop Street, Suite 1765
Los Angeles, CA 90071
Phone: 213/485-0160
FAX: 213/626-5526

Japanese Chamber of Commerce
and Industry of Chicago
401 North Michigan Avenue,
Room 602
Chicago, IL 60611
Phone: 312/332-6199
FAX: 312/822-9773

Japanese Chamber of Commerce
of New York, Inc.
145 West 57th Street, Sixth Floor
New York, NY 10019
Phone: 212/246-8001
FAX: 212/246-8002

KOREA

Korean Chamber of Commerce
3350 Wilshire Boulevard, Suite 660
Los Angeles, CA 90010
Phone: 213/480-1115
FAX: 213/480-7521

U.S.-Korea Society
750 Third Avenue, 8th floor
New York, NY 10022-2705
Phone: 212/759-7525
FAX: 212/759-7530

MEXICO

Confederation of National Chambers
of Commerce
Services and Tourism
USHCC
1030—15th Street, N.W.
Suite 206
Washington, DC 20005
Phone: 202/842-1212
FAX: 202/842-3221

United States-Mexico Chamber
of Commerce
1730 Rhode Island Ave., N.W.
Suite 1112
Washington, DC 20036
Phone: 202/296-5198
FAX: 202/728-0768

United States-Mexico Chamber
of Commerce
400 East 59th Street, Suite 8B
New York, NY 10022
Phone: 212/750-2638
FAX: 212/750-2149

United States-Mexico Chamber
of Commerce
720 Kipling, Suite 201
Lakewood, CO 80215
Phone: 303/237-7080
FAX: 303/237-5568

United States-Mexico Chamber
of Commerce
555 S. Flower Street, 25th floor
Los Angeles, CA 90071-2236
Phone: 213/623-7725
FAX: 213/623-0032

United States-Mexico Chamber
of Commerce
3000 Carlisle Street, Suite 210
Dallas, TX 75204
Phone: 214/754-8060
FAX: 214/871-9533

United States-Mexico Chamber
of Commerce
150 N. Michigan Ave., Suite 2910
Chicago, IL 60601
Phone: 312/236-8745
FAX: 312/781-5925

THE NETHERLANDS
Netherlands Chamber of Commerce
in the United States, Inc.
One Rockefeller Plaza, Suite 1420
New York, NY 10020
Phone: 212/265-6460
FAX: 212/265-6402

Netherlands Chamber of Commerce
in the United States
233 Peachtree Street, N.E., Suite 404
Atlanta, GA 30303-1504
Phone: 404/523-4400
FAX: 404/522-7116

NORWAY
Norwegian-American Chamber
of Commerce
Upper Midwest Chapter
800 Foshay Tower
821 Marquette Ave.
Minneapolis, MN 55402-2961
Phone: 612/332-3338
FAX: 612/332-1386

Norwegian-American Chamber
of Commerce
20 California Street, Sixth Floor
San Francisco, CA 94111-4803
Phone: 415/986-0770
FAX: 415/986-6025

Norwegian-American Chamber
of Commerce
800 Third Avenue, 23rd Floor
New York, NY 10022
Phone: 212/421-9210
FAX: 212/838-0374

PERU
Peruvian-American Chamber
of Commerce
3460 Wilshire Blvd., Suite 1006
Los Angeles, CA 90010
Phone: 1-800-737-8226;
213/386-7378
FAX: 213/386-7376

THE PHILIPPINES
Philippine-American Chamber
of Commerce
711 Third Avenue, 17th Floor
New York, NY 10017
Phone: 212/972-9326
FAX: 212/867-9882

Philippino-American Chamber
of Commerce
310 David Drive
Alamo, CA 94507
Phone: 510/831-9257
FAX: 510/831-8728

PUERTO RICO

Puerto Rican Economic
Development Administration
666 Fifth Ave.
New York, NY 10103-1599
Phone: 212/245-1200
FAX: 212/581-2667

SAUDI ARABIA

Saudi Arabia Commercial Office
c/o Abdullah Alathel,
Commercial Attache
The Royal Embassy of Saudi Arabia
601 New Hampshire Avenue, N.W.
Washington, DC 20037
Phone: 202/337-4088
FAX: 202/342-0271

SPAIN

Spain-U.S. Chamber of Commerce
350 Fifth Avenue, Room 2029
New York, NY 10118
Phone: 212/967-2170
FAX: 212/564-1415

SWEDEN

Swedish-American Chamber of
Commerce
599 Lexington Avenue, 12th Floor
New York, NY 10022
Phone: 212/838-5530
FAX: 212/755-7953

Swedish-American Chamber
of Commerce
230 California Street, Suite 405
San Francisco, CA 94111-4319
Phone: 415/781-4188
FAX: 415/781-4189

SWITZERLAND

Swiss-American Chamber
of Commerce
608 5th Ave., Room 309
New York, NY 10020
Phone: 212/246-7789
FAX: 212/246-1366

TRINIDAD AND TOBAGO

Trinidad and Tobago Consulate
c/o Ms. George, Consul
733 Third Avenue, Suite 1716
New York, NY 10017
Phone: 212/682-7272
FAX: 212/986-2146

UNITED KINGDOM

British-American Chamber
of Commerce
52 Vanderbilt Avenue, 20th Floor
New York, NY 10017
Phone: 212/661-4060
FAX: 212/661-4074

British-American Chamber
of Commerce
41 Sutter Street, Suite 303
San Francisco, CA 94104
Phone: 415/296-8645
FAX: 415/296-9649

REGIONAL ORGANIZATIONS

ASIA

U.S.-ASEAN Trade Council
425 Madison Avenue
New York, NY 10017
Phone: 212/688-2755
FAX: 212/371-7420

Asia Society
725 Park Avenue
New York, NY 10021
Phone: 212/288-6400
FAX: 212/517-8315

Asia Society
1785 Massachusetts Avenue, N.W.
Washington, DC 20036
Phone: 202/387-6500
FAX: 202/387-6945

LATIN AMERICA

Council of the Americas
680 Park Avenue
New York, NY 10021
Phone: 212/628-3200
FAX: 212/517-6247

Inter-American Chamber
of Commerce
510 Bering Drive, Suite 300
Houston, TX 77057-1400
Phone: 713/975-6171
FAX: 713/975-6610

Latin Chamber of Commerce
1417 West Flagler Street
Miami, FL 33135
Phone: 305/642-3870
FAX: 305/642-0653

Latin American Manufacturing
Association
419 New Jersey Avenue, S.E.
Washington, DC 20003
Phone: 202/546-3803
FAX: 202/546-3807

Association of American Chambers
of Commerce in Latin America
(AACCLA)
1615 H Street, N.W.
Washington, DC 20062
Phone: 202/463-5485
FAX: 202/463-3126

U.S. Hispanic Chamber of Commerce
1030 15th Street N.W., Suite 206
Washington, DC 20005
Phone: 202/842-1212
FAX: 202/842-3221

MIDDLE EAST

National Council on U.S.-
Arab Relations
1140 Connecticut Avenue, N.W.,
Suite 1210
Washington, DC 20036
Phone: 202/293-0801
FAX: 202/293-0903

National U.S.-Arab Chamber
of Commerce
1100 New York Avenue, N.W.,
East Tower, Suite 550
Washington, DC 20005
Phone: 202/289-5920
FAX: 202/289-5938

National U.S.-Arab Chamber
of Commerce
420 Lexington Avenue, Suite 2739
New York, NY 10170
Phone: 212/986-8024
FAX: 212/986-0216

U.S.-Arab Chamber of Commerce,
Pacific
P.O. Box 422218
San Francisco, CA 94142-2218
Phone: 415/398-9200
FAX: 415/398-7111

INTERNATIONAL TRADE ORGANIZATIONS

Trade associations, like export-import clubs and world trade centers, can serve as gateways to small businesses interested in exporting. Many of these associations maintain libraries, data banks and other resources including established relationships with foreign governments to assist their members in exporting ventures. Associations can be an excellent avenue to market programs, as most have monthly or quarterly newsletters.

Listed below are a selected group of organizations that help businesses engage in international trade. In addition, local international trade organizations are abundant throughout the United States. These groups usually meet on a regular basis, sponsor seminars and support their members' international trade interests. Contact the national Federation of International Trade Associations (*see below*) for the international trade association in your area.

American Association of Exporters and Importers (AAEI)
11 West 42nd Street
New York, NY 10036
Phone: 212/944-2230
FAX: 212/382-2606

AAEI provides its member firms with information on trade regulations, legislation and international developments affecting business through weekly and quarterly publications. AAEI also testifies before Congress and other levels of government to address international trade related problems. Membership consists of multinational, medium- and small-size firms representing a broad cross section of industry sectors.

U.S. Chamber of Commerce of the United States
International Division
1615 H Street, N.W.
Washington, DC 20062-2000
Phone: 202/463-5460
FAX: 202/463-3114

The U.S. Chamber of Commerce represents American business. It lobbies the U.S. government for specific trade policies and sponsors a number of conferences. The U.S. Chamber also supports a number of country—or regional-specific Chambers of Commerce.

> National Association of Export Companies (NEXCO)
> P.O. Box 1330, Murray Hill Station
> New York, NY 10156
> Phone: 212/725-3311
> FAX: 212/725-3312

Membership consists of exporting companies. The organization holds monthly meetings in New York, although membership is nationwide, and communicates through a monthly newsletter.

> National Customs Brokers and Forwarders Association of
> America (NCBFAA)
> One World Trade Center, Suite 1153
> New York, NY 10048
> Phone: 212/432-0050
> FAX: 212/432-5709

NCBFAA, a membership organization of customs brokers and forwarders, sells its membership list, which can assist in locating customs brokers and freight forwarders in your area.

> National Foreign Trade Council (NFTC)
> 1625 K Street, N.W.
> Washington, DC 20006
> Phone: 202/887-0278
> FAX: 202/452-8160

NFTC's membership consists of about 500 U.S. manufacturing corporations and service companies having international operations or interests.

Small Business Exporters Association (SBEA)
4603 John Taylor Court
Annandale, VA 22003
Phone: 703/642-2490
FAX: 703/750-9655

SBEA is a trade association representing small- and medium-size exporters.

United States Council for International Business
1212 Avenue of the Americas, 21st Floor
New York, NY 10036
Phone: 212/354-4480
FAX: 212/575-0327

The Council, a membership organization, is the U.S. affiliate of the International Chamber of Commerce, which monitors and facilitates trade worldwide. The Council also oversees the Interstate Commerce Commission's Temporary Admission Carnet System (ATA Carnet), which simplifies customs procedures governing the temporary exportation of commercial product samples.

World Trade Centers Association (WTCA)
One World Trade Center, Suite 7701
New York, NY 10048
Phone: 212/432-2626
FAX: 212/488-0064

WTCs are located around the world, including Centers throughout the United States and Mexico. One of the ways WTCs encourage global trade is through the World Trade Centers' trade lead data bank and message system, NETWORK. World Trade Center members receive office support services, consultant services, conferences and reciprocal membership services at WTCs globally.

Federation of International Trade Associations (FITA)
1851 Alexander Bell Drive
Reston, VA 22091
Phone: 703/620-1588
FAX: 703/391-0159

FITA is a national organization of international trade associations. FITA can assist you in locating an international trade association in your geographic area.

SECTION 8

Publications/Information Sources

U.S. Government Hotlines

Publications/Information Sources

The following publications and information sources, organized by chapter as they are referred to in *Breaking Into The Trade Game*, are of interest to small business exporters. Other publications and information sources not referred to directly, but of relevance to each chapter heading, are also included.

CHAPTER 1: MAKING THE EXPORT DECISION

> U.S. Small Business Administration
> International Trade Assistance
> *SBA Fact Sheet #42*
> Available through your nearest SBA District Office or
> U.S. Export Assistance Center
>
> SB*Atlas*
> Small Business *Automated Trade Locator Assistance System*
> Available through your nearest SBA District Office or
> U.S. Export Assistance Center

SB*Atlas* data reports provide specific product information on the top 35 importing and exporting countries; and specific country information on the top 20 imported and exported products. A market share trend analysis is presented in 3D graphics.

PERIODICALS

Agexporter
United States Department of Agriculture
Foreign Agricultural Service
Information Division, Room 5074-S
14th St. & Independence Avenue
Washington, DC 20250-1000
Phone: 202/720-3329

Magazine on international trade and trade opportunities overseas. Published monthly by the Department of Agriculture.

Business America
Superintendent of Documents
P.O. Box 371954
Pittsburgh, PA 15250
Phone: 202/512-1800
FAX: 202/512-2250
Price: $32.00 per year; $3.00 each issue

Magazine on international trade issues and business opportunities overseas. Published monthly by the U.S. Department of Commerce.

Export Today
733 15th Street, N.W., Suite 1100
Washington, DC 20005
Phone: 202/737-1060
FAX: 202/783-5966
Price: $49.00 per year

The "how to" international business magazine for U.S. exporters. Published monthly.

The Exporter
34 West 37th Street
New York, NY 10018
Phone: 212/563-2772
FAX: 212/563-2798
Price: $160.00 per year

Monthly reports on the business of exporting.

Foreign Trade Magazine
6849 Old Dominion Drive, #200
McLean, VA 22101
Phone: 703/448-1338
FAX: 703/448-1841
Price: $45.00 per year (12 issues)

Features trade briefs, information on financing, shipping, air cargo, trucks and rails, and current legislation.

Global Trade Talk
Superintendent of Documents
P.O. Box 371954
Pittsburgh, PA 15250
Phone: 202/512-1800
FAX: 202/512-2250
Price: $11.00 per year (bi-monthly)
$13.75 foreign

Magazine about international trade and the role of the U.S. Customs Service in facilitating international trade while enforcing U.S. laws.

International Business Magazine
500 Mamaroneck Avenue, Suite 314
Harrison, NY 10528
Phone: 914/381-7700
FAX: 914/381-7713
Price: $35.00 per year (12 issues)

Reports on overseas market opportunities, global corporate strategies, trade and political developments to assess their impact on U.S. imports, exports, joint ventures and acquisitions.

Journal of Commerce
Two World Trade Center, 27th Floor
New York, NY 10048
Phone: 212/837-7000
FAX: 212/837-7045
Price: $349.00 per year (Daily M-F)

Information on domestic and foreign economic developments plus export opportunities, agricultural trade leads, shipyards, export ABCs and trade fair information. Features articles on tariff and non-tariff barriers, licensing controls, joint ventures and trade legislation in foreign countries.

World Trade Magazine
17702 Cowan
Irvine, CA 92714
Phone: 714/640-7070
FAX: 714/798-3501
Price: $24.00 per year

Profiles of successful exporters and reports on international trade developments.

BOOKS

A Basic Guide to Exporting
Superintendent of Documents
P.O. Box 371954
Pittsburgh, PA 15250
Phone: 202/512-1800
FAX: 202/512-2250
Publication number: 003-009-00604-0
Price: $9.50

The steps involved in exporting and sources of assistance.

The Dos and Taboos of International Trade—
A Small Business Primer
by Roger E. Axtell
John Wiley and Sons, Inc.
Professional, Reference and Trade Group
605 Third Avenue
New York, NY 10158-0012
Price: $16.95

A book about international trade practices for small businesses.

Export Sales and Marketing Manual
by John Jagoe
Export USA Publications
6901 West 84th Street, Suite 157
Bloomington, MN 55438
Phone: 612/893-0624; 1-800-445-6285
FAX: 612/943-1535
Price: $295.00 for manual
$175.00 for quarterly updates

Step-by-step procedural manual for marketing U.S. products worldwide. The manual contains illustrations, flow charts, worksheets and samples of export contracts, shipping documents and effective international correspondence.

Exportise
The Small Business Foundation of America
1155 15th Street, N.W.
Washington, DC 20005
Phone: 202/223-1103
FAX: 202/467-6534
Price: $19.95

Instructional manual on conducting international business, with detailed information on the process of exporting.

Fast-Track Exporting
by Sandra L. Renner and
W. Gary Winget
American Management Association
135 West 50th Street
New York, NY 10020
Price: $29.95

A step-by-step process for assessing your company's readiness to export and details for developing strategic plans for entering international markets.

World Business Directory
Gale Research Inc.
835 Penobscot Building
Detroit, MI 48226
Phone: 313/961-2242
FAX: 1-800-414-5043
Price: $495.00

Directory of trade-oriented businesses. Included is coverage of emerging trade regions. Four volumes.

Building an Import/Export Business—
Revised and Expanded Edition
by Kenneth D. Weiss
John Wiley and Sons, Inc.
1 Wiley Dr.
Somerset, NJ 08875-1272
Phone: 1-800-225-5945
Price: $16.95 paperback; $37.95 cloth
ISBN: 0-471-536-27X paperback; 0-471-536-261 cloth

A handbook designed to guide the novice through complexities of foreign trade. Discussion includes source and outlet management, suppliers and distributors, goods and currencies.

*Profitable Exporting: A Complete Guide to Marketing
Your Products Abroad, 2nd edition*
by John S. Gordon
John Wiley and Sons, Inc.
1 Wiley Dr.
Somerset, NY 08875-1272
Phone: 1-800-225-5945
Price: $70.00
ISBN: 0-471-575143

A step-by-step guide on how to enter and succeed in the export market-place. Topics include markets, strategies, organizational management, risk analysis and controls.

CHAPTER 2: MAKING THE CONNECTION

EDI World
2021 Coolidge Street
Hollywood, FL 33020-2400
Phone: (305) 925-5900
FAX: (305) 925-7533
Price: $45.00 per year

A monthly magazine about electronic commerce management and technology integration.

Guide to Internet Resources: U.S. Federal Government
Margaret Parhamovich, University of Nevada, Las Vegas
Updates: magoo@nevada.edu
Access information: Gopher at University of Michigan
gopher@una.hh.lib.umich.edu
(choose the following items):
inet directories
all guides
U.S. Federal Gov. Info.

Federal Government World Wide Web—WWW
Americans Communicating Electronically—ACE
Instructions for locating this information on-line:
gopher ace.esusda.gov or
mail: almanac@ace.esusda.gov

Access to FedWorld, National Technical Information
Service via:
Telnet fedworld.gov
modem: 703/321-8020

CHAPTER 3: IDENTIFYING INTERNATIONAL MARKETS

United States Merchandise Trade: Exports, General
Imports, and Imports for Consumption
Superintendent of Documents
P.O. Box 371954
Pittsburgh, PA 15250
Phone: 202/512-1800
FAX: 202/512-2250
Price: $127.00 per year.

A monthly country-specific breakdown of imports and exports by
Standard International Trade Classification (SITC) number.

Department of Commerce Economic Bulletin Board
(EBB)
U.S. Department of Commerce
14th and Constitution Avenue, N.W.
Washington, DC 20230
Phone: 202/482-1986
FAX: 202/482-2164 or try EBB as a guest user by dialing
202/482-3870 with PC and modem
(2400 baud, 8 bit words, no parity, 1 stop bit)

EBB is a personal computer-based electronic bulletin board providing
trade leads and up-to-date statistical releases from the Bureau of Census, the
Bureau of Economic Analysis, the Bureau of Labor Statistics, the Federal

Reserve Board and other federal agencies. The Trade Opportunities Program (TOP) is available on EBB.

Price: Annual subscription fee of $45.00

National Trade Data Bank (NTDB)
U.S. Department of Commerce
14th and Constitution Avenue, N.W.
Washington, DC 20230
Phone: 202/482-1986
FAX: 202/482-2164
Price: $40.00 per disk or $360.00 for one year

The NTDB is an international trade data bank compiled by 15 U.S. government agencies. It contains the latest census data on U.S. imports and exports by commodity and country, the complete CIA *World Factbook*, current market research, *Foreign Commercial Service Country Commercial Guides*, the *Foreign Traders Index* and many other data series. The NTDB is available at over 800 federal depository libraries, or can be purchased on CD-ROM for personal PC use.

World Factbook
Superintendent of Documents
P.O. Box 371954
Pittsburgh, PA 15250
Phone: 202/512-1800
FAX: 202/512-2250
Price: $29.00

Produced by Central Intelligence Agency, this book gives geographic and demographic information about each country around the globe.

Gammon Directory for Eastern Europe and the Newly Independent States
18860 U.S. 19 North, Suite 168
Clearwater, FL 34624
Phone: 813/531-7664
FAX: 813/530-5692
Price: $98.00

Four-hundred page, loose-leaf directory on doing business in Eastern Europe and the Newly Independent States.

> *World Bank Atlas*
> The World Bank
> Publication Department, 1818 H Street, N.W.
> Washington, DC 20433
> Phone: 202/473-2209
> FAX: 202/676-0581
> Price: $7.95 plus $5.00 shipping and handling

Gives population, gross domestic product and average growth rates for every country.

> *U.N. Statistical Yearbook, 39th Edition*
> United Nations Publications
> Two UN Plaza, Room DC2-853
> New York, NY 10017
> Phone: 212/963-8302; 1-800-253-9646
> Price: $110.00

Economic and demographic data for 220 countries. Most recent statistics through 1993.

> *International Trade Statistics Yearbook*
> United Nations Publications
> Two UN Plaza, Room DC2-853
> New York, NY 10017
> Phone: 212/963-8302; 1-800-253-9646
> Price: $135.00

Statistical analysis of overall foreign trade by regions and countries, as well as world exports by origin, destination and product category.

Demographic Yearbook, 45th edition
United Nations Publications
Two UN Plaza, Room DC2-853
New York, NY 10017
Phone: 212/963-8302, 1-800-253-9646
Price: $125.00

Demographics for 220 countries. Most recent statistics through 1993.

UNESCO Statistical Yearbook
Unipub
4611-F Assembly Drive
Lanham, MD 20706-4391
Phone: 1-800-274-4888
Price: $86.00

Economic and demographic data for 200 countries.

Hispanic Yearbook
T.I.Y.M. Publishing Company, Inc.
8370 Greensboro Dr., #1009
McLean, VA 22102
Phone: 703/734-1632; 734-1716
FAX: 703/356-0787
Price: $14.90

A state-by-state reference and referral guide featuring Hispanic organizations, media and scholarships.

International Marketing Handbook
Gale Research Incorporated
835 Penobscot Building
Detroit, MI 48226
Phone: 313/961-2242
FAX: 1-800-414-5043
Price: $235.00

Detailed marketing profiles for 141 nations. Includes country reports averaging 31 pages in length. 4,400 pages in three volumes.

Worldcasts
Predicasts North America
362 Lakeside Dr.
Foster City, CA 94404
Phone: 1-800-321-6388
FAX: 415/358-4759
Price: $1,375.00 for entire set; regional and product edi-
tions, $975.00 each; single editions $500.00. Plus
$75.00 for shipping & handling charges.

Abstracts over 60,000 forecasts for products and markets in countries outside the United States. Published annually.

Exporter's Encyclopedia
Dun & Bradstreet Information Services
5107 Leesburg Pike, Suite #2501
Falls Church, VA 22041
Phone: 1-800-526-0651
Price: $534.00 per year

An annual handbook covering more than 220 world markets.

Economic Outlook
Organization of Economic Cooperation and
Development Publication
2001 L Street N.W., Suite 650
Washington, DC 20036-4910
Phone: 202/785-6323; 1-800-456-6323
FAX: 202/785-0350
Price: $27.00 per issue or $61.50 per year
(delivered directly from France)

Provides economic summaries of OECD's 25 member countries. Published semi-annually.

Doing Business in . . . Series
Matthew Bender and Company
1275 Broadway
Albany, NY 12204
Phone: 1-800-424-4200
Cost range: $165.00 to $1075.00

A series of multiple-volume manuals on doing business in a number of foreign countries. Information includes legal environments, product liability, foreign investment, tax considerations, local forms of business incorporation, foreign investment and intellectual property.

World Trade Resources Guide
Gale Research Incorporated
835 Penobscot Building
Detroit, MI 48226
Phone: 313/961-2242
FAX: 1-800-414-5043
Price: $169.00

Eighty of the world's largest trading nations as well as many smaller countries. Includes country profiles, vital statistics on population, currency exchange rates, GNP/GDP, import/export/trade balance figures, major trading partners, principal commodities and imported and exported.

Culturegrams
Kennedy Center Publications
Brigham Young University
P.O. Box 24538
Provo, Utah 84602-4538
Phone: 801/378-6528
FAX: 801/378-7075
Price: $90.00 (full set); $3.00/each (1-5);
$1.50/each (6-19); prices for individual briefings
decrease the more ordered

Four-page briefings on 128 countries that feature the customs, culture, background, taboos of each country.

Flash Facts—To Get Export Information Instantly

For several areas of the world, the information is at your fingertips from the U.S. Department of Commerce, if you have a touch-tone telephone and a fax. Dial the number, follow instructions and the requested information will automatically be faxed to you. The *Automated Fax Delivery System Flash Facts* are available 24 hours-a-day, seven days a week, free of charge.

Flash Facts *are available for the following regions:*

Eastern Europe Business Information Center (EEBIC) 202/482-5745. Information is available on specific Eastern European countries including Albania, Bosnia-Hercegovina, Bulgaria, Croatia, Czech Republic, Estonia, Hungary, Latvia, Lithuania, Macedonia, Poland, Romania, Slovak Republic and Slovenia.

Office of Latin America and the North American Free Trade Area 202/482-4464. Current trade-related documents concerning Mexico and countries of Latin America are available. Information is also available on the North American Free Trade Agreement; tariffs, permits and customs regulations; marketing, distribution and finance; investment; statistics and demographics. The same type of information is available for Canada by calling 202/482-3101.

Asia Business Center 202/482-3875 or 202/482-2522. Categories include general export information, regional and country information (Australia, Cambodia, Indonesia, Korea, Laos, Malaysia, New Zealand, Philippines, Singapore, Taiwan, Thailand and Vietnam).

Offices of Africa, Near East and *South Asia* 202/482-1064. Categories include general and country information (Nigeria and South Africa). For the Office of the Near East, categories include general and country information (Algeria, Bahrain, Egypt, Iran, Iraq, Israel, Jordan, Kuwait, Lebanon, Libya, Morocco, Oman, Qatar, Saudi Arabia, Syria, Tunisia, United Arab Emirates and Yemen). Categories for the Office of South Asia include general and country information (Afghanistan, Bangladesh, Bhutan, India, Nepal, Maldives, Pakistan and Sri Lanka).

Business Information Service for the Newly Independent States (BISNIS) 202/482-3145. Categories include U.S.-Newly Independent States trade statistics, current export and investment opportunities and upcoming trade events, general investment and defense conversion opportunities, World Bank and European Bank for Reconstruction and Development (EBRD) opportunities, export and trade opportunities and BISNIS publications.

CHAPTER 4: FOREIGN MARKET ENTRY

> *Export Trading Company Guidebook*
> Superintendent of Documents
> P.O. Box 371954
> Pittsburgh, PA 15250
> Phone: 202/512-1800
> FAX: 202/512-2250
> Price: $11.00

Produced by the Department of Commerce Office of Export Trading Company Affairs. Provides essential information on the functions and advantages of establishing or using export trading companies.

> *Bergano's Register of International Importers*
> Bergano Book Co.
> P.O. Box 190
> Fairfield, CT 06430
> Phone: 203/254-2054
> FAX: 203/255-3817
> Price: $95.00

Contains thousands of entries of importing firms and major distributors in Europe, North America, the Middle East, Asia, Africa and Latin America.

Manufacturers' Agents National Association
European Distributors
P.O. Box 3467
Laguna Hills, CA 92654
Phone: 714/859-4040
Price: $92.50

Maintains a data bank of European distributors.

Commercial News USA
U.S. Department of Commerce
14th and Constitution Avenue, N.W.
Washington, DC 20230
Phone: 202/482-4918
FAX: 202/482-5362
Price: $3.99

U.S. companies can list a photo and description of their product in Commercial News USA, which is distributed to more than 100,000 companies and government officials overseas.

Export Magazine
Johnston International Publications
25 Northwest Point Blvd., Suite 800
Elk Grove Village, IL 60007
Phone: 708/427-9512
FAX: 708/427-2013
Price: $50.00 for 6 issues, additional $25.00 for airmail
(international)

Lists products of U.S. firms. Distributed worldwide.

American Literature Review
Five Penn Plaza
New York, NY 10001
Phone: 212/629-1173
FAX: 212/629-1140

Sent to businesses around the world, ALR is a catalog of the product catalogs of hundreds of U.S. exporters.

American Export Register
Five Penn Plaza
New York, NY 10001
Phone: 212/629-1173
FAX: 212/629-1140
Price: $120.00

A two-volume, 3,000-page guide featuring names of U.S. exporters, their product listings in more than 4,200 categories, and where they export, by region.

*The World Trade System: A Comprehensive
Reference Guide*
Gales Research, Inc.
835 Penobscot Building
Detroit, MI 48226
Phone: 313/961-2242
FAX: 1-800-414-5043
Price: $165.00

Provides trade activity for every country of the world. Information on principal exports, principal imports, principal trading partners, international economic relationships, membership in regional trading organizations and political data.

Trade Shows Worldwide, 9th edition
Gale Research, Inc.
835 Penobscot Building
Detroit, MI 48226
Phone: 313/961-2242
FAX: 1-800-414-5043
Price: $225.00

Over 5,700 scheduled exhibitions, trade shows, association conventions and similar events around the world are listed.

CHAPTER 5: THE EXPORT TRANSACTION

The Export Operation: Putting the Pieces Together
Unz & Company
190 Baldwin Avenue
Jersey City, NJ 07306
Phone: 1-800-631-3098
Price: $55.00

Arranged as a series of recommendations from an industry expert to an imaginary shipper. Provides the guidance needed to avoid many of the pitfalls of foreign trade.

Export Documentation
International Trade Institute, Inc.
5055 North Main Street
Dayton, OH 45415
Phone: 1-800-543-2453
Price: $67.50 plus $5.00 shipping & handling

Examines steps that must be taken to process any international order.

Export Documentation and Procedures
Unz & Company
190 Baldwin Avenue
Jersey City, NJ 07306
Phone: 1-800-631-3098
Price: $55.00

Leads the new exporter through every element of the export process and introduces the experienced exporter to ways of doing things perhaps not yet considered.

Incoterms 1990
ICC Publishing, Inc.
156 Fifth Avenue, Suite 308
New York, NY 10010
Phone: 212/206-1150
Price: $24.95

Defines the thirteen 1990 trading terms and specifies the respective rights and obligations of buyer and seller in an international transaction.

Treaties and International Documents Used in
International Trade Law
ICC Publishing, Inc.
156 Fifth Avenue, Suite 308
New York, NY 10010
Phone: 212/206-1150
Price: $75.00

Complete text of the most useful instruments in international trade. Contains documents concerning contractual relations and documents related to the regulation of international litigations.

International Exporting Agreements
Matthew Bender & Company
1275 Broadway
Albany, NY 12204
Phone: 1-800-424-4200
Price: $140.00

Guide to the negotiation and the drafting of contracts for export sales.

CHAPTER 6: FINANCING EXPORT SALES

International Finance Library
Unz & Company
190 Baldwin Avenue
Jersey City, NJ 07306
Phone: 1-800-631-3098
Price: $189.95 for 7 titles; individual title prices are
approximately $55.00

Package includes seven titles that offer practical information about issues involved in financing international trade, getting paid by overseas customers and accounting for international ventures.

Dictionary of International Finance, 2nd edition
John Wiley & Sons
1 Wiley Dr.
Somerset, NY 08875-1272
Phone: 1-800-225-5945
ISBN: 0-471-836-540
Price: $65.00

Definitions of over 300 trade-related terms.

Financing and Insuring Exports:
A User's Guide to Eximbank Programs
Eximbank Business Development Office
811 Vermont Avenue, N.W.
Washington, DC 20571
Phone: 202/565-3900
FAX: 202/565-3931
Price: $50.00 plus $5.00 shipping & handling

The Global Financial Handbook
Business International
111 West 57th Street
New York, NY 10019
Phone: 212/554-0600
FAX: 212/586-1181
Price: $195.00

A reference manual including rules on remitting dividends and profits, repatriation of capital, trade financing, borrowing and investing instruments, tax rates, risk management tools and import and export controls.

Guide to Documentary Credit Operations
ICC Publishing Corporation
156 Fifth Avenue, Suite 308
New York, NY 10010
Phone: 212/206-1150
Price: $34.95

Export letters of Credit and Drafts
International Trade Institute, Inc.
5055 North Main Street
Dayton, OH 45415
Phone: 1-800-543-2453
Price: $67.50, plus $5.00 shipping & handling

Explanation of letters of credit (LCs) transactions. Includes information on how to read LCs, examples of various types of LCs, and what to do when you cannot collect or comply.

Uniform Rules for Collections
ICC Publishing Corporation
156 Fifth Avenue, Suite 308
New York, NY 10010
Phone: 212/206-1150
Price: $8.95

Lists international guidelines for collections.

CHAPTER 7: TRANSPORTING GOODS INTERNATIONALLY

Dictionary of Shipping Terms
Unz & Company
190 Baldwin Avenue
Jersey City, NJ 07306
Phone: 1-800-631-3098
Price: $49.95

Lists all terms and abbreviations used in the movement of goods by water.

Export Administration Regulations
Superintendent of Documents
P.O. Box 371954
Pittsburgh, PA 15250
Phone: 202/512-1800
FAX: 202/512-2250
Price: $88.00 with updates

Provides in-depth information on export licenses, restrictive trade practices or boycotts, import regulations, documentation requirements and related information.

Export and Import Procedures and Documentation Series
Unz & Company
190 Baldwin Avenue
Jersey City, NJ 07306
Phone: 1-800-631-3098
Price: $55.00 for each document book

Series of document reference books for the most commonly used import/export and hazardous goods forms, includes, but not limited to, Shipper's Export Declaration, Shipper's letter of instructions, pro forma invoice, commercial invoice and Certificate of Origin.

Export Reference Manual
Bureau of National Affairs
Distribution Center
9435 Key West Avenue
Rockville, MD 20850
Phone: 1-800-372-1033
FAX: 1-800-253-0332
Price: Three manuals $630.00 plus tax for one year
    subscription. Update every week as information
    changes.

Export Shipping
International Trade Institute
5055 North Main Street
Dayton, OH 45415
Phone: 1-800-543-2453
Price: $67.50 plus $5.00 shipping & handling

Guide to understanding ocean/air tariffs, usage of ocean/air containers, how to obtain an international freight quotation, port marks on international cargo, international ocean/air shipping documents, basic trade terms and service organization.

Incoterms 1990
ICC Publishing S.A.
International Chamber of Commerce
38, Cours Albert 1$^{er.}$
75008 Paris, France

ISBN-92-842-0087-3

The official guide to terms used to specify obligations for delivering goods in international contracts, to eliminate any possibility of misunderstanding and subsequent dispute.

International Shipping
Unz & Company
190 Baldwin Avenue
Jersey City, NJ 07306
Phone: 1-800-631-3098
Price: $75.00

Comprehensive exploration of the shipping industry.

Schedule B Statistical Classification of Domestic and Foreign Commodities Exported from the United States
Superintendent of Documents
P.O. Box 371954
Pittsburgh, PA 15250
Phone: 202/512-1800
FAX: 202/512-2250
Price: $77.00 with updates and supplements.

PERIODICALS

Journal of Commerce Shipcards
Two World Trade Center, 27th Floor
New York, NY 10048
Phone: 212/837-7000
FAX: 212/837-7045
Price: $349.00 (for the journal)

Shipcards is a supplement to the Journal of Commerce. It lists scheduled sailings of vessels worldwide.

Shipping Digest
Geyer-McAllister Publications
51 Madison Avenue
New York, NY 10010
Phone: 212/689-4411
Price: $46.00 per year (52 issues)

Explores current topics related to international transportation.

CHAPTER 8: STRATEGIC ALLIANCES AND FOREIGN INVESTMENT OPPORTUNITIES

Licensing Law Handbook-Europe
Clark Boardman, Ltd.
155 Psington Rd.
Deerfield, IL 60015
Phone: 1-800-221-9428
Price: $110.00

General information on European licensing law.

Investing, Licensing and Trading Conditions Abroad
Business International
111 West 57th St.
New York, NY 10019
Phone: 212/554-0600
FAX: 212/586-1181
Price: $1,975.00 for entire package;
      $1375.00 for regional package;
      $225.00 for one country.

Includes information on operating conditions and practices for 60 countries.

International Trade and the U.S. Antitrust Law
Clark Boardman, Ltd.
155 Psington Rd.
Deerfield, IL 60015
Phone: 1-800-221-9428
Price: $145.00

Looseleaf binder covering federal international trade regulations as they pertain to antitrust law.

Worldwide Government Directory
7979 Old Georgetown Rd, #900
Bethesda, MD 20814
Phone: 1-800-332-3535 or 301/718-8770
FAX: 301/718-8494
Price: $697.00 for the updated monthly;
      $497.00 for the update quarterly;
      $347.00 for the annual hardcover edition.

A 1,400-page reference guide to virtually every key elected and appointed government official in 195 nations including all former Soviet Republics.

Worldwide Directory of Defense Authorities
7979 Old Georgetown Rd, #900
Bethesda, MD 20814
Phone: 1-800-332-3535 or 301/718-8770
FAX: 301/718-8494
Price: $897.00 for the updated quarterly;
$647.00 for the annual hardcover edition.

A 1,100-page reference guide that covers every ministry of defense, general staff and service branches in-depth, with a special emphasis on procurement departments and their officials in 195 nations.

Profiles of Worldwide Government Leaders
7979 Old Georgetown Rd, #900
Bethesda, MD 20814
Phone: 1-800-332-3535 or 301/718-8770
FAX: 301/718-8494
Price: $297.00

A 850-page reference guide to more than 3000 world ministers and heads of states. Coverage includes private and public career, education, birthdate, political party and office address.

Worldwide Government Report
7979 Old Georgetown Rd, #900
Bethesda, MD 20814
Phone: 1-800-332-3535
FAX: 301/718-8494 or 301/718-8770
Price: $247.00 for 1 year

Provides analysis of ongoing changes in governmental structures and personnel around the world plus biographical information on the people involved. Bi-weekly.

HOTLINE NUMBERS

U.S. Small Business Administration
Answer Desk
Dial 1-800-8-ASK-SBA
For the hearing impaired, the TDD number is (202) 205-7333.

SBA ON-LINE
Electronic Bulletin Board
From Washington, DC—202/205-7265
Toll free—1-800-859-4636 for a 2400 baud modem; 1-800-697-4636 for a
9600 baud modem. Set communications software protocol for N (no parity), 8
(data bits), and 1 (stop bit). This is a 24-hour-a-day service with information
on SBA export and financial assistance, speakers, SBA's women's mentor program, minority programs and a mail box for electronic conversations.

U.S. Agency for International Development
Center for Trade and Investment Services (CTIS). Tailored country-specific
information. 9:00-5:30 EST Monday through Friday
202/663-2660; 1-800-USAID-4-U
FAX: 202/663-2670

U.S. Department of Agriculture
Trade and Promotion Office (TAPO) of the Foreign Agricultural Service (FAS):
202/720-7420

U.S. Customs
Customs will help you identify your product's code under the Harmonized
System (HS). Call 202/927-0370 for the phone number of the Customs office
nearest you. U.S. Customs has a NAFTA hotline, too. Call 202/927-0066.

U.S. Department of Commerce
Trade Information Center
1-800-872-8723
TDD 1-800-833-8723

National Trade Data Bank
Help # 202/482-1986
8:30-4:30 Monday-Friday EST

Economic Bulletin Board (EBB)—202/482-3870. This is a 24-hour service with information on trade leads and statistics. Compatible with 300, 1200, 2400 or 9600 bps using standard communications software. With 9600 bps service, call 202/482-1986. Staff available Monday-Friday 8:30 to 4:30; 202/482-1986. Subscribe through the Office of Business Analysis 202/482-1986.

U.S. Center for Standards and Certification Information on product standards, testing and certification. 301/975-4040

Export-Import Bank of the United States 1-800-565-EXIM

Overseas Private Investment Corporation 1-800-336-8799.

EXPORT HOTLINE: 1-800-USA-XPORT

Presented by AT&T and the Hotline Referral Network in cooperation with the U.S. Department of Commerce. The Export Hotline, a corporate-sponsored, nationwide fax retrieval system providing international trade information for U.S. business. Its purpose is to help find new markets for U.S. products and services.

THE EXPORT OPPORTUNITY HOTLINE
The Small Business Foundation of America
1155 15th Street, N.W.
Washington, DC 20005
Phone: 1-800-243-7232
In Washington, DC: 202/223-1104

Answers questions about getting started in exporting. Advice on product distribution; documentation; licensing and insurance; export financing; analyzing distribution options; export management firms; customs; currency exchange systems and travel requirements.

SECTION 9

INTERNATIONAL CALLING CODES

INTERNATIONAL CALLING CODES

ALBANIA 355	Merlo 220
Durres 52	Posadas 752
Elbassan 545	Resistencia 722
Korce 824	Rio Cuatro 586
Shkoder 224	Rosario 41
Tirana 42	San Juan 64
	San Rafael 627
ALGERIA 213	Santa Fe 42
Adrar 7	Tandil 293
Ain Defla 3	
Bejaia 5	ARMENIA 7
Guerrar 9	All cities 885

AMERICAN SAMOA 684	ARUBA 297
	All cities 8
ANDORRA 33	
All cities 628	ASCENSION ISLAND 247

ANGOLA 244	AUSTRALIA 61
Luanda 2	Adelaide 8
	Ballarat 53
ANGUILLA 809	Brisbane 7
	Canberra 6
ANTARCTICA 672	Darwin 89
	Geelong 52
ANTIGUA 809	Gold Coast 75
	Hobart 02
ARGENTINA 54	Launceston 03
Bahia Blanca 91	Melbourne 3
Buenos Aires 1	Newcastle 49
Cordoba 51	Perth 9
Corrientes 783	Sydney 2
La Plata 21	Toowoomba 76
Mar Del Plata 23	Townsville 77
Mendoza 61	Wollongong 42

NON-DIAL COUNTRIES

Afghanistan
Cuba
Easter Island
Midway
Pitcairn Island
Somalia
Spanish Sahara
Sudan
Wake

SECTION 10

GLOSSARY OF INTERNATIONAL TRADE ACRONYMS AND TERMS

GLOSSARY OF INTERNATIONAL TRADE ACRONYMS AND TERMS

ACCEPTANCE:
An agreement to purchase goods at a stated price and under stated terms.

ACCESSION:
The process of becoming a member of the General Agreement on Tariffs and Trade (*see* GATT).

ACTUAL TOTAL LOSS:
A marine insurance term; a ship is usually considered an actual total loss for insurance purposes when it has been listed as missing.

ADB:
Asian Development Bank. ADB was created to foster economic growth and cooperation in the region of Asia and the Far East and to help accelerate economic development for the countries of the region.

AD VALOREM RATE:
An import duty rate determined "according to the value" (ad valorem) of the commodity entering a country, as opposed to the weight or other basis for calculation. An ad valorem tariff is a tariff calculated as a percentage of the value of the goods when clearing customs.

ADVANCE AGAINST DOCUMENTS:
A loan secured by turning over shipment documents of title to the creditor; an alternative to acceptance financing.

AFDB:
The African Development Bank and Fund. Established to foster economic and social development of the independent African nations and to promote their mutual economic cooperation. AFDB membership is limited to African countries. The African Development Fund (AFDF), a loan facility, directs its loan resources towards social development projects.

AFFREIGHTMENT, CONTRACT OF:
An agreement between a shipping company and an importer or exporter for cargo space on a vessel at a specified time for a specified price. The importer/exporter is liable for payment whether or not the shipment is made at the time agreed upon.

AFTER DATE (A/D):
A payment on a draft or other negotiable instrument due a specified number of days after the date the draft is presented to the payee.

AFTER SIGHT (A/S):

A payment on a draft or other negotiable instrument due upon presentation or demand to the payee.

AIR WAYBILL:

A bill of lading covering both the domestic and international portions of flights to transport goods to a specific destination. The air waybill serves as a non-negotiable receipt for the shipper.

ALL-RISK CLAUSE:

An insurance clause providing that all loss or damage to goods is insured except that caused by shipper.

AMCHAMS:

American Chambers of Commerce in foreign countries. As affiliates of the U.S. Chamber of Commerce, 84 AmChams, located in 59 countries, collect and disseminate extensive information on foreign markets. While membership fees are usually required, the small investment can be worth it for the information received.

ANTI-DUMPING DUTY:

A tariff imposed to discourage the underpriced (below foreign country's domestic market) sale of foreign goods in the U.S. market, which might hurt U.S. manufacturers.

APEC:

Asia-Pacific Economic Cooperation. A forum to advance economic cooperation and trade and investment liberalization in the Asia-Pacific region, chaired by Indonesia. APEC goals in addition to trade liberalization include human resource development, growth of small- and medium-sized businesses and infrastructure development.

ARBITRAGE:

The practice of buying foreign currency, stocks and bonds and other commodities in one country or a number of countries and selling them in another market at a higher price to gain an advantage from the differences in exchange rates.

ARBITRATION CLAUSE:

A clause in a sales contract detailing how any contract disputes will be settled.

ASEAN:

The Association of Southeast Asian Nations, an economic cooperation which includes Thailand, Indonesia, Malaysia, Singapore, Philippines and Brunei. The ASEAN Alliance for Mutual Growth (AMG) is a multilateral initiative to encourage mutually beneficial trade relations between the United States and the ASEAN countries.

BUYER CREDIT:

Term to provide the exporter with prompt payment by the overseas importer, who borrows the necessary funds from the bank. The payment is usually made directly by the importer's bank to the exporter.

BANKER'S ACCEPTANCE:

A draft drawn on and accepted by the importer's bank. Depending on the bank's creditworthiness, the acceptance becomes a financial instrument which can be discounted.

BILL OF EXCHANGE:

Also a draft. A written unconditional order for payment from a drawer to a drawee, directing the drawee to pay a specified amount of money in a given currency to the drawer or a named payee at a fixed or determinable future date.

BILL OF LADING:

A document establishing the terms of a contract between a shipper and a transportation company for freight to be moved between specified points for a specified charge. Usually prepared by the shipper on forms issued by the carrier, it serves as a document of title, a contract of carriage and a receipt for goods.

BONDED WAREHOUSE:

A warehouse authorized by customs authorities for storage of goods where payment of duties on the goods is deferred until they are removed from the warehouse.

CARNETS:

Customs documents permitting the holder to carry or send merchandise temporarily into certain foreign countries for trade shows or sales meetings, without paying duties or posting bonds.

CARIBBEAN DEVELOPMENT BANK (CDB):

CDB, founded in 1970, provides financing to foster economic development and integration in the Caribbean. The CDB's members are the governments of Antigua, Bahamas, Barbados, Belize, British Virgin Islands, Canada, Cayman Islands, Colombia, Dominica, Grenada, Guyana, Jamaica, Montserrat, St. Kitts-Nevis, St. Lucia, St. Vincent, Trinidad and Tobago, Turks and Caicos Islands, the United Kingdom, and Venezuela. Headquarters are located in Barbados.

CARICOM:

The Caribbean Community and Common Market, founded in 1973. Member countries are Antigua, Bahamas, Barbados, Belize, Dominica, Grenada, Guyana, Jamaica, Montserrat, St. Kitts-Nevis, St. Lucia, St. Vincent, Trinidad and Tobago and Anguilla. Headquarters are in Guyana. Related organizations are the Caribbean Investment Corporation and the Caribbean Monetary Fund.

CASH AGAINST DOCUMENTS (C.A.D.):

A payment method by which title to the goods is given to the buyer when the buyer pays cash to an intermediary acting for the seller, usually a commission house.

CASH IN ADVANCE (C.I.A.):

A payment method for goods in which the buyer pays cash to the seller before shipment of the goods. Usually required by the seller when the goods are customized, such as specialized machinery.

CASH WITH ORDER (C.W.O.):

A payment method for goods by which cash is paid at the time of order and the transaction then becomes binding for both the buyer and seller.

CERTIFICATE OF ORIGIN:

A certified document detailing the origin of goods used in foreign commerce. Usually required to qualify for reduced tariffs or duties, specified in the terms of a trade agreement, such as the North American Free Trade Agreement.

CHARTER PARTY:

Renting of an entire vessel or part of its freight space for a specified voyage or stipulated period of time.

C&F NAMED PORT:

Cost and freight. The seller must pay all costs of goods and transportation to the named port; these costs are included in the price quoted. Buyer pays risk insurance once the goods are aboard the ship up to overseas inland destination.

C.I.F. NAMED PORT:

Cost, insurance, freight. Same as C&F except seller also provides insurance up to the named destination.

C.I.F. & C.:

Price includes commission as well as C.I.F.

C.I.F. DUTY PAID:

The seller includes in the final price to the buyer, in addition to C.I.F., the estimated U.S. duty.

C.I.F. & E.:

Price quoted includes currency exchange from U.S. dollars to foreign money as well as C.I.F.

CLEAN BILL OF LADING:

A document specifying that the goods were received in "apparent good order" by the carrier.

COCOM:

Coordinating Committee on Multi-lateral Export Controls, a committee of all NATO countries (except Iceland) plus Japan to coordinate and control exports of member countries, especially in high-technology equipment.

COLLECTION:

An exporter draws a bill of exchange on a customer abroad and gives the bill to his/her bank to collect funds. The importer must be willing to pay. The bank charges a fee to collect payment, but is not liable should the importer refuse to release the funds.

COLLECTION PAPERS:

All documents, including bills of lading, invoices and other papers, submitted to a buyer to receive payments for a shipment.

CONDITIONAL FREE:

Merchandise free of duty under certain conditions, if the conditions can be satisfied.

CONFIRMED LETTER OF CREDIT:

A letter of credit issued by a foreign bank with payment confirmed by a U.S. bank. An exporter who requires a confirmed letter of credit from the buyer is assured payment from the U.S. bank in case the foreign buyer or bank defaults. (*See* Letter of Credit.)

CONSIGNMENT:

The delivery of merchandise from an exporter to a distributor specifying that the distributor will sell the merchandise and then pay the exporter. The exporter retains title to the goods until the buyer sells them. The buyer (distributor) sells the goods, retains a specified commission and then pays the exporter.

CONSUL:

A government official residing in a foreign country charged with representing the interests of his country and its nationals.

CONSULAR DECLARATION:

A formal statement describing goods to be shipped, made out to the consul of the country of destination. Approval from the consul must be obtained prior to shipment.

CONSULAR INVOICE:

A document required by some foreign countries showing exact information about the consignor, consignee, value and description of shipment.

CONVENTIONAL TARIFF:

A tariff established in the agreements resulting from tariff negotiations under the GATT (*see* GATT).

CREDIT RISK INSURANCE:

Insurance which protects the seller against loss due to default on the part of the buyer.

CUSTOMHOUSE BROKERS:

A person or firm, licensed by the U.S. Treasury Department, engaged in clearing goods through U.S. Customs. A broker's duties include preparing the entry form and filing it; advising the importer on duties to be paid; advancing duties and other costs; and arranging for delivery to the broker's client, the trucking firm or other carrier.

CUSTOMS TARIFF:

Charges imposed by the U.S. government and most other governments on imported and/or exported goods.

DATE DRAFT (D/D):

A draft payable a specified number of days after the date it was issued, regardless of the date of acceptance.

DELIVERED AT FRONTIER:

Term referring to the seller's obligation to supply goods which conform with the contract. At his/her own risk and expense, the seller must deliver the to the buyer at the specified time and the specified frontier. The buyer is responsible for complying with import formalities and payment of duties.

DELIVERY DUTY PAID:

Term referring to the seller's obligation to supply goods according to the terms of the contract. At his/her own risk and expense, the seller must deliver the goods, duty paid, at the specified time and the specified frontier, after complying with all necessary formalities at that frontier.

DEMURRAGE:

Excess time taken to load or unload a vessel. A sum agreed to be paid to the shipowner for the excess time taken for loading or unloading not caused by the vessel operator, but due to the acts of a charterer or shipper. Also refers to imported cargo not picked up within prescribed time.

DESTINATION CONTROL STATEMENT:

One of a number of statements required by the U.S. Government to be displayed on export shipments specifying the authorized destinations for the shipments.

DIRECT EXPORTING:
Sale by an exporter directly to a buyer located in a foreign country.

DISTRIBUTION LICENSE:
A license given to an export to replace numerous individual validated licenses when there is continuous shipping of authorized products.

DISTRIBUTOR:
A foreign agent who sells directly in the foreign market for a U.S. supplier and maintains an inventory of the supplier's products.

DOCUMENTS AGAINST ACCEPTANCE (D/A):
Instructions by a shipper to a bank indicating that documents transferring title to the goods should be given to the buyer only after the buyer's signing a time draft. Thus the exporter extends credit to the importer and agrees to accept payment at a named future date.

DOCUMENTS AGAINST PAYMENT (D/P):
Payment for goods without a guaranteed form of payment in which the documents transferring title to the goods are not given to the buyer until he/she has signed a sight draft.

DOCUMENT OF TITLE:
Evidence of entitlement or ownership, such as a carrier's negotiable bill of lading, which allows a party to claim title to the goods in question.

DUTY:
A tax levied by a government on an import, an export or the use and consumption of goods.

DUTY DRAWBACK:
A partial refund of duties paid on importation of goods which are further processed and then re-exported, or exported in same condition as imported.

EMBARGO:
A restriction or prohibition upon exports or imports, for specific products or specific countries. Embargoes may be ordered by governments due to warfare, or are intended for political, economic or sanitary purposes.

ENTRY PAPERS:
Documents which must be filed with U.S. Customs officials describing goods imported, such as the commercial invoice, Ocean Bill of Lading or Carrier Release.

EUROPEAN ECONOMIC COMMUNITY (EEC):

An economic grouping of countries also known as the European Common Market, organized by the Treaty of Rome in 1957. Member countries are Belgium, Denmark, France, Germany, Greece, Ireland, Italy, Luxembourg, the Netherlands, Portugal, Spain and the United Kingdom. The EEC was the largest trading bloc in the world until the North American Free Trade Agreement created a larger market beginning in January 1994.

EX MILL (EX WAREHOUSE, EX MINE, EX FACTORY):

Obligates the seller to place a specified quantity of goods at a specified price at his warehouse or plant, loaded on trucks, railroad cars or any other specified means of transport. Obligates the buyer to accept the goods in this manner and make all arrangements for transportation.

EXPORT DECLARATION:

A formal statement made to Customs at the exit port declaring full particulars about goods being exported.

EXPORT LICENSE:

A permit required to export certain commodities and certain quantities to certain destinations. The purpose is to control the transfer of technologies such as hardware, software, technical data and services. Lists of goods requiring an export license are listed in the official U.S. government publication *The Export Administration Regulations* of the Bureau of Export Administration (BXA) of the U.S. Department of Commerce.

EXPORT MANAGEMENT COMPANY (EMC):

A firm that acts as a complete export arm for a company's exporting needs. Usually an EMC will pay all expenses and receive compensation in the form of a discount off the U.S. price of the product. An organization which, for a commission, acts as a purchasing agent for either a buyer or seller.

EXPORT QUOTAS:

Restrictions or set objectives on the export of specified goods imposed by the government of the exporting country. Such restraints may be intended to protect domestic producers and consumers from temporary shortages of certain materials or as a means to moderate world prices of specified commodities. Commodity agreements sometimes contain explicit provisions to indicate when export quotas should go into effect among producers.

EXPORT RATE:

A freight rate specially established for application on export traffic and generally lower than the domestic rate.

EXPORT TRADING COMPANY (ETC):

A business that acts as a complete export service house and, in addition, takes title to a company's exported goods.

EX SHIP:

An international trade term meaning that the seller shall make the goods available to the buyer on board the ship at the destination named in the sales contract. The seller must bear the full cost and risk involved in bringing the goods to the buyer.

EX WORKS:

An international trade term meaning that the seller's only responsibility is to make the goods available at seller's premises. The seller is not responsible for loading the goods on the vehicle provided by the buyer, unless otherwise agreed. The buyer bears the full cost and risk involved in bringing the goods from there to buyer's desired destination. This term thus represents the minimum obligation for the seller.

FACTORING HOUSES:

Types of companies which purchase international accounts receivable at a discount price, usually about two to four percent less than their face value. The fee charged the exporter is offset by the immediate availability of payment, plus the reduction in risk for the exporter. (*See* Forfaiting.)

F.O.B. FREIGHT ALLOWED:

The same as F.O.B. named inland carrier, except the buyer pays the freight charges of the inland carrier and the seller reduces the invoice by that amount.

F.O.B. FREIGHT PREPAID:

The same as F.O.B. named inland carrier, except the seller pays the freight charges of the inland carrier.

F.O.B. NAMED INLAND CARRIER:

Seller must place the goods on the named carrier at the specified inland point and obtain a bill of lading. The buyer pays for the transportation.

F.O.B. NAMED PORT OF EXPORTATION:

Seller is responsible for placing the goods at a named point of exportation at the seller's expense. Some European buyers use this form when they actually mean F.O.B. vessel.

F.O.B. VESSEL:

Seller is responsible for goods and preparation of export documentation until actually placed aboard the vessel.

FOREIGN-BASED AGENT/DISTRIBUTOR:

An individual or firm serving as the foreign representative of U.S. suppliers, locating buyers for them in the foreign market.

FOREIGN BRANCH OFFICE:

A sales (or other) office maintained in a foreign country and staffed by direct employees of the exporter.

FOREIGN FREIGHT FORWARDER:

A corporation carrying on the business of forwarding who is not a shipper or consignee. The foreign freight forwarder receives compensation from the shipper for preparing documents and arranging various transactions related to the international distribution of goods. Also, a brokerage fee may be paid to the "forwarder" from steamship lines if the forwarder performs at least two of the following services: (1) coordination of the movement of the cargo to shipside; (2) preparation and processing of the Ocean Bill of Lading; (3) preparation and processing of dock receipts or delivery orders; (4) preparation and processing of consular documents or export declarations; and (5) payment of the ocean freight charges on shipments.

FOREIGN SALES AGENT:

An agent residing in a foreign country who acts as a sales representative for your company's products.

FOREIGN TRADE ZONE ENTRY:

A form declaring goods which are brought duty-free into a Foreign Trade Zone for further processing or storage and subsequent exportation and/or consumption.

FORFAITING:

Forfaiting, similar to factoring, is an arrangement under which exporters actually forfeit their rights to future payment in return for immediate cash. The arrangement is commonly used for sales of capital equipment with terms of one-to-five years.

FREE ALONGSIDE (F.A.S.):

(or free alongside steamer)
The seller must deliver the goods to a pier and place them within reach of the ship's loading equipment. The buyer arranges ship space and informs the seller when and where the goods are to be placed.

FREE OF CAPTURE AND SEIZURE (F.C. & S.):

An insurance clause providing that loss is not insured if due to capture, seizure, confiscation and like actions, whether legal or not, or from such acts as piracy, civil war, rebellion and civil strife.

FREE TRADE ZONE:

An area designated by the government of a country to which goods may be imported for processing and subsequent export on duty-free basis.

FREIGHT TO (NAMED DESTINATION):

The seller must pay to forward the goods to the agreed destination by road, rail or inland waterway and is responsible for all risks of the goods until they are delivered to the first carrier.

GATT:

General Agreement on Tariffs and Trade, now renamed the World Trade Organization. A multilateral treaty adhered to by over 124 nations which provides a set of rules for trade policies and a means for settling disputes among member nations. After eight years of negotiations, the Uruguay Round Agreement of the GATT nations, creating a global trade accord, was voted on by the U.S. Congress in December, 1994 and approved for American participation. The pact is expected to lower world tariffs by 40 percent, cut subsidies globally, expand protection for intellectual property and set rules for investment and trade in services.

GENERAL AVERAGE:

A deliberate loss or damage to goods in the face of a peril, which sacrifice is made for the preservation of the vessel and other goods. The cost of the loss is shared by the owners of all goods on board up to time of peril.

GENERAL LICENSE (EXPORT):

Authorization to export goods or services without specific documentary approval.

GENERAL LICENSE, LIMITED VALUE (GLV):

Authorization to export a limited value amount of a good without specific documentary authorization.

GENERAL ORDER:

A Customs term by which if proper entry has not been made for merchandise within five working days after arrival in a port of entry, the goods are sent to a general order warehouse. All costs are charged to the importer.

GROSS WEIGHT:

Entire weight of goods, packing and container, ready for shipment.

HARD CURRENCY:

A currency expected to remain at stable value or to increase in relation to other currencies; also, a freely convertible currency may be called "hard."

HARMONIZED SYSTEM:

The harmonized system (HS) is a classification system for goods in international trade that provides a uniform system of product classification for all major trading countries.

IMPORT:

To bring foreign goods or services into a country.

IMPORT LICENSE:

A license required and issued by some governments authorizing the entry of foreign goods into their countries.

IMPORT QUOTA:

A restricted amount of certain types of goods entering a country, usually maintained through licensing importers, assigning to each a quota, after determining the amount of goods or commodities allowed for that period. The license may also state the country from which the importer is allowed to buy, thus restricting free trade, but many times adopted by governments because of internal pressures from certain industries worried about competition.

INDENT:

A requisition for goods, stating conditions of the sale. Acceptance of an indent by a seller means his agreement to the conditions of the sale.

INDIRECT EXPORTING:

Sale by the exporter to the buyer through an intermediary in the domestic market.

INLAND BILL OF LADING:

A bill of lading used in transporting goods overland to the exporter's international carrier, where the ocean bill of lading becomes applicable. Although a *through* bill of lading can sometimes be used, it is usually necessary to prepare both an inland bill of lading and an ocean bill of lading for export shipment.

INLAND CARRIER:

A transportation line which hauls export or import freight between ports of entry and inland destinations.

INTEGRATED CARRIERS:

Carriers that have both air and ground fleets. Since they usually handle thousands of small parcels an hour, they have more competitive prices and offer more diverse services than regular carriers.

INTELLECTUAL PROPERTY:

The patents, trademarks, service marks, copyrights and trade secrets of a business are considered intellectual property.

INTER-AMERICAN DEVELOPMENT BANK (IDB):

The Inter-American Development Bank provides resources to finance Latin American development. The IDB also serves as administrator for special funds provided by several member and nonmember countries. The largest of these funds is the U.S. Social Progress Trust Fund.

INTERNATIONAL CHAMBER OF COMMERCE:

Established in Paris in 1919, this is a non-governmental organization serving world business. The ICC has members in 110 countries that include companies, industrial associations, banking bodies and chambers of commerce. The ICC International Court of Arbitration was founded in 1923 to settle international business disputes; it is the leading international arbitration institution.

INTERNATIONAL FINANCE CORPORATION (IFC):

A separately organized member of the World Bank group, receiving its funds through stock subscriptions from member countries, revolving loans, and earnings. The IFC encourages the flow of capital into private investment in developing countries. It makes loans at commercial interest rates, usually as a lender of last resort when sufficient capital cannot be obtained from other sources on reasonable terms.

IRREVOCABLE LETTER OF CREDIT:

A letter of credit which obligates the issuing bank to pay the exporter provided all the terms and conditions of the letter of credit have been met. None of the terms and conditions may be changed without the consent of all parties to the letter of credit. (*See* Letter of Credit.)

LAY TIME:

The time allowed a ship to load or unload. If this number of days is exceeded, demurrage is incurred.

LEGAL WEIGHT:

The weight of the goods plus any immediate wrappings which are sold along with the goods; e.g., the weight of a tin can as well as its contents. (*See* Net Weight.)

LETTER OF CREDIT (L/C):

A method of payment for goods by which the buyer establishes his/her credit with a local bank, clearly describing the goods to be purchased, the price, the documentation required and a limit for completion of the transaction. Upon receipt of documentation, the bank is either paid by the buyer or takes title to the goods themselves and then transfers funds to the seller. The bank will insist upon exact compliance with the terms of the sale, and will not pay if there are any discrepancies.

LIQUIDATION:

The final determination of the duties due.

MARINE INSURANCE:

Insurance which will compensate the owner of goods transported overseas in the event of loss which cannot be legally recovered from the carrier.

MULTIPLE EXCHANGE RATES:

A number of countries operate systems by which different exchange rates are used for different transactions.

NAFTA:

The North American Free Trade Agreement, the largest free trade area in the world, 340 million people and $6 trillion in GDP, encompassing Canada, the United States and Mexico. This free trade pact was passed by the U.S. Congress in November 1993 and began implementation in January 1994. NAFTA follows the model of the U.S.-Canada Free Trade Agreement and will lower trade barriers among the three countries over the next 15 years to zero in most categories of goods and services.

NET WEIGHT (ACTUAL NET WEIGHT):

The weight of the goods without any immediate wrappings; e.g., the weight of the contents of a tin can without the weight of the can. (*See* Legal Weight.)

NON-TARIFF BARRIERS:

These are factors, other than tariffs, inhibiting international trade, meant to discourage imports. They may include requiring advance deposits in import payments, requiring excessive customs adherence and excessive administrative procedures.

NON-VESSEL OPERATING COMMON CARRIER (NVOCC):

A cargo consolidator of small shipments in ocean trade, generally soliciting business and arranging for or performing containerization functions at the port.

OCEAN BILL OF LADING:

A contract between an exporter and an international carrier for transportation of goods to a specified foreign port. Unlike an inland bill of lading, the ocean bill of lading is a collection document, an instrument of ownership which can be bought, sold or traded while the goods are being shipped. There are two types of ocean bills of lading used to transfer ownership:

- Straight (non-negotiable): provides for delivery of goods to the person named in the bill of lading. The bill must be marked "non-negotiable."
- Shipper's Order (negotiable): provides for delivery of goods to the person named in the bill of lading or anyone designated.

The shipper's order is used with draft or letter-of-credit shipments and enables the bank involved in the export transaction to take title to the goods if the buyer defaults. The bank does not release title to the goods to the buyer until payment is received. The bank does not release funds to the exporter until conditions of sale have been satisfied.

OPEN ACCOUNT (O/A):

A trade arrangement in which goods are shipped to a foreign buyer without guarantee of payment, with 30-45 days accounts payable, for example. The buyer's integrity must be unquestionable, or the buyer must have a history of payment practices with the seller.

OVERSEAS PRIVATE INVESTMENT CORPORATION (OPIC):

A wholly owned government corporation designed to promote private U.S. investment in developing countries by providing political risk insurance and some financing, including project financing.

PERFORMANCE BOND GUARANTEE:

If a company is undertaking a contract, it may be asked to give a performance bond for part of the value of the contract. If the customer considers the company's performance under the terms of the contract has been unsatisfactory, payment of the bond can be demanded from the banker guaranteeing the bond. The bond is issued by the bank on behalf of the company, and therefore increases the bank's potential exposure to the company.

PIGGYBACK ARRANGEMENT:

An arrangement whereby one company—sometimes a smaller one—uses the already established distribution channels of another company, which is effective when the two companies wish to sell complementary products.

PORT OF ENTRY:

A port where foreign goods are admitted into the receiving country.

PRIVATE EXPORT FUNDING CORPORATION (PEFCO):

A U.S. company owned by the Export-Import Bank and a number of U.S. commercial banks and industrial corporations. It works with Ex-Im Bank by purchasing foreign buyers' medium. PEFCO funds itself by public issues of long-term secured notes, unsecured medium-term obligations, short-term notes sales, and by credit lines from the banks and from Ex-Im Bank.

PRO FORMA INVOICE:

An invoice prepared by an exporter before the shipment of merchandise informing the buyer of the kinds of goods to be sent, their value and important specifications such as size, quantity and weight.

Resources

QUOTA:
The quantity of goods which may be imported without restriction or additional duties or taxes.

QUOTATION:
An offer to sell goods at a stated price and under stated terms.

SCHEDULE B:
Refers to "Schedule B, Statistical Classification of Domestic and Foreign Commodities Exported from the United States."

SHIPPER'S EXPORT DECLARATION (SED):
A form required by the U.S. Treasury Department and completed by a shipper showing the value, weight, consignee, destination, etc., of export shipments, as well as Harmonized Schedule B identification number.

SIGHT DRAFT:
A draft payable upon presentation to the drawee. A sight draft is used when the seller wishes to retain control of the shipment, either for credit reasons or for the purpose of title retention. Money will be payable at *sight* of the completed documents.

STANDARD INDUSTRIAL CLASSIFICATION (SIC):
A standard numerical code system used by the U.S. government to classify goods and services.

STANDARD INTERNATIONAL TRADE CLASSIFICATION:
A standard numerical code system developed by the United Nations and used in international trade to classify commodities, primarily designed for statistical and economic purposes.

STANDBY LETTER OF CREDIT:
A letter of credit issued to cover a particular contingency, such as foreign investors guaranteed payment for commercial paper. (*See* Letter of Credit.)

STRIKES, RIOTS AND CIVIL COMMOTIONS (S.R.& C.C.):
A term referring to an insurance clause excluding insurance of loss caused by labor disturbances, riots and civil commotions or any person engaged in such actions.

SUE AND LABOR CLAUSE:
A provision in marine insurance obligating the insured to take necessary steps after a loss to prevent further loss and to act in the best interests of the insurer.

TARE WEIGHT:
The weight of packing and containers—without the goods to be shipped.

TARIFF:

A tax on goods which a country imports. The rate at which imported goods are taxed. A tariff schedule usually refers to a list or schedule of articles of merchandise with the rate of duty to be paid to the government of importation.

TARIFF QUOTAS:

Setting a higher tariff rate on imported goods after a specified, controlled quantity of the item has entered the country at the usual tariff rate during a specified period.

THROUGH BILL OF LADING:

A single bill of lading covering both domestic and international passage of an export shipment.

TRANSPORTATION AND EXPORTATION ENTRY:

A form declaring goods entering the United States for the purpose of exportation through a U.S. port. Carriers and any warehouse must be bonded.

UNIFORM CUSTOMS AND PRACTICE:

Standardized code of practice issued by the International Chamber of Commerce in Paris covering Documentary Credits. (*See* International Chamber of Commerce.)

UNIFORM RULES:

Standardized rules issued by the International Chamber of Commerce in Paris covering collections, Combined Transport Documents, and Contract Guarantees. (*See* International Chamber of Commerce.)

URUGUAY ROUND:

The most recent (1989-1994) round of trade talks of the member countries of the General Agreement on Tariffs and Trade (*see* GATT).

VALIDATED EXPORT LICENSE:

A document issued by the U.S. Government authorizing the export of commodities for which written export authorization is required by law.

VALUE ADDED TAX (VAT):

An indirect tax assessed on the increase in value of a good from raw material stage to final product for consumption. The tax is paid by those who increase the value of the items before they resell them. A system used by the European Community.

WORLD TRADE ORGANIZATION (WTO):

This organization was the former General Agreement on Tariffs and Trade (GATT) and was created and named by the Uruguay Round in 1994.

WAREHOUSE ENTRY:

A form declaring goods imported and placed in a bonded warehouse. Duty payment may not be required until the goods are withdrawn by the importer.

WITHOUT RESERVE:

A shipping term indicating that a shipper's agent or representative is empowered to make definitive decisions and adjustments abroad without approval of the group or individual represented.

WORLD BANK:

The World Bank assists the development of member nations by making loans when private capital is not available at reasonable terms to finance productive investments.

PART 3
INDEX

INDEX

INDEX